Ken. McFarle

# LIVING

### IN THE

# SUPERNATURAL
# DIMENSION

RIGHT CHOICE NOW—BEST LIFE FOREVER

## JOHN ABRAHAM

WESTBOW
P R E S S
A DIVISION OF THOMAS NELSON

Scripture quotations marked AV are from The Holy Bible, King James Version. Copyright ©1977, 1984, Thomas Nelson Inc., Publishers. All rights reserved. Scripture quotations marked NKJV are taken from the New King James Version. Copyright ©1979, 1980, 1982. Thomas Nelson Inc., Publishers. All rights reserved. Scripture quotations marked NASB are taken from the New American Standard Bible. Copyright ©1960, 1962, 1963, 1971, 1972, 1973. The Lockman Foundation. Used by permission. All rights reserved. Scripture quotations marked NIV are from the New International Version. Copyright ©1973, 1978, 1984. Used by permission of Zondervan Publishing House. All rights reserved. WestBow Press books may be ordered through booksellers or by contacting:

WestBow Press
A Division of Thomas Nelson
1663 Liberty Drive
Bloomington, IN 47403
www.westbowpress.com
1-(866) 928-1240

Because of the dynamic nature of the Internet, any web addresses or links contained in this book may have changed since publication and may no longer be valid. The views expressed in this work are solely those of the author and do not necessarily reflect the views of the publisher, and the publisher hereby disclaims any responsibility for them.

Certain stock imagery © Thinkstock.
Any people depicted in stock imagery provided by Thinkstock are models, and such images are being used for illustrative purposes only.

The design of the Holy Spirit and Bible symbols on the front cover and book jacket is by Kyle Van Kleek. Used by permission.

ISBN: 978-1-4497-3968-3 (sc)
ISBN: 978-1-4497-3969-0 (hc)
ISBN: 978-1-4497-3967-6 (e)
Library of Congress Control Number: 2012901981

Library of Congress Cataloging-in-Publication Data
Abraham, John, 1937-
        Living in the supernatural dimension : right choice now – best life forever / John Abraham.
        p. cm.
        Includes bibliographical references and indexes.
        ISBN: 978-1-4497-3968-3 (sc); ISBN: 978-1-4497-3969-0 (hc);
        ISBN: 978-1-4497-3967-6 (e)
        1. Abraham, John, 1937-    2. Abraham, Shirley.  3. Evangelists--Biography--Canada.  4. Missionaries--Biography--Canada.  5. Evangelists--Biography--Northern Ireland. 6. Miracles. I. Van Kleek, Laurence M., 1944-  ed.  II. Pentecostal Assemblies of Canada. III. Title.
BX8762.Z8A159 2012                                                           289.9

Printed in the United States of America
WestBow Press rev. date: 03/07/2012

# CONTENTS

# PART 3: PERSEVERING

# PART 4: FULFILLING

*Dedicated
to
the glory of God.
For His perpetual love, His sustaining power,
and His endless patience toward
me.*

*To Shirley, the love of my life.
For your trust and devotion, which have been
faultless in every circumstance of our lives
together. For your part in making me who I
am as a husband, father, and His servant, I
thank you from the bottom of my heart. You
have faithfully carried an equal share in
ministry, which made our missions' call, and
this book, possible.*

*To our four children.
For Alden, William, Grant, and Shirleen, their
spouses, children, and grandchildren, whose
circumspect walks with God and their own
ministries for the Kingdom richly bless me.*

# PREFACE

As a Pentecostal family we joyfully acknowledge the presence and work of the Holy Spirit in the Church as promised by Jesus. This understanding is not simply to be theoretical or theological, but is to be our daily reality.

John and Shirley Abraham have experienced that reality as they have pursued the Lord's call on their lives and have shared the Gospel in the power and demonstration of the Spirit worldwide. *Living in the Supernatural Dimension* is an inspiring, challenging, and instructional account of how God took a couple who were prepared to listen to His voice and live by faith. As a result they have seen God at work in ways they could only have imagined.

Knowing John, as I do, his goal in writing this book is to give glory to God for His faithfulness, while encouraging all of us to trust the Spirit to be at work in our daily lives in a naturally, supernatural manner. I am happy to commend this book to you.

Rev. David R. Wells
General Superintendent
The Pentecostal Assemblies of Canada

# FOREWORD

What a privilege and honour I have experienced to be invited by John Abraham to assist him by editing the story of the ministry God has given him! As I have read through, edited, and revised many written drafts of this project, my life has been transformed. I have been made more aware and challenged to live my life in the supernatural dimension through the enabling power of the Holy Spirit.

First and foremost, for most of his life John has been an evangelist and moves easily in other ministry giftings. During the past twenty-five years, he has served and continues to serve overseas as a missionary evangelist, teacher, and church planter. A quarter of a century ago, I first heard him preach at our home church in Abbotsford, British Columbia, and have since observed God's unusual leading in his ministry. He and Shirley, his wife, are some of the most hospitable people I know.

I have witnessed John Abraham to be a man of sincerity, honesty, integrity, and intensity, with deep dedication, devotion, love, and passion for our Lord and Saviour, Jesus Christ. John both mirrors and models the love of God.

Also, John has a heart that loves and cares deeply for people and for their welfare. He continues to give of himself and spend his life so that those who haven't yet heard the gospel of Jesus Christ may have the opportunity to do so and commit their lives to Him and live for Him.

I immediately identified with the author's choice of a sports analogy to give structure to the story; with his love for the Bible through internalizing the gospel or good news message; with his value and emphasis on prayer and fasting; with his sacred conversion and baptism in the Holy Spirit experiences; and with his passion for Christ's missionary and evangelistic cause.

Through the course of John's ministry as a missionary evangelist, God has spoken into virtually every area of human need. Is God perhaps speaking into a needy aspect in your life?

If you are an agnostic, a humanist, an atheist, religious or a theist, but without Jesus Christ in your life; if you are hungry for more of God or to be filled with the Holy Spirit; if you are physically sick; if you have an unforgiving or broken heart; if you feel alienated; if you are financially in need; if you have a strained or broken marriage; if you are the victim of abuse; if you are addicted, if you are physically or mentally challenged; if you are a prisoner; if your life is in ruins; if you are demonized; if you are dying of a terminal illness; or if you are a backslidden or relapsed prodigal son or daughter, you may want to read this book.

It is for the young, the teenager, the young and older adult, and the senior. It is for the moral and immoral individual; for the single person, the married, the separated, the divorced, and the remarried; for the one living common law; for the nuclear, extended, or blended family member; for the rich, the poor, and the middle class individual; for the executive, businessperson, professional, paraprofessional, tradesperson, labourer, or the unemployed; for the individual who holds to a politically left, right, or center position; and for all cultures, races, nationalities, and religions. God has used John in a ministry that is global and inclusive.

—Laurence M. Van Kleek, Editor

# ENDORSEMENTS

During these many years, what an honour it has been to work alongside such precious people of God! These are workers whose hearts of compassion and love brought them to the spiritual harvest fields of their calling to accomplish great things for God. On many mission fields, we have been blessed to have continued fellowship with them.

Some of these workers have honoured us by taking time to share briefly, in an introductory way and from their perspective, what great things God has done during those times of demonstrating His supernatural dimension and intervention. The following are excerpts from their endorsements.

## Taiwan Report

"The sixty meetings in twenty-four days conducted by Evangelist Abraham were the most powerful visible manifestation of God's power that I have ever seen in my life. John is a premier evangelist, a man set aside by God who is more sensitive to the moving of the Holy Spirit than any I have known before. He was powerfully used of God in healing, the gifts of the Holy Spirit (in remarkable ways), and casting out of demons. This was the first time I saw evidenced within a series of meetings all nine gifts of the Holy Spirit . . . Thanks, John, for impacting my life."

Donald S. Young, Shanghai, China

## Philippine Report

"John's energy, his heart, and the anointing on his life have always amazed me. I personally considered it a rich privilege to sit under his teaching. My own life was enriched, and my personal ministry benefited. John is a superb evangelist who moves powerfully in the Holy Spirit, with many coming to Christ, being filled with the Holy Spirit, and receiving physical healing in every service. The altars were always full, and the Holy Spirit was always powerfully present and working in people's lives. However, John's greatest legacy may well be as a teacher and trainer of national workers for the harvest field."

Henry C. Borzel
Senior Pastor
Vancouver Chinese Pentecostal Church
Formerly PAOC Asia Regional Coordinator

## Sri Lanka Report

"'God Has a Miracle for You' was the theme of the crusade. John Abraham was the speaker. In thirty-nine meetings, we had over twenty-three hundred recorded responses. A mighty move of God brought many forward for salvation, physical healing, and deliverance. The big miracle, however, was the sudden influx of people into our churches, virtually all of them new converts. One church grew from fifteen to seventy in a matter of six weeks."

Rainer Mittelstaedt
PAOC Missionary to Sri Lanka

## Ukraine Report

"A number of years ago, John and Shirley came to Ukraine to teach a week-long course on the Holy Spirit and His gifts. It was a wonderful time as the Word was both taught passionately and demonstrated with power; even in class the sick were prayed for and words of knowledge were given to many. Most of those students are now in leadership positions in the church and regularly minister both in deliverance and healing ministries.

"What I remember the most of this time, however, is how John ministered personally to the senior pastor. The Holy Spirit gave him some key words of knowledge—of both correction and encouragement. They came at a decisive time in his life, and I believe they were vital for this pastor to remain focused and fruitful. The church has more than quadrupled since then, with well over two thousand members . . . and they are always asking for John to come back!"

Jonathan Willoughby
PAOC Missionary

# ACKNOWLEDGMENTS

It has been said, "We are the product of the people we know and the books we read." In the natural realm, this is often true. In the spiritual dimension, in my case, it is certainly true.

Thanks, first, to all the many great men, some of whom are now deceased, in my youth and early ministry who poured lavishly of their spiritual maturity and wisdom into my life, majoring on focus and balance in foundational Christian values. Each, in his own way, encouraged, strengthened, and stretched me to newer and higher heights. Each played a significant role in the outworking of God's hand on my life from which *Living in the Supernatural Dimension* was birthed.

The late Dr. Andrew Ghi, then of China Inland Mission, which is now known as OMF International, spoke into my life with passion for Asian missions in the late 1940s. Running his fingers through my then mop of dark, curly hair, he said, "One day you will minister to my people in Asia," and we still are.

The late Lindsay Glegg of Keswick and Filey Bible Week was probably Britain's best-known evangelist of the twentieth century, and he continually encouraged young men to ministry. That distinguished, respected, and elderly saint of God, with a full head of pure white and lengthy hair, always encouraged me to "do the work of an evangelist."

The late Dr. F. F. Bruce (Rylands Professor of Biblical Criticism and Exegesis, Manchester University, 1959) was an author and theologian. He invested much time in me over lengthy periods in the library of his home and helped me hone the finer points of theology that have provided a lifetime of learning. It was such an honour to sit under his tutelage.

The late Rev. Glen S. McLean, Principal of the Full Gospel Bible Institute, now Eston College, played a vital role in my moulding. He was a busy little man with a massive heart and time for everyone. Not only was his lecture time a great highlight in those years, but his private mentoring in impromptu sessions was also excelled only by hours of private discussions as he and I traveled to different cities and on occasion, preached together. Those encounters still play out in daily life and in this writing.

Dr. John Wesley White (D. Phil. Oxon) was a Billy Graham associate evangelist for forty years. He invited me, just ordained in 1958, to be his associate evangelist in Britain. His preaching was to me an art form in communicating to the heart of the hearer. With John, I enjoyed six life-moulding and fruitful ministry years. Our lifetime relationship continues. I love you, John and Kathleen!

In more recent years, the late Rev. William Cornelius, Executive Director of Overseas Missions for the Pentecostal Assemblies of Canada and who was instrumental in our appointment to PAOC Missions, also played a major role in our lives. He showed us great understanding, patience, and love, fanning the mission flame that we are honoured to hold high as we continue to be credentialed with that great fellowship.

The Rev. Calvin C. Ratz, our former pastor, mentor, and long-time friend, was always an encourager and always affirming. Thank you, Cal, for the long sessions, the great counsel, your patience, and making me much of what this volume is about!

The Rev. Henry C. Borzel for several years was our PAOC Asian Regional Coordinator. His sound spiritual judgement, open-hearted dialogue, and love and friendship made our mission years productive and exciting. Thank you, Henry, for your quiet encouragement to put pen to paper in this writing venture!

The Rev. Laurence M. Van Kleek, BA, MDIV, MA, MLS, is Librarian/Administrator of the Hudson Memorial Library of Summit Pacific College in Abbotsford, British Columbia. He has proofread, edited, and revised the manuscript for this book. Without his literary skills, this project would have been overwhelming. For hundreds of hours, he has worked tirelessly on this assignment. I have personally appreciated his input, patience, and tenacity to get the manuscript to press. He has done an admirable job, for which I have the deepest appreciation. I could never repay him for this great ministry service. Thank you, Laurie!

# INTRODUCTION

We often speak in the corporate world of the glass ceiling. It is that invisible barrier beyond which one rarely rises, for a myriad of reasons, such as education, ethnicity, or gender. In a similar way, in the Christian world there is a perceived glass ceiling. Going beyond it to higher levels with God can also, for many reasons, be a challenge.

As I have spoken with numerous Christian leaders around the world, they recognize that their congregations, pastoral staff, or they themselves have at some time in their Christian lives faced that proverbial ceiling.

To understand better this perceived barrier and walk in a closer and more powerful union with God, some basic principles should be noted. Those foundational concepts resemble the threads woven together to create a fabric. Each of these threads represents a biblical concept. When the threads are fully woven into God's pattern, they produce His perfect plan for removing the imagined glass ceiling.

The Bible is God's plan, and He longs for us to reach our highest levels by following it. For me there is no shortcut in following His manual. In the spiritual world, for many the glass ceiling represents the limitations many believers sense in experiencing an intimate relationship with God. For some it is a challenge to know to a greater degree His power or to overcome a deep personal hurdle.

As I searched my heart before God and catalogued my personal forks in the road that keep me on track with His will for my life, I wrote this book. During overseas leadership experiences, I learned valuable lessons as God, on occasion, took me apart and then put me back together again. I now share those experiences with you.

Of the many books I read each year, some tell me *what* to do for a deeper, richer, and more powerful walk with God. Seldom will an author reach into the depths of his own heart to teach *how* to achieve those goals. Only by revealing my major encounters with God, by bearing my own soul, and by sharing what God is teaching me in the spiritual and supernatural dimension can I help others who face glass ceilings to remove them. This, then, is my desire for you. If you are not experiencing all that God has planned for your life, will you let Him move you from where you are to where He desires for you to be?

Hopefully you will walk this journey with me, letting God take you each step in His plan for you. Sometimes as we travel together, it will demand strenuous *training*. Often the pace will quicken to a *sprint*. Many times the demand will be gruelling, as in a *marathon*. As we press on together with endurance, there will be a *fulfilling* reward. In this way, you will scale the new heights He has planned for you. New vistas of richer fellowship with Him are your inheritance to enjoy a life fully empowered by the Holy Spirit. Claim your inheritance now by following His divine plan, and walk in total obedience to His Word. He waits to transform you with a fresh baptism of His divine love, peace, and power and to energize you for greater kingdom exploits.

*Living in the Supernatural Dimension* is not intended to be a literary masterpiece or a theological dissertation but by the Spirit, to speak from my heart to your heart. Each chapter may be read as a standalone unit in that each addresses a notable miracle or event, often contrasting a dimension of our Christian faith or principles. For example, the biblical directive on forgiveness is addressed together with real-life parallels of deliverance that directly result from obedience to His command for us to forgive.

Some autobiographical background is included to apprise you of the Potter's hand that prepared, moulded, and led me into child evangelism and later, to witness miraculous, supernatural ministry that was considered, from my teaching as a teenager, a dispensational impossibility.

Facing a mission's call was catastrophic for me. Western evangelism was my calling. My flesh was diametrically opposed to a missions' lifestyle. Even as a teenager in Bible college, it seemed dishonest for me to sing missions' hymns about a calling I had no intention to follow.

For security reasons, details of countries, cities, pastors, workers' names, and dates have mostly been omitted. Many nationals who work to arrange for our ministry in their countries risk great danger to themselves, their families, and their congregations. For this reason, although you may find this minor security measure somewhat of a distraction, I trust that in a spirit of love and understanding, you will accept it for the greater good of all concerned.

PART ONE

# TRAINING

# 1

# FLASHBACK

## How It All Started

Like watching a vignette, my life flashed before me. Everything of consequence that had brought me to that moment now begged the questions, *how did I get here?* and, *what am I doing?* as the crowd before which I stood warmly received me.

A few years ago in an African city late one afternoon, a pastor asked me to speak in his weeknight service. I imagined a small church-plant on the edge of town with fifty people; I agreed to speak.

As we talked, he indicated that he was trained in another discipline and was not a seminary graduate. I took that to mean he was a lay worker ministering in his free time. After further discussion, he left the room and said to his other colleague, "Have him speak this evening." Returning to our billet, we refreshed, ate, and then left for the location. Arriving just before the appointed time, we entered a tiny room through a small side door.

Following a brief word of prayer, the colleague led us up a few narrow steps to a large open space. As my eyes adjusted to the darkness beyond the dazzling spotlights, a packed auditorium and balcony emerged. Upward of thirty thousand people, we were told, filled the place. Since this was their regular teaching meeting, within a few minutes it was my turn to speak. As I walked to the pulpit, I was able to see the whole crowd, which, until that time, may have been my largest audience. I learned that the pastor was a medical doctor and that his sizable ministry team were doctors or lawyers, none of whom were seminary graduates.

In this chapter, I will briefly share what led me to that point.

## A Different Childhood

I grew up an only child in a small farming community in Northern Ireland and was allowed to have a carefree life. My mother, father, and I lived on a small working farm that kept my father very busy. He also had a full-time job. With dairy cows, a herd of pigs, thousands of laying hens, and a massive greenhouse to care for, even I was put to work. Later, my father built three fabric factories in our district. My childhood days were happy and full. My Christian parents practised their faith in the home and trained me in the way that I should live.

Bible stories from a giant family Bible were part of the bedtime routine, together with prayer. My extended family of many uncles, aunts, and an army of cousins on both sides of the family all attended the Plymouth Brethren Gospel Hall in their communities. The Gospel Hall that I attended was about a mile away and across several farmers' fields and ditches, which separated the fields and often overflowed in the rainy season. Sunday school, only for children, was held in the afternoons. As a small child, going alone to Sunday school was not a pleasant journey for me and would be unheard of in our culture today. But I really did enjoy the classes.

On more than one occasion, I intentionally dawdled, making myself late. Sometimes when I crossed the ditches between farms, I would "accidentally" get wet or slip into a water-filled ditch and then return home to change my clothes. By then it was decided that I was too late to go. On one occasion, I was dressed in a new suit when I attempted such a ploy. My father became furious with me and exclaimed, "Look at your new suit!" As I pulled off my trousers, his trusty razor strap connected with my vulnerable posterior. I quickly redressed, but in older clothes. Then I was on my way again to Sunday school. This time, as my father was watching me, I made better progress and successfully navigated the troublesome ditch.

In the 1940s, my Gospel Hall had special gospel meetings. A young man, Harold Paisley, came and preached the gospel for many weeks. He preached clear, strong gospel messages of God's love, man's total depravity, heaven and hell, and the sovereign grace of God. He preached that salvation was achieved only by faith in the finished work of Jesus Christ on the cross. Only through His shed blood was cleansing from sin possible. Then salvation was to be received as a gift, not by works. As one is empowered by Christ's resurrection, one is enabled to live in victory as a new creation. That was his nightly message, the old-fashioned kind of preaching that we seldom hear today in our seeker-sensitive and politically correct world.

One Saturday night soon after those meetings, while playing marbles using a small hole in the kitchen floor left from an air bubble in the cement during pouring, something unusual happened to me. With my father reading the evening paper in a large lounge chair beside a roaring log fire, I began crying inconsolably. Dropping to his knees, he picked me up in his arms and asked, "John, son, what is wrong with you?"

At first I couldn't speak. Then I was able only to speak in an indecipherable stutter. Minutes later, with both parents crouching beside me and with a measure of composure, I sobbed, "If I die in sin, I will go to hell." With my father's strong arms comforting me, he placed me on one knee and guided me in giving my life to Christ. "This is how you need to pray," he said. Quietly my salvation prayer was whispered. I gave my life to Christ by confessing my sin and receiving His love, forgiveness, and cleansing for my sin. By His blood alone, the everlasting work was done. As Scripture assures, ". . . whoever calls on the name of the LORD shall be saved" (Rom. 10:13 NKJV). That was and still is a Saturday night highlight in my life.

The next day, seemed to me like a new world. Although I was only seven years old, I felt that a heavy weight of sin was lifted from me. Now, I cleared every ditch without falling or slipping and gladly made it to Sunday school on time. In the following week, my father took me to town to a Christian bookstore where I was allowed to choose my very own Bible. When I arrived home, my first task was to open the front page of the Bible and print in it my name and date of my salvation.

So many Brethren relatives came to our home and were delighted to hear the good news of my conversion. They grilled me with questions to confirm that I really understood what had transpired in my life. They were overjoyed that I had come to faith in Christ.

The next couple of years were uneventful, consisting of an orderly and prioritized life of school and homework, and then chores and play. At that time, there was one more activity: as time permitted, my dog, MacWhurter, and I would hide in the most deserted spot of the fields. He would lie on his stomach with his chin on his outstretched paws and was obliged to listen to me ramble, as I practised preaching from my new Bible.

At ten years old, I walked home the three miles from school and often with a friend. As I preached to my dog, I would also witness to my friend. Sometimes he would feel convicted or cry, and then we would pray together for his salvation.

One time, as my parents and I were eating supper, my father started chatting with me. He said, "I was talking with Mrs. Brown and she told me that recently her son gave his life to Christ as you prayed with him on the way home from school. Is this true?" Excitedly, I concurred and related to him the event. "Go to your room!" was his response. He followed me, accompanied by his reliable razor strap. After what he considered was adequate correction, he explained that I was too young to attempt praying with others to receive Christ, and I was not to do it again. We resumed our evening meal.

Perhaps a year later, and again at an evening meal, my father began, "Since we last spoke of Mrs. Brown's son, have you led anyone else to Christ?" Immediately, it was as though Satan jumped on my right shoulder, saying, "Tell him no! Tell him no!" Instead, I answered, "Yes!"

Again my father sent me to my room—where I experienced the same disciplinary treatment. But this time it was a little different. After I received several strokes to my backside, something else happened. Instead of crying, I began quietly laughing. So my father turned me over and demanded, "Why are you laughing when I am strapping you?" I explained that the first time he gave me one spanking for leading one boy to Christ. This time I only received one spanking, but I had since led several children to Christ. What a good discount! He began to laugh and said, "You be careful; you're too young to know what you're doing."

Before the era of television, sometimes I was allowed to listen to the radio, but not for very long because the acid-filled battery didn't last long in the days before electricity came to our district. One evening, I found a station on 208 Meters Medium Wave, from Radio Luxemburg. I heard a preacher who really fascinated me. It was a program relayed from the United States. The minister had a huge tent and traveled the country preaching the gospel and deliverance. The gospel I knew, but deliverance, what was that about? My parents allowed me to stay up until after nine p.m. to finish the program. As they went for solitude to another room, they left me with my ear glued to the radio program.

I settled back in my huge lounge chair in which, as a small boy, I felt lost. This preacher's message was different. His name was Oral Roberts. After preaching the gospel, he sat on the platform and prayed for sick people as they filed past. The sick people gave testimonies when some, and often many, were healed. As the weeks passed and I became attached to him and more comfortable with his message of deliverance, something began to happen to my spirit.

Although I was only twelve years old at the time, I sensed a presence—the presence of God. What a good and rich feeling that was! Warmth accompanied His presence. Often it felt like warm oil flowing from my head to my shoulders and upper body. Sometimes I had the urge to cry softly, even though there was nothing wrong. At other times I would begin to laugh gently. After weeks of listening to the preacher, it seemed that at times what he said about God, Jesus, or the Holy Spirit would cause one of those laughing or crying emotions to rest on my spirit. In addition to all of these experiences that were new to me, as Oral Roberts preached, and while the warmth of oil seemed to be flowing from my head, my spirit was lifted out of my body to the ceiling of the room. It remained there for the rest of the program, and I could view my body sitting in the big chair.

Those evidences of the Holy Spirit's presence continued regularly and reminded me of when I started laughing during the spanking my father gave me for leading my friends to Christ. In retrospect, it was the same anointing. In His own way, God was quietly and unknown to me preparing me to understand the moving of His Spirit for later use, while, at the time, I only knew a fundamental faith.

As I recall, about this time, a Bible correspondence course was offered by M. R. De Hahn of Back to the Bible Broadcast from Lincoln, Nebraska. It was intended for new adult believers. Over several weeks, I completed these and mailed them back. Then they were corrected, and when a passing mark was achieved, after a few weeks, I would receive the next segment. About eighteen months later, I received an impressive certificate of achievement. They never questioned that I was a child graduate.

## The Beginning of Children's Ministry

Two teachers working with Child Evangelism Fellowship, Sam Doherty and David McQuilkin, came to a community hall two fields across from my home to begin children's meetings. For me, attending them was great fun. We all loved singing choruses, playing games, hearing Bible stories, and more. After a few weeks, we were asked if anyone would like to tell a Bible story. My hand shot up. After all, MacWhurter and I had rehearsed dozens of stories and sermons over the past five years.

The leader called me up and asked me to tell the story of David and Goliath. As I did so, the story came so much to life that it even captivated me, as did hearing my voice telling it in public for the first time. I did this several times over the next months, and I felt comfortable doing it. One day Sam Doherty asked me to tell the story while they left to do another meeting. That room became my meeting and my place, but the leaders continued to provide ongoing oversight. What an exciting and fulfilling time for me as many children my age of twelve and younger gave their lives to Christ!

One evening as I was standing in an open-air circle, without warning, the leader put the microphone in my hand and asked me to testify. Later when I arrived home, I realized that the huge cone-shaped loud speaker was facing in the direction of our house. My father greeted me by saying, "Even though I told you, you were too young, you did a good job; carry on!"

## Teenage/Adult Ministry Begins

At age thirteen, I had a brilliant idea. Having done children's meetings for about a year and then open-air meetings, why not conduct evangelistic crusades? The thought simmered for weeks, and finally I had a plan. Many of my similar-aged friends loved the Lord and testified with me. Perhaps we could form a preaching team. *Why not preach to adults?* I thought. Knowing that young people don't preach to adults, I tried to suppress the thought but without success. Week by week, I felt prompted to preach.

Later the idea of a ministry team made up of my Christian friends seemed workable. As I spoke to several of them and met once a week for prayer with them, ideas began to germinate. Over several months we decided to save our pocket money and raise whatever we could from sympathetic family members and from whatever extra jobs we could find. All expenses would be paid from the proceeds of our work activities.

We purchased material to build a portable platform. We needed a piano, so I went in search of one. When I found a store that sold pianos, I asked about their prices. All of them were too expensive for us, but the salesman suggested he send another man to try and help me.

The man who came to assist me further was a well-dressed and distinguished gentleman, not tall but commanding. Looking at me over his horn-rimmed glasses, his first question was, "How much *can* you pay?" Then he asked, "How much do you have?" When I replied, he smiled and walked away. Minutes later he returned with a small book the size of a large postage stamp. Then he showed me a massive, battered old piano, saying it was "substantial." He was right; it was the largest, heaviest, most ornate and ancient piano I had ever seen. Its price was thirty-five pounds or seventy dollars. He wrote that amount into the book and deducted my paltry amount of five pounds or ten dollars and said, "Pay me the rest as you can." The piano was ours.

Unknown to me at the time, that store belonged to one of the most successful Christian businessmen in the area. When he learned that the piano would be for gospel meetings, he sold it to me on trust. From that day forward and for the rest of his life, until just recently when God took him to glory, George Allen of Portadown and I remained lifetime friends.

Now we were in business—or more accurately, in ministry. We printed song books and chorus sheets; distributed hand bills and posters; and booked meeting places. We were now ready to begin our evangelistic venture to adults. We had a pianist, Sam Elliott, and a quartet made up of Cecil Hutchinson, Raymond McDowell, Joshua Sloan, and Stanley Robb, who also functioned as master of ceremonies and song leader. Preaching was mostly left to me. Other key members were Tom Gilchrist, Raymond Cairns, Fred Douglas, and others, who also played leading roles in keeping with their giftings.

From time to time over the years and for various reasons, there were changes in team members. Until today, those of us who are still alive are serving God and have remained lifetime friends.

The very first crusade was close to our homes, and everyone knew us. The place was packed nightly, as the whole community wanted to see the *performance.* Everything went smoothly until they called me to preach. Within three minutes, I had finished all I knew to say. Then, as though it were part of the program, I called upon a team member to testify and then on another, until all had testified. Then I continued preaching and finished with a small measure of dignity.

One evening two boys came from school. One was tall for his age and the other one shorter. At the altar call time, the shorter one stood to be saved, but the taller one pulled him down by his coat. This action happened twice. Later, the shorter boy waited behind, and we led him to Christ. What became of him after those years, I had never heard. As the crusade continued, several gave their lives to Christ.

Recently, sixty years after these meetings, I received a phone call, and a voice said, "This is Sandy Beckett!" It was the shorter boy who gave his life to Christ at the crusade. He asked me if I remembered who he was. I did. Not knowing what had become of him over the years, I asked how things had been going and if he had been living for Christ. He related how, following school, he had prepared for ministry and had just retired after fifty-plus years as a pastor. Only in the last few years did the taller boy give his life to Christ. Our group of young evangelists visited community after community, and many committed their lives to Christ and today are faithful believers in pastoral ministries or missions.

During this ministry to adults, I had the opportunity, in obedience to the Lord Jesus Christ, to follow His example in the waters of baptism by immersion according to Scripture. This was another milestone in my life and gave me a real sense of fulfillment.

As time passed, we became a closely knit team, functioning well together in ministry. We were still teenagers, but as we saw God at work in honouring His Word, we did our best.

At one stage, one of the young men in the quartet was Pentecostal. Since all the rest of us were fundamentalists, we thought that since he was only singing, it would be okay to include him. As I continued to preach, periodically he would remind me that I was not preaching the *whole* gospel.

One night the situation came to a head. In the course of the message I said, "We serve a God who can do anything." I simply meant that He created and controls the universe and His creation.

At the end of the service an elderly lady to us as teenagers—perhaps in her forties—came forward by saying, "You said God could do anything."

I agreed with her. She continued, as she removed a large kerchief from her neck, "Then I would like Him to remove this, please!"

As I looked in horror, she uncovered a massive goitre the size of a grapefruit on her neck. Because I believed that the dispensation for healing had passed with the New Testament church and with the death of the apostles and realizing that the Pentecostal member of the quartet, Tom Gilchrist, was listening, I asked myself, *What should I do? Should I have him pray? What if she is healed?* With confidence that she would not be healed, I decided to pray for her myself. That would send a statement to Tom. Closing my eyes tightly, I prayed, "God heal her according to *her* faith!" While my eyes were still closed, I heard her say, "Oh God, it's gone!" God did heal her, and Tom pointed his finger and said to me, "If God healed her, the fullness of the Holy Spirit is also a question you better search from Scripture!"

## My Holy Spirit Encounter

Sometime later after a crusade meeting, Tom Gilchrist and I rode our bicycles from where the taxi dropped us off to his little church. As we arrived very late, from the foyer I heard the pastor say, "Now I have taught you about the fullness of the Holy Spirit, so come forward and receive from Him." As though a warm, gentle hand was placed on my back encouraging me to go through the swinging double doors and down and aisle of a church I had never attended, I went. I stood alone to the left of the platform and waited for the pastor to pray for me, but it didn't happen.

Instead, and almost immediately, as I had often experienced before, I began to sense the presence of the Holy Spirit. As my body became unsteady, I placed one leg behind me for stability, which didn't help. Soon I rested softly on the floor, as though I was on a mattress. Until three in the morning, my Pentecostal encounter was full of the presence of the Holy Spirit. He anointed and blessed me. At times it seemed that I could contain no more. He evoked prayer and praise, singing and weeping, and words so sacred, I still can't relate them.

As the apostle Paul testified, "I will pray with the spirit, and I will also pray with the understanding. I will sing with the spirit, and I will also sing with the understanding" (1 Cor. 14:15 NKJV). The prayer language of that evening gave expression in praise and worship and set the stage for my personal worship and most intimate relationship with Him.

The worship and praise that exuded from me that night were beyond my description and capacity to understand, as were the sounds and words that I had never before heard or spoken. It was a euphoric mountaintop visitation I have always treasured and will always treasure as sacred. This visitation was God, the Holy Spirit, in His Pentecostal capacity. This was my Pentecost. This was my epiphany to own for the rest of my life.

Hours passed, as I seemed to be there, without any pastoral prayer. As the anointing eased and I became aware of my natural surroundings again, I tried to get to my feet but felt like what a drunken person would likely feel after a heavy drinking binge. It was almost impossible to stand to my feet, and I still had miles to ride on a bicycle to return home. The lights were still on in the church, and there was a man waiting for me to compose myself, but he was now asleep on the back pew; it was after three in the morning!

By the time I had biked home, it was almost 4:00 a.m., and I was still lost in the same praise and worship mode as when I was resting in the Holy Spirit on the church floor.

When I arrived home, the front door, which was not usually locked, was locked. My dad let me in and asked me, "Where have you been until this hour of the morning?" I made a feeble, thick-tongued attempt to answer my father with the details; it now seemed that from the extended periods of my spirit praying, praising, and worshiping, my enunciation had become slurred to a considerable degree. He had heard enough and concluded from my verbal account that something had gone terribly wrong with his normally on-track son and dismissed me to my bed, saying, "I think you're drunk!" not unlike the response of the crowd on the day of Pentecost. "They are full of new wine," said the crowd. In reply Peter stated, "For these are not drunk as you suppose" (Acts 2:13, 15 NKJV).

From my vantage point of that evening, it seemed to me he was more correct than he knew. Nothing more was said at home the next morning. The fallout, however, with the extended family of fundamental preachers, teachers, and elders was another matter. Those same men who were delighted with my profession of faith in Christ as a seven-year-old when they tested me to be sure that I really understood the magnitude of my decision were now anything but encouraging.

More than half a century later, I have been blessed to accept warm apologies from several of those chief antagonists to my eventful experience. Some of their children and grandchildren are paying the greatest subliminal compliment to me by now embracing the same doctrinal position and experience with their families for which their forefathers castigated me.

The most significant of those who opposed this development in my spiritual life was my maternal grandfather. He was a serious Bible student and elder in his assembly and majored in eschatology. As a professional designer in textiles, he used this skill to design and paint wall-size dispensational charts depicting every aspect of transition since creation until then. He was persuaded that numbers in the Bible were significant and held part of the key to understanding end times prophetic fulfillment. For many years he worked laboriously figuring and re-figuring what he considered to be biblical mathematical formulae in preparation of the manuscript for his prophetic book.

On one occasion, he became intensely frustrated when no combination of numbers would produce the result he felt necessary to prove a prophetic date. Keep in mind that he was ultra-fundamental and diametrically opposed to any Pentecostal dispensational carryover after the apostles. One evening, in exasperation from his mathematic stalemate, he asked God to help him resolve this problem.

Many hours into a sound sleep, he was awakened by brilliant supernatural light that flooded his otherwise dark bedroom. Becoming fully awake and sitting up, he noticed on the bare wall, beyond the foot of his bed, as though projected there, his lines of formula. As he looked in disbelief, the shadow of a hand wrote in the blank spaces that he himself could not supply. When the equations were completed and he had copied them down, giving him the answers to his prolonged search, the hand and the numbers faded, and the room returned to its former darkness.

Many years after my Holy Spirit encounter, and many more years after my grandfather's "handwriting on the wall" revelation, and as a very elderly man, he spoke to me one day. "John," he said, "I must tell you what that vision meant to me. Not only did it solve years of research, but it also proved to me that God can and will still reveal Himself to those who seek. I must apologise to you for the reaction all of us had when you had your Holy Spirit revelation. I am an old man now, and God will soon take me home. God has now shown me the supernatural, and you were right; go on believing and preaching your message for His glory."

More than forty years after his last statement to me, there is a sequel to the story. Recently, when I removed a book from my library for study, a very old copy fell forward with it. I was about to replace it on the shelf when the title caught my eye: *Signs and Wonders*[1] by M.B. Woodworth-Etter. This book was signed on the flyleaf by my grandfather, when he would have been in his mid-thirties and only recently born again.

Maria Woodworth-Etter had been active in ministry for some time, but 1885 appears to be the beginning of her ministry in a Pentecostal dimension. In America her ministry was marked with outstanding healings, the Baptism of the Spirit with the evidence of speaking in tongues as the Holy Spirit gave utterance, and visions and the gifts of the Spirit in operation. In his book entitled, *Canadian Pentecostals: A History of the Pentecostal Assemblies of Canada,* Thomas William Miller refers to Woodworth-Etter[2] and Aimee Semple McPherson[3] numerous times as being leaders[4] in ministry.

Throughout the book, my grandfather had noted and underlined significant Holy Spirit passages, each relating to God's power being available to believers today, as initially found in the book of Acts. These notations indicate to me that, although he never publically identified with this position, he had embraced, to some considerable degree a dispensational shift in his theology before God took him to glory. This, to me, is God; He moves in majesty!

I can't understand why any Christian today cannot embrace such empowerment of the Holy Spirit for ministry, and I question why anyone still believes that the dispensation of the operation of the gifts of the Holy Spirit ceased with the New Testament church and the death of the apostles. Could it be that the reason for one's denial of the Holy Spirit experience and empowerment is because it has not been one's experience?

As G. Campbell Morgan asks in his book, *The Acts of the Apostles,* "Have we not some kind of subconscious heresy in our minds that Pentecost is passed, and that Pentecostal power has weakened in the process of the centuries? It is not so. The resources are as limitless now as they were in the dawning of that great day. The question for our hearts should be: Is Christ limited in us?"[5] Morgan continues, "Finally we learn from this study that the Christian messenger must know by experience, or he cannot preach; that he must be filled with the Spirit if there are to be any results from his preaching; and that he must be wise, for 'he that winneth souls is wise.'"[6]

## Canada: College on the Horizon

## A Fork in the Road

After six years with the team, plans were forming in my spirit to consider Bible college. I chose a fundamental college in London.

At that time, there was a great stir in the community and in the press that an American evangelistic team was coming to our town. That was big news. Now we could see how it really should be done. The day came, and the streets around the venue were gridlocked. For us, such a traffic situation was mind blowing!

The auditorium was filled to capacity long before the event began, and the overflow halls also were filled. Each event segment was fast paced, and the song leading and singing were vigorous. The quartet's rendition of hymns and spirituals left us breathless. The preacher was John Wesley White, a Canadian from Pangman, Saskatchewan, with a Chicago accent, probably resulting from his Moody Bible Institute study years, and he kept all of us on the edge of our seats.

His message was sound and homiletic to a greater degree than any of us had ever heard. The invitation for salvation brought people from every corner of the auditorium and overflow area in response to the call to faith in Jesus Christ.

The crusade had early morning prayer meetings that were well attended, with each one of us praying from the back left corner to the front right of the prayer room. He asked for brief first-person prayers, with no lectures. The preacher singled me out one morning, asking why I prayed as I did. Not knowing how to answer, he asked if I was Pentecostal. I replied in the negative, saying that my background was Brethren. Pressing me further, he asked about the experience of the Holy Spirit in my life, which I acknowledged had just recently occurred. I shared about the team ministry and my plan to go to a Bible college in London. He challenged me by saying that if I was walking in a Holy Spirit experience I should consider attending a Holy Spirit-endorsed Bible college.

He pulled a used, dog-eared envelope out of his jacket pocket and wrote about six lines on it. This was my recommendation to his friend, Glen McLean, the Principal of the Full Gospel Bible Institute in Eston, Saskatchewan, which was later renamed Eston College. He assured his friend that he would be responsible for any of my indebtedness. After that encounter and in the middle of the crusade, John Wesley White's mother passed away in Canada. In an incredible turn of events, when he arrived at his mother's home, he was met by the young lady who, many years later, but unknown to me at the time, would become my wife.

The following weeks were a blur as our team finished our scheduled crusades. At the age of eighteen, I busied myself with completing emigration papers for Canada and prepared for my departure to "the new world," which displeased my parents.

Departure meant that I needed to say my farewells. We left for the forty-minute drive to the Belfast Ferry. Believing we had departed without fanfare, about halfway there, I looked around and saw a familiar car behind us and another and then another. As the motorcade eventually parked dockside near the ship, there was pandemonium. My personal friends, team members, extended family, and probably sixty or more of our factory employees filled the wharf.

I smoothly completed my documentation shipside and threw my travel trunk and cases on a conveyer. I watched them being swallowed into the bowels of the ship. Hugging those closest to me, I escaped quickly up the gangplank. After a peek at my cabin, my next stop was the departure deck.

My appearance at the ship's railing triggered the total group in singing. For thirty minutes, they sang memorized hymns and choruses. Finally the heavy hawsers were pulled aboard, and the ship slipped softly into the dusk. Those I loved most in the world stood singing, "God Be with You till We Meet Again." Their features blurred, whether from the misty night or my clouded vision, I don't know.

Armed with that special envelope of endorsement, I embarked on a life-changing journey. Air flights in those days were prohibitively expensive, so I traveled by boat. The Belfast Ferry took me to Liverpool, where I left on the Cunard's *Saxonia* for Quebec City, the first major destination of my journey and into the unknown. It was fortunate for me because that October was the first winter the deepened St. Lawrence River had accommodated year-round ocean liners to navigate it. Otherwise it would have been a much longer route. Also, it was the first winter in the crew's memory that vicious Atlantic gales had delayed the five-day trip by almost another two days. For several days in the mid-Atlantic Ocean, the dining rooms that accommodated over one thousand people were almost empty. Dishes slipped back and forth from side to side and along the length of the tables as the ship corkscrewed through the storm.

After I arrived in Quebec City, it took time for me to get back my land legs. Recently on a trip to that city, Shirley and I were able to visit and look down from the Chateau Frontenac to the dock where I arrived in Canada over fifty years earlier. I stood at the same spot with Shirley and my cousin Margaret and her husband, George Willey. He was an extended part of the original teen-team. Together they have continued to be an integral part of present day ministry in the United Kingdom. As we surveyed the scene together, no doubt they wondered at my expression of emotion as I silently replayed the memory of this scene from the distant past. I reflected on the rich provision, protection, and guidance of God at every major fork in the road. As a teenager I last surveyed this vista. What a great God we serve!

On my first arrival in Quebec City, I transferred to the intercontinental train that would whisk me across three time zones and four provinces in four days to the Canadian prairies. How breathtaking was the scenic panoramic view from the train's vista dome lounge! I experienced a never-to-be-forgotten trip. I appreciated the unfolding splendour of my Creator's handiwork that was tantamount to a high degree of worship.

I traveled to Saskatoon and then to Eston, Saskatchewan, as I witnessed the site of the golden stubble after harvest had blended at the horizon with blue sky. The train ground to a halt and hung over both ends of a short and almost-deserted platform. As my name was called from a distance, I looked around and saw a tall, handsome young man approaching, saying his name was Donny. He was the son of Glen McLean, the principal of the college. My travel trunk and cases were dumped in the back of a '48 GM half-ton, and after a few minutes of chatting, we were on campus. Fourteen days of travel and half a world away from home, was this for me the end of the world or a new beginning?

## The Thrill of Bible College

My major journey from Britain to Bible college in Canada had ended. Now great expectations filled my spirit, and I was ready for the thrill of whatever God had planned for me. Six years of preaching as a teenager without formal Bible college training repeatedly reminded me of the urgent need for this time and place in my life. Many times while I was preaching teaching or in a one-on-one debate, I felt that my knowledge was insufficient, and with Bible college training, I was preparing to rectify my deficiencies.

Students came from everywhere. We all became settled, and for me, it was exactly the right fit. One evening as we all sat in the men's lounge chatting, someone spoke of this being their year of college. I had never thought in such terms. What was that about? Was someone coming for one year? The thought to me was preposterous. Bible college was the opportunity I had anticipated for such a long time. I wanted to finish my program and return to my calling of evangelism.

This was it, a place to bury myself in the challenge to work, study, and sit at the feet of those who knew what I didn't but had the ability to communicate what I needed to learn. For me Bible college was such an incredible experience. With vigour, everyone adjusted to the task at hand. As we made new friends that would develop into lifetime relationships, the weeks passed like days. Full lecture days with study evenings kept us busy, as did special gratis assignments, which meant campus work. The rotation changed weekly as we did whatever chores were required, usually without question.

In many ways each Bible college year was akin to a juggling plates act. We had to keep our grades high and our deportment demerits low. Behaviour, attitude, decorum, and many other minor breaking of rules, when accumulated, would cost us dearly, even to expulsion from the college. If our monthly one hundred credits were depleted, we would put ourselves in jeopardy. Dating and casual relationships were also closely monitored but without the high-technology surveillance gadgetry of today.

Classes sped by, and Christmas break came, with students scattering in all directions, but what about the orphan Irish student? Someone took pity on me and invited me to their friend's home. For me, the long drive to Regina was a rigorous adventure on treacherous roads. As we parked in front of the cosy house at 2501 Atkinson, I had a good feeling. There Gordon and Mabel Mitchell instantly became everyone's mom and dad. They welcomed us, a car load of exhausted and half-frozen students, with hugs and hot chocolate and for that holiday, with endless food, fun, and fellowship.

What a home away from home those ten days at Christmas were! As we bundled ourselves back into the cars in atrocious winter weather, I tried to thank my hostess for her incredible hospitality in my best British manner. "Mabel," I said, "you have been so homely."

To this Gordon quickly interjected, "John, surely you mean 'homey'!"

His western definition of "homely" left me red-faced with embarrassment as I stuttered my profuse apology. In Britain my word meant exactly the same as homey does in Canada.

We arrived safely back on campus. As the next four months galloped past, my first year was completed.

College was out, and we were off for summer activities. Some went on choir tour with the director and others to itinerate in children's work, then called DVBS (Daily Vacation Bible School). Several of the men formed a team with me (this time not thirteen— and fourteen-year-olds) and evangelized throughout the province until college recommenced.

We preached and sang through the small towns of Northern Saskatchewan. As I wrote to my family while on that trip, I mentioned that I was in Love. Quickly a hurried reply came from Ireland telling me not to act on impulse and to take my time because I was still young. My next letter home explained that Love was the name of the town in which we were to preach.

In my experience, beginning a new school year was better than the first year; this time we knew one another and what was expected of us. Study came easily for me. Everything I learned at college informed me as to what I was missing in my earlier years of preaching. Now I had learned the details of dotting the Is and crossing the Ts in the process of my college learning experience.

One Monday each month was a full day of prayer. Classes were suspended, and after a brief devotional, we found ourselves alone with God. These were special days. In those hours battles were fought, victories won, mountains climbed, and direction for a lifetime downloaded. Often the Holy Spirit would brood or hover over the student body as we were enveloped in the warmth and gentleness of His very presence. At times we would have wished that those moments would last forever. As David prayed, "Do not take Your Holy Spirit from me" (Ps. 51:11 NKJV).

On young, mouldable lives those were memorable days of God's sovereignty moving. The clay was still pliable in the Master Potter's hand, readily formed to His touch and pattern. From some of us with harder clay, the Potter had to work more laboriously as He chiselled our characters. Destinies were revealed to those whose hearts responded, destinies that had been in His plan from the beginning of time. Now the human vessel was being prepared to contain the oil of gladness and in due time, it would be poured out on a parched, sad, and hurting world.

Those were days when there was liberty in the Spirit. As the Scripture reminds us, ". . . where the Spirit of the Lord *is* there *is* liberty" (2 Cor. 3:17b NKJV). Without inhibition, there was freedom to move in the Spirit and to minister in the gifts of the Holy Spirit. Students who had received the fullness of the Spirit ministered freely in their gifts to others and were themselves finding the direction in the Spirit they sought.

Some students were new believers and anxious for real sustenance, like Peter instructed, "As new born babes, desiring the sincere milk of the word, that ye may grow thereby" (1 Peter 2:2 AV). Others, like me, were first-generation Pentecostals coming from fundamental backgrounds and were paying a price from family, with strained, if not severed, relationships with their former circle of believers for their stand in their newfound empowerment in Christ. Each student had a relentless drive for growth and development and an insatiable desire to be stronger in Him and to go deeper in His Word.

Today I wonder if the Pentecostal message is being diluted, if the salt is losing its savour (Matt. 5:13 AV). Are there not fewer first-generation Holy Spirit—filled believers who are willing to engage in spiritual warfare and pay the price to carry the full gospel banner? As they do so, they will be replicating the Pentecostal model from the book of Acts of the same evidence that produced historical moves of God through the centuries.

Has the cutting edge been dulled by second-, third-, and now fourth-generation Pentecostals who prefer to conform to mainline denominational respectability and acceptance rather than commit to the power and demonstration of the Spirit? Is it not a sad commentary, if from our pulpits in the West the new generation is hearing about the good old days of Pentecost, pointing back to historical roots, like the Azusa Street Revival[7] in Los Angeles over a century ago rather than living in the continuing day of Pentecost today and until Christ returns? Why not live in the dimension of the supernatural?

The Azusa Street Revival was a sovereign move of God—a God moment that birthed the modern full-gospel explosion that had positive changing effects across North America and around the world. Was that move of God only a historical landmark to be visited by this generation and remembered, with nostalgia, by earlier generations? Instead, the earlier generations of Pentecostals need to mentor the new generation, through the Holy Spirit, to live in the power of God's today experience.

As God intended, the Great Commission needs to be empowered by Pentecost in its fullest sense, supplying that same empowerment that will for this and future generations "pour out this which you now see and hear" (Acts 2:33 NKJV).

College occupied our every waking moment. Once a month the total student body drove to the hills on the prairie by the South Saskatchewan River for a much-needed outing. Whatever we felt like doing within reason to reduce stress and burn off energy—

yes, even play ice hockey on the frozen Saskatchewan River—was acceptable. The wrap-up of those hilarious events was a campfire barbecue or wiener roast. The evening concluded with a sing-along and meaningful current testimonies from students who were making breakthrough strides in their Christian development. We had a time of praise and worship around a crackling, warm, marshmallow-roasting, dying-ember fire to stave off the now-chilling prairie fall evening. As we bundled into a convoy of assorted vehicles, we were soon back at the college.

During all three years at the college, preaching points were made available, allowing teams to minister on weekends. Towns within driving range like Lacadena, Leader, Elrose, Glidden, and others welcomed us as we practised and sharpened our ministry skills.

Since I came from the usually mild British winters, this exercise of battling treacherous winter driving did not come easily to me. Almost to the end of the spring term, my final preaching assignment was at Leader, which was a considerable distance in normal temperatures by road and across a bridge but only a short distance across the frozen river.

On one occasion at spring time, the driver decided to take the direct route. Halfway across the river, as I looked out the rear window, sheets of broken ice were folding out behind the rear wheels of our vehicle as we sped across the river, which we managed to cross without harm but dangerously.

Again, while we were visiting at the Leader church, we enjoyed a great service. A young local man led the worship, and I preached. Following the service, we were both invited to a home for lunch a few miles away. As I was driving on the deserted highway, he suddenly pulled out from behind, and as he passed us, he gestured to me to pull over. Thinking he had a problem, I did as he had requested. When he walked over to my driver window, he cited me for speeding as he handed me a ticket. We continued to the home for fellowship and a delicious lunch. Unknown to me, he was an off-duty policeman.

## Billy Graham: The New York Crusade

The college term finished, and the students scattered for the summer. During my itinerary that year, I went home for a few weeks, but on my way home, I traveled through the United States by Greyhound bus. What an incredible journey! My experience included stopping, starting, eating, and sleeping. The days and nights merged, and time almost stood still. Finally the journey ended, and I reached my destination. The large, dirty silver Greyhound bus that had been my accommodation for days now deposited me on the sidewalk, alone in the "Big Apple"—New York City. I had just turned twenty years old, and at that moment, no one in the world knew my whereabouts.

It was there for many nights that I would sit enthralled listening to Billy Graham who preached his first sermon in a Baptist church in Bostick, a close by community of Palatka, Florida, at age nineteen on Easter Sunday evening 1939.[8] At age thirty-nine, Billy Graham was instrumental in holding crusades in Madison Square Garden and Times Square, for that moment the crossroads of the Christian world. The Sunday finale had an estimated attendance of one hundred thirty thousand people. He extended his meetings from a six—to a sixteen-week crusade from May 15 until September 1, 1957.[9] The nightly crowds filled up the auditorium's capacity of eighteen thousand and swelled to perhaps twenty-six thousand, considering the outdoor overflow area. In silence, everyone listened as the over fifteen hundred-voice choir, led by Cliff Barrows, would render the most uplifting selections of traditional and contemporary music of the day. Barrows would then introduce the beloved George Beverly Shea to thrill and bless the crowd as many were held spellbound by his baritone voice.

Billy Graham followed Beverley Shea's last solo that prepared the crowd for his message. Then he preached the gospel in its purest and simplest form and with the most profound gentleness of Christ's love. The anointing of the Holy Spirit energized Graham, the servant of God, with amazing results from responsive audiences nightly. Whatever the sermon title, night by night, it always uplifted Jesus Christ, the Son of God, who loved us and gave

Himself for us. The apostle Paul personalized this blessed truth of Christ by declaring, ". . . who loved me and gave Himself for me" (Gal. 2:20f NKJV).

The fullness of the Holy Spirit evidenced in Billy Graham's preaching was rooted in his experience resulting from "his visit to Britain in October 1946."[10] At that time while at Hildenborough Hall in Kent, he met Stephen Olford after Stephen preached a message on "Be not drunk with wine . . . but be filled with the Spirit."[11] Graham told Stephen, "You've spoken of something that I don't have. I want the fullness of the Holy Spirit in my life too."[12] The two men arranged to meet later at a hotel in Pontypridd in Wales.[13]

As a result of those two days in their study of the Word and praying together, "Billy prayed, 'Lord, I don't want to go on without knowing this anointing You've given my brother.'"[14] Stephen "then told Billy how God had completely turned his life inside out. It was, he said, 'an experience of the Holy Spirit in His fullness and anointing.'"[15] Later, as Stephen "explained that 'where the Spirit is truly Lord over the life, there is liberty and release—the sublime freedom of complete submission of oneself in a continuous state of surrender to the indwelling of God's Holy Spirit.'"[16] According to Olford, "Billy cried, 'Stephen I see it. That's what I want.'" [17] Wirt continues, "the two men went to their knees praying and praising."[18] "It was . . . on the second day that Billy began pouring out his heart 'in a prayer of total dedication to the Lord.' According to Stephen, 'all heaven broke loose in that dreary little room.'"[19] "Billy exclaimed, 'My heart is so flooded with the Holy Spirit!' They alternately wept and laughed, and Billy began walking back and forth across the room, saying, 'I have it! I'm filled. I'm filled. This is the turning point of my life. This will revolutionize my ministry.'"[20]

"Said Olford, 'That night Billy was to speak at a large Baptist church nearby. When he rose to preach, he was a man absolutely anointed.'"[21] His Welsh audience "came forward for prayer even before the invitation was given. Later when it was given, Olford said, 'The Welsh listeners jammed the aisles. There was chaos. Practically the entire audience came rushing forward.'"[22]

This endowment, this anointing, empowers the Word that Billy Graham preaches, producing the legendary results that have accompanied his lifetime ministry.

At the Itinerant Evangelist Congress in Amsterdam in 1983,[23] Billy Graham "spoke to more than 4,000 evangelists."[24] At the Congress, Graham said, "'Jesus is the message. Jesus Christ, by His death and resurrection, became the Gospel. It is not a new set of morals or a guide for happy living. It's the solemn message that we are alienated from God, and only Christ, by His death and resurrection, can save us.'"[25] Because Jesus came as God in the flesh, lived to reveal God to man, was crucified upon a cross for our sin, offered cleansing through His blood as a gift without price, and rose from the dead, He has shown Himself to be the gospel personified. He *is* the *good news,* and as ministers, it is our responsibility to declare it with integrity or face the consequences.

The challenge facing those of us who work to hone our skills in presenting the gospel message is to step back sufficiently to allow the power of the Holy Spirit to do His good work and lead the penitent to Christ. "You also gave Your good Spirit to instruct them" (Neh. 9:20 NKJV). It is "the kindness of God leads you to repentance" (Rom. 2:4c NASB).

The gospel should be preached with *promptness.* "Behold, now *is* the accepted time; behold, now *is* the day of salvation" (2 Cor. 6:2 AV). The gospel should be preached with *plainness.* Jesus calls for simplicity, using a child as the example. "Except ye be converted, and become as little children" (Matt. 18:3 AV). The gospel should be preached with *power.* "For he taught them as *one* having authority, and not as the scribes" (Matt. 7:29 AV). "No man ever spoke like this Man!" (John 7:46 NKJV). In referring to the gospel during his ministry, the apostle Paul spoke of it with increasing degrees of respect.

In writing the letter to the church at Rome, Paul referred to the gospel as "*the* gospel" (Rom. 1:1 AV, emphasis mine). To the Galatians Paul spoke of the gospel as "*that* gospel" (Gal. 2:2 AV, emphasis mine). In his second Corinthian letter, Paul called the gospel "*our* gospel" (2 Cor. 4:3 AV, emphasis mine).

In AD 67, Paul's final letter from prison in Rome was addressed "To Timothy, a true son in the faith" (1 Tim. 1:2a NKJV). Recognizing the end was imminent, Paul, having had a lifetime of victories with hardships because of his unflinching stand for the gospel, assured Timothy that his fight was a good fight. He had finished the race. He had kept the faith. The time of his departure was near (2 Tim. 4:6-7). Then Paul chose to escalate his affection for the gospel to his highest and most emotional level when he declared it to be "*my* gospel" (2 Tim. 2:8c AV, emphasis mine).

The awesome responsibility that rests upon the shoulders of those of us who presume to proclaim the gospel must be to strive, as Paul did, to move to that highest form of gospel—not to be satisfied with "*the* gospel" or "*that* gospel" or even "*our* gospel." Is it not only as we have internalized the gospel as "*my* gospel" that it will become our personal possession and we will approach the degree to which the apostles evidenced their selflessness in declaring a total or full gospel? Paul stated in writing his last instruction to Timothy, ". . . so that the message might be preached fully through me" (2 Tim. 4:17b NKJV).

It was "*the* gospel" that, at the end of each disciple's life, became "*my* gospel" and for which, according to tradition, ten of the twelve original disciples of Jesus Christ became martyrs. (The other two were Judas Iscariot, who hanged himself, and the apostle, John, who died a natural death). "Matthias" took Judas Iscariot's place and "was numbered with the eleven apostles" (Acts 1:25-26 NKJV). "*My* gospel," which Paul lived and died for, is one of power. It was that gospel, of which Paul was not ashamed, and he declared it to be "the power of God unto salvation for everyone who believes" (Rom. 1:16b NKJV).

To preach the gospel is to preach the cross of Christ; it is to preach the blood of Christ shed for our sin; it is to preach the power of the resurrection of Christ by His endless life, enabling us to live in total victory; and it is to preach His anticipated second coming. We are reminded that by the ". . . preaching of the cross . . . is the power of God" (1 Cor. 1:18 AV). Could it be that the absence of a full declaration of the gospel from our western pulpits is impeding the release of God's power that we so desperately need? For over half a century, the Christian world has evidenced, through the simplicity and fullness of the gospel declared in Billy Graham's preaching, the power of the gospel by the Spirit to lead men and women to repentance and faith in Jesus Christ.

One memorable night, as I recollect over fifty years later, Billy Graham came to the pulpit and began to describe the events that led to his conversion. In his mid-teens at the time, sports, especially baseball, may have become a passion, but he was instead arrested by the claims of Christ to run in the spiritual race of races. "'Come to Jesus while there's time,' cried Mordecai F. Ham, and quiet penitents walked slowly down the shavings trial to faith and hope and God. They reached the closing verse when Billy Frank, barely sixteen—said, 'I'm going down.'"[26]

He then proceeded to describe the preacher responsible for his conversion by saying that he was in Madison Square Garden that evening. The crowd waited with intense anticipation finally to see the man who was instrumental in leading Billy Graham to Christ. Finally, he asked the evangelist to please stand to his feet, and Graham introduced him as Mordecai Ham.[27] My eyes scanned the massive audience for a glimpse of this distinguished guest. As he stood to his feet, everyone recognized that God had used him to give the world the next great soul winner. Through His faithful servant, God had, by His grace, produced a new generation's servant of God. Billy Graham preached to more people face to face and led more to Christ through his total ministries than any other in recorded history to date. We need to realize that because of one convert, no matter how many weeks we preach for that result, the gospel may reach another Billy Graham, who also changed his world. All my weeks in the Garden in New York were worth that moment.

That New York Crusade was a hands-on learning experience. I watched every step of the program, the song and solo content, and then the message, all of which were, it seemed to me, choreographed to perfection. Yes, it was planned by man, but it was orchestrated by the Holy Spirit. Everything flowed toward the message and altar call, which took many minutes to process, as hundreds, if not thousands some nights, streamed to a massive altar area. Counsellors fell in stride beside each seeker, sharing and praying with them, registering their decision, and leaving them with meaningful literature.

Now the memory of those days and the lessons learned replay on a regular basis as I still work to lift Christ higher and minimize in myself the hindrances of the flesh that can so subtly inhibit the preaching of "*my* gospel."

This intense learning experience at the Garden provided a lasting template or pattern for my ministry. From that crusade, I could trace workable formats for today's changing world to present the same unchanging gospel. In declaring "*my* gospel," we, who do so must be mindful that we live in continually changing cultures and times. This may require modification in presentation of the message, but it must not dilute, modify, or change the forthright and lucid declaration of a comprehensive gospel through which a seeking sinner may find the forgiving Saviour.

The time at Madison Square Garden was quickly coming to an end. Those lessons learned at the Garden resembled for me something of how the apostle Paul may have felt sitting at the feet of Gamaliel (Acts 22:3).

## A Super Finish and the New Beginning

My final college year began with a difference; I was in the senior class. This status brought behavioural responsibility. We were being observed by the other students. This year's academic load was heavier, plus all of the seniors wanted to make better grades to balance any deficiency in our earlier years.

January saw everyone returning to college following the Christmas break. As this year's graduating class, we were excited to prepare for graduation, which would be held the first week in April. Dresses were measured for the ladies and suits for the men, graduation outfits we had waited weeks to see and that actually arrived only hours before the event. Final exams were intense, not because they were more difficult but because of extra assignments and less study time available to do them. The pressure was really on us, but we were on the home stretch.

During my final exams, reports, essays, and rehearsals, of all things imaginable, I succumbed to measles and had to be quarantined in a blacked-out room for several days. Finally, when graduation day arrived, I was certified safe and remained composed in my debilitated state and masqueraded as healthy in my new "grad garb" as I graduated.

An added personal blessing for me was that it had been confirmed that upon graduation, because of my eight years of ministry before and during Bible college, and having satisfied the Examining Ordination Board, that they would ordain me in Saskatoon the following day.

In addition to that unprecedented gesture, it was also confirmed that, as a result of my continuing contact with the man who wrote my recommendation to the college on the back of a used envelope, following my graduation, Evangelist John Wesley White had invited me to become his associate evangelist. I would be working with him in Britain. My super Bible college days were over, and a new ministry was beginning.

The flashback of the vignette from childhood to ordination played in my mind and lasted but a second as I walked to the pulpit.

When the African weeknight service concluded, I asked myself, *how did I get here?* And, *what am I doing?*

The message concluded with a prayer of opportunity for those willing to accept Christ or those with personal needs to respond. In respect to the massive audience, the altar area was woefully inadequate. All we could do was to invite seekers to stand where they were for prayer. Conservatively, about 40 percent of the crowd stood and prayed an audible prayer.

This review has highlighted some of the forks in the road that moulded me as a boy, teenager, and adult and has traced the pattern of my life that has, in sixty years of ministry, fulfilled my every aspiration and has allowed me to be God's servant for Jesus' sake.

# 2

# BRITISH EVANGELISM

As I completed college and was ordained by age twenty-one and launched immediately into ministry in Britain, a great sense of achievement welled up in my spirit. In my absence, the family textile business had continued to grow and would require any free time I might be available to give to it.

My beginning ministry in Britain with John Wesley White brought back memories of my teenage years with the team, but this time it was a major project. My new status as an associate now entailed wearing different ministry hats as circumstances dictated. Being a rookie evangelist working with seasoned ministers of many mainline denominations presented to me a major learning curve. Days were filled with nonstop activity. I preached sometimes in a little chapel to a few believers or up the spiralling cast iron stairs to an Anglican pulpit and addressing a small congregation in a massive architectural edifice.

A major part of my job description was to do advance committee work with churches wishing to unite for a citywide crusade, perhaps a year or more in advance. In different British cities, the events would be scheduled as spokes in a wheel, designed as citywide evangelistic thrusts that would, in addition to reaching those communities for Christ, raise awareness of the bigger picture for major future mega Billy Graham crusades that would become the hub of the wheel. This peripheral evangelism resulted in greater support of those mega-crusades as hundreds of coaches plied the spokes of the proverbial wheel, emptying thousands into the vast hub arenas of Harringay and Earls Court Billy Graham events.

Since the advance support crusades would be launched at different times, it entailed traveling on a regular basis throughout the country to each city, assuring that timely progress was being made by each subcommittee as it related to prayer, publicity, venue, program, and finances. At any given time, there could be five or more crusades in the planning stages over twelve or more months. On some occasions it was necessary to work with up to four yearly planners.

The crusade was always the central event, the hub of the wheel, so to speak, with many spokes emanating in the form of prayer meetings, crusade committees, public school assemblies, and ladies' and men's meetings. Executive noon business luncheon meetings were an extension of ministry in factories. Leadership of this dimension of evangelism was given by Martin Higginbottom, who founded Outreach to Industry. Through this ministry, major industrial plants opened their doors, or more accurately, their factory floors and outside work yards, for the gospel to be preached to their employees. Often we spoke from the deck of a truck or a low-bed trailer for thirty or forty minutes at a time, which usually culminated in many people surrendering their lives to Jesus Christ.

On some occasions where management preferred, they allowed their workers or staff to be witnessed to at their own work stations. This method could require a number of work days in order to speak to each person. Several of Britain's car manufacturers were also sympathetic to this approach to benefit their employees.

Upper and middle management in large industrial plants often had private dining rooms. This would also be an avenue for brief ministry during or after the meal. These presentations were always challenging and Christ-centered and provided the hearer with a clear gospel message and an invitation to respond to the claims of Christ on their lives.

Many major companies of domestic name food processors, engineering, and electronics welcomed this type of ministry for their employees. Statistics at the time indicated that employees with a personal commitment to Christ had a high standard of work ethic, often out-producing other employees. This single fact made this overture to management most attractive.

Through contacts of the team's ministry, a number of distinguished individuals who were industrial titans, military leaders, university chancellors, and theologians stood with us and lent us the influence of their positions to the overall success of these crusades. Some of them chaired the local crusade committee or were masters of ceremonies in the crusade venues.

One such contact who benefited the evangelistic thrust beyond measure was J. Arthur Rank, who then owned the Odeon theatre chain throughout Britain. He gave us full freedom to present the gospel in the theatres. Sometimes this permitted us to speak for a few minutes before the movie, during the intermission, or after the show and enabled us to present a concise gospel message, usually in not more than six or seven minutes. Anyone who wished to respond could meet later a team member in the lobby. Even though we preached in churches at every opportunity that only represented a minimum percentage of our ministry time. Daytime evangelism substantially exceeded all church-related ministries.

Typically a day would begin at four or five in the morning to share the gospel with the sanitation department's employees. Twenty minutes before they left the depot to sweep the city streets, we could present the claims of Christ to them.

Often we were allowed to speak to school children during their assembly between eight and nine each morning. It was left to the discretion of principals whether to permit such bookings. In those days, after presenting a complete, brief gospel, we would close the presentation in a very meaningful prayer of commitment. Following a gospel presentation and if needed, a room would be made available for prayer or counselling. Depending on the location of a school and the time of its assembly, sometimes it would be possible to speak in two or three assemblies in one morning.

In the afternoon, we finalized preparation for the program of the crusade service. This required details for each part of the service. We would interview and confirm as available for a particular evening service those who would participate as speakers, choir members, and singers and players of special musical numbers. We would meet visiting guest testimonials and local dignitaries, who needed to be introduced, like the lord mayor or government officials, at the venue and brief them as to their part in the program.

Evangelist John Wesley White always brought the gospel message. He was an incredibly energetic individual and on occasion, accepted more speaking engagements than seemed practical, sometimes cutting it very close to be on time to preach. More than once, as I was ready to introduce him, he would arrive, having just preached at an earlier, close-by meeting.

Hearing John preach was a not-to-be-forgotten experience. He was anointed in his spirit, articulate in his delivery, and very human in his approach. I traveled with him for about six years, and while we worked, prayed, and preached together, he became the single greatest mentor of my ministry life. During this time, I learned many of the finer points that made the man. Personal, private prayer was a vital, intrinsic, and foundational part of his daily ministry. Bible reading for his own edification, apart from reading to build a message, was a must for him. John Wesley White practised what he preached and often reminded me that as gospel preachers, we can only remain at the cutting edge of our calling by consistently doing certain things. White took time to do personal evangelism each day and instilled in me, by his example, that we can only stand in front of an audience and preach with passion to the individual heart, if we have developed perceptive and gentle one-on-one witnessing skills. In this way we develop a love and concern for each lost soul to whom we witness.

For this reason, John would disappear for lengthy periods while he took one side of a row of houses, knock on each door, and invite them to the crusade or present the love of Christ to them. On one such occasion, he knocked on a door that was opened by an elderly man who had recently buried his wife. As John witnessed to him at length, sharing with him the love of God and the gift of God that was available to him, he finally led the man in a salvation prayer. The man accepted Christ as his personal Saviour. Within the next day or so, John returned to visit and encourage him in his newfound faith. After knocking on the door several times with no response, a neighbour next door said, "He passed away yesterday." This is the lesson of importunity in soul winning. It was this ingredient in John's gospel preaching that enabled him to preach to thousands as though he was speaking into the heart of an individual.

Every afternoon during crusades, John would closet himself for many hours to be alone with God to build and fine tune every point and sub-point of his message. His message was always relevant, always current, and often included illustrations and news items from that day's newspaper headlines. He worked tirelessly to reinforce each gospel point, driving it home as his message progressed to a preaching masterpiece uplifting Christ as the answer to man's total depravity.

Generally as he prepared a message, it would begin with a blank sheet of white paper about sixteen inches square. When finished, it would be completely covered in boxed points, illustrations, Scripture references, and newspaper or literary quotations. In some ways it resembled a sketch of a brick wall each brick strategically placed for its fullest effect. John would sit on the platform reviewing this paper until I announced him to preach, at which time he would drop it to the floor, move to the podium, and begin his message extemporaneously. On occasion I would pick it up and follow his preaching, watching as his current point concurred with his boxed notes; the two dovetailed like two interlocking pieces of a puzzle.

Occasionally the "human" side of this man of God would become transparent, and we would enjoy a good joke. One such occasion occurred when a lady approached him in a crusade and volunteered to share a solo in a future meeting. She assured him this would be a real contribution to the event. He referred the lady to me, saying that was my department and I would see to the details. She assured me on all points, and I approved her part and gave her a date to sing. The evening came, and she was there in her finery. I announced her to sing, and she floated to the podium and microphones, only to give the most horrendous rendition of a beloved gospel song. After the program, she presented herself to the evangelist, who was himself a musician and singer, thanking him for the opportunity to minister to such an adoring audience and breathlessly awaiting his accolades. Standing nearby, I awaited John's response with bated breath. It came without hesitation and went something like this: "Madam, it was just out of this world," which said it all without saying anything.

As my ministry load increased, the family business saw less of me. It continued to provide for my financial support, which allowed me to minister in almost a fulltime capacity without charge to the crusades. It also provided me with much-needed transportation in the form of a vehicle.

While working on the "Ringing Barking" crusade in the run up to a future Billy Graham crusade, and while using my Northern Ireland registered vehicle in greater London, on one unforgettable day there was a dramatic aside to my normal activities. As the custom was, I was always billeted with a local family who supported the advance planning of their local crusade. Over many weeks of accommodation with them, we developed good relationships. When I was able, I would attend their assembly on Sunday mornings.

On this memorable occasion, as I went about the normal activities to produce an event of this nature, the senior gentleman of the home where I resided and a leading elder in his assembly accompanied me as I drove into the city of London. During the course of the day, as I drove the car we fellowshipped and enjoyed lunch. I also made the various calls necessary to fulfill my appointments for the day. In the mid-afternoon, as we were about to return to Barking and while waiting at a red traffic light in a center lane of heavy traffic, our conversation was pleasant and engaging. Suddenly, and seemingly from nowhere, my car was surrounded by heavily armed police, one of whom was knocking vigorously on my driver's window. As I rolled down my car window, he said, as I recall, "You are surrounded. When this light changes, move very, very slowly to your right, as we will hold the traffic in the inside lanes to allow you to park around the corner. You are completely surrounded by police; do not make a sudden move." I did exactly as he said.

As I looked across the car at my senior conservative brother, he was ashen white. Seconds later, we were both pulled out and spread-eagled against opposite sides of the car, face down on the roof and vigorously searched. Without explanation, we were bundled into separate police vehicles and driven at breakneck speeds with sirens screaming for what seemed to me to resemble an eternity until we reached New Scotland Yard. He and I each enjoyed the dubious distinction of our own private interrogation rooms while my officer demanded answers to questions, for which I could provide no satisfaction. I would later learn that my friend in his own cubicle was experiencing a similar process and was equally mystified. The afternoon passed like a month, and late evening brought no respite to the relentless barrage of rapid-fire questions.

One of my greatest concerns was for my senior friend, who appeared to be in a state of shock, and how he was coping with it I was certain, in his conservative assembly life, a situation that he would never before have encountered. By now he would no doubt think that, under the guise of being an evangelist and living under his roof, he in fact had been harbouring a felon or worse, not to mention what subliminal damage may have been done to his impressionable teenage sons, each of whom have now become successful in their respective careers and cornerstones of character in their communities.

The interrogation became a blur for me as the hours passed, with no food or drink, and officers working in relay without respite. The torrent of questions was relentless: "Where are you from? Why are you here? What are you doing? Who is your friend? Where do you live? Where does he live? What does he do? Why is he with you? What do you have in common? Who are your accomplices?" So the questions continued.

Then my vehicle became the focal point; its ownership. It was not in my name but in the company's. It was not registered in England: "Why? Although it is a new car, why has it been repainted? Why was the number-plate switched when the car was repainted?" My honest answers never satisfied them. The truth was that it was a new car, it was never repainted, and the number-plate was original to the car and had never been switched. The plot thickened, and I became fatigued, which added to their frustration. Half a day into a mind-boggling nightmare, it began to emerge that they believed my vehicle had been used in a major crime and was now being disassembled and dissected in their garage under a forensic microscope.

Although I knew I was innocent, my mind raced through my own list of questions: *What of my friend? Can he physically handle this? What will it do to our relationship and the crusade he is involved with me in? What about my own long-term ministry? Is this its end, while it is just beginning? How could I be so foolish not to know my new car has been repainted?* I almost began to mistrust my own cognitive ability.

The endless barrage of questions without having the answers they wanted left me at my wit's end. Without changing expression, somehow between answering them, my inner self, the spiritual man, talked to God. I breathed a silent thought prayer: "Please, God, show them we are not suspects. Show me how to handle this mess. Give me direction. Help! Help!"

In the later evening, as they hammered away at me in an attempt to justify, in my thinking, what must be the beginning of World War III, in which we were emerging as crucial pawns in their legal chess game, I was nearing exhaustion. Suddenly, I had a eureka moment. No, it was not I who had a eureka moment—this was the Holy Spirit. It was a God moment! In a moment, I was lucid, my mind fresh and clear for the first time in hours, and I knew exactly what to say.

I interrupted the interrogator and said, "Since you will not believe anything I have told you, if I could produce an independent third-party witness who could corroborate my movements and activities in the period of time in question, would that satisfy you and allow our release?" To this he replied, "Yes!" I then told him that in the boot (trunk) of my car there was yesterday's edition of a *London Daily* that carried a story that would exonerate us. This article detailed my work in relation to the crusades, which would ultimately feed into the larger proposed Billy Graham mega-crusade.

At that moment I felt something of what the disciples must have felt as Christ assured them that when they would be brought before kings and rulers, he would give them a mouth and wisdom to speak, "and your *interrogator* will not be able to resist" (Luke 21:12-15).

The simple reason the vehicle presented such a problem for them in relation to re-painting and the switched number plate was this: When our company purchased my cream-coloured car, it also purchased an identical one for my father on the same date, except in the colour green, and it had a number plate with identical numbers except for the last digit. Both cars were registered in the company's name.

When they checked the registration of my vehicle with the licensing department in Northern Ireland, it was done with a phone call. When the Londoner's accent said "cream" car, the Irish understood, "green" and gave the green car registration number as mine, which meant the British police believed the plates had been switched or the car repainted cream from green. They constantly called me by my father's name and refused to call me by my own name. All of this confusion arose from the English Irish accent that neither party clearly understood.

After my suggestion about a third-party witness and the article, he retrieved the newspaper, read the article a couple of times, and moments later, we were released with a tongue-in-cheek apology.

The reason for our unceremonious detention was part of a nationwide sweep for the perpetrators of what was at the time Britain's largest heist. Even as this was being written, Ronnie

Briggs, considered by many the mastermind, was still making headlines relating to his incarceration.

For more than fifty years, numerous books have been written and documentaries and movies made in an endless effort to portray more fully the Great Mail Train Robbery. At that time, for our moment of notoriety, we were seen by New Scotland Yard as major players in what would be for decades to come one of their major cases.

The drive to my friend's home late that night was almost silent. Confused and exhausted, we were relieved to be free of our prison rooms and to breathe again as free men. Also, we understand that the event of our detention and release made the press.

For the ensuing years of ministry in Britain, at any time it became difficult for me to penetrate a reluctant principal's hesitation in allowing me to speak to his student assembly, my perceived involvement in the Great Mail Train Robbery always opened that door of opportunity for me.

The senior brother, who was my un-witting "accomplice" that day, has remained my lifetime friend, as has his son, Peter, for over half a century. His very conservative assembly, which I sometimes attended, became a second place of fellowship for me. Sometimes I was permitted to share in their meetings, which, if nothing else, attested to my exoneration in his mind.

# 3

# A Fork in the Road

The significance of God's leading with each step of a believer's life cannot be overestimated. The intent of this chapter is to use personal examples of how, with divine intervention, God arrested me and spoke into my spirit at major junctures, each representing a crucial state for my future.

It was on a relaxed autumn day and after a church Sunday dinner early in September in Ireland that I was interrupted by a phone call that would forever change the direction of my life. I was surprised to hear the voice of A. D. Marshall (affectionately known as "AD"), my former dean of the Full Gospel Bible Institute in Eston, Saskatchewan, Canada, from which I had graduated in 1958. After a few pleasantries, he asked me to consider coming to the college in October as their guest convention speaker.

Remembering that they scheduled their speakers a couple of years in advance, I asked, "For what year?" To this he replied, "This year—in six weeks!" Then I asked, "Why the invitation at such short notice, and why me?" He replied that I was their second choice. The speaker they had booked had just passed away. As he shared the circumstances of the tragedy, I asked if I would know him, to which he replied, "Yes, he was a former student, Louis Peskett, married to Shirley Mills." I remember asking how many children they had, to which he responded, "Two fine boys."

Louis Peskett was the popular leader and executive director of Youth for Christ in Edmonton.[28] He was also the founder of Frontier Lodge at Nordeg, Alberta, a summer camping program providing leadership for young people needing healthy Christian principled guidance. The camp also included hiking, mountain climbing, and wilderness camping experiences. There, for many summers in the demanding program, he and Shirley worked side by side. Scores of teens, and especially teens in trouble, found help and salvation at this camp.

While leading a group of campers on a mountain climb in the Canadian Rockies to an area known as the Box Canyon in proximity to the camp, the tragedy occurred. Louis was struck on the temple by a small falling rock. As he continued climbing for some time, he became unwell and received assistance from other capable climbers. It was eventually necessary to improvise a stretcher for him and climb down the mountain to an ambulance to take him to the hospital. Everything possible was done to save him. But one week later, God, in His wisdom, took Louis to be with Himself. Several thousand people attended his memorial service, and during the altar call, substantial numbers of people responded for salvation.

After such devastating news, it was pointless to continue the earlier conversation about the convention. I asked him to call me the following day for an answer. My intention was to pray about it and see how I could fit it into my already heavy schedule. On my bedroom dressing table was a travel wallet containing tickets for the tropical Southern Canary Islands off West Africa. That trip was scheduled to end on the day the convention was to begin, half a world away in the frozen Canadian north.

As I was preoccupied with sadness over the news, the rest of Sunday was a blur. I searched my bookcase for old Bible college yearbooks with pictures of Louis and Shirley. My mind raced ahead with emotions and mental pictures of my first recollections of this couple. On occasion they returned to Eston for special events. I had always enjoyed his sincere preaching or sharing with the students in devotions and Shirley's ministry in song.

What was usually a pleasant Sunday-evening meal with family, was now, for me, solitude. As my family conversed, I escaped in my mind to memories of happier times. After muttering something that must have sounded to them as a feeble excuse about turning in for the night, I went to my room. It seemed best for me to be alone with my thoughts, settle my emotions, pray about this travel change, and try to sleep. Strategizing was useless. The flesh said, "Go to the tropics!" The Spirit said, "Go to the frozen north!" Prayer didn't seem to work, mostly because it was flavoured with my carnal preference. Why go from the mild climate of the UK to freeze in the winter in Eston, Saskatchewan, when I could go down to the tropics for a warm and pleasant rest?

Wrestling with these choices frustrated and exhausted me, and in exasperation, I prepared to go to sleep. Sleep usually came quickly, but not then. Twisting and turning, I told God how I thought it ought to go, which only heightened the drama, and fatigue finally induced sleep.

Suddenly, in the *wee hours* of the morning, sleep vanished as a soft, brilliant light flooded the room—but not from my night light. This was a different experience, a light from nowhere! But it was accompanied by a warm, good feeling. A presence filled the room—God's presence. It brought to my mind the incident when God spoke to Moses about evacuating the children of Israel from Egypt when He promised in Exodus 33:14, "My Presence will go with you, and I will give you rest" (NIV). I heard no voice. Suddenly the room was dark again. What was this about? Was it the emotion of yesterday? Was it too much food? No, this was God doing a new thing just for me. As I lay down, sleep vanished again. An hour or more passed while the silent rural night was interrupted by the town clock chiming in the distance to mark the passing hour.

A night table with a reading lamp and my travel wallet with tickets for the trip to West Africa were at my bedside. The table also held my Thompson chain reference Bible, which I purchased sixteen years earlier when I began preaching in earnest at thirteen. Having traveled with me to hundreds of meetings and attended every Bible college class, it was an old and trusted friend. My Bible was heavily underlined in multi-coloured markings as special passages stood out during my personal study or were highlighted for preaching purposes. It had withstood Irish open-air winters, helped lead many to the Saviour, and witnessed countless theological debates by first-year students who thought they knew all the answers.

*The Bible, that's it; the Bible—read the Bible; that will help!* I thought. As I reached across the bed in the now-darkened room, my hand felt for the Bible. As I pulled it to me in the darkness, it fell open on the bed, where my jabbing fingers poked the well-worn and fragile pages. When I turned on the swivel light, a brilliant beam fell on me, the disobedient Jonah. *Read where it opened,* I thought.

As the story of Jonah unfolded, I was reminded that God told him to go northeast to Nineveh. Instead, he went down to Joppa, found a ship going to Tarshish, paid the fare, and in wilful disobedience, went in the opposite direction to that city. So began his journey of disobedience to God and away from the presence of the Lord. *Enough!* I thought. In the opposite direction from where God was calling me to minister, my heart desired to go down from the presence of the Lord. Immediately I came to my senses. "Never!" I exclaimed.

Following this holy encounter with God, I fell into a sound sleep. Upon awaking, I reworked my travel plans that allowed the convention to fit my new schedule. Now everything was going God's way instead of my way. This choice proved to be a significant event, a fork in the road, an important juncture in my life where God supernaturally intervened. Since then, and in similar circumstances in which I had to make major decisions that could have adversely affected me, God has intervened in my life. In retrospect, had I decided to go to the Canary Islands, my whole future would have been built on God's second best for my life and ministry. Later I will speak more about a fork in the road and God's intervention.

At the time of this call to Eston's convention, I was heavily involved in ministry in the UK and carried the additional load of the family business. The textile embroidery trade was thriving, expansion was continuous, demand exceeded supply, and on a regular basis, employees were being hired. The factory was rebuilt and extended three times, with a second factory a few miles away from the first one. For a time a third factory was leased to accommodate the crushing demand for production. For long periods and in rotation, employees worked two or three eight-hour shifts. Everything was prospering.

As I re-scheduled some meetings, it allowed me to attend the convention and to make arrangements to be absent from management in the factory for a brief ten-day period, things came smoothly together. I had come from the tropics via London to the frozen plains of Saskatchewan in one day. What a shock to my system! What a tiring journey as I flew from London's Heathrow Airport to Saskatoon, Saskatchewan! Then I experienced a hair-raising trip to Eston on *skating-rink* roads. The driver, Lorne Pritchard, my former Bible college teacher, said that upon arrival, "We're going straight on the platform!" This information, together with my exhausted body, blew my mind as I was frantically trying to format the message for the assembled crowd awaiting us.

We made it! We were late, but we arrived safely. Until we arrived, the audience had an extended worship service. Strangely, Glen McLean, the college Principal and good friend, introduced me humorously as "a former graduate and (coming from ten days in the tropics) the only black Canadian with an Irish accent."

The five-day conference went by quickly, and God honoured His Word with a precious refreshing and great fellowship. Although I was deeply saddened with Louis' death I felt really grateful to have been chosen to stand in for him. Eleven years earlier I had been a *first-year* student at the same institution. Now I was an ordained minister and speaker to the students, which gave me a sense of accomplishment.

Close to the end of these meetings, AD came to me with his usual demure look, holding a sheaf of loose papers. Pushing them toward me he announced that, as I had preached during the week, pastors visiting the convention had come to him inquiring about the possibility of having a meeting with me in their assembly. Remembering my promised return to the UK within ten days, the lengthy list raised many questions in my mind. "How do I handle this development?" The flesh recoiled as the filled pages were turned one by one to reveal a proposed schedule of several months, but the Spirit seemed to prompt me with a good feeling inside me toward acceptance.

I recalled God's supernatural intervention that had brought me to this point in my life and ministry. I was determined not to have another restless night so soon. I promised to provide a decision the next day, committed it to the Lord, and had a good night's sleep.

The next day brought a new freshness and readiness to commit myself to the impromptu schedule. This time it was not about me or my wants but about God and His will for me.

The pastors were contacted, and suitable itineraries were promptly arranged. On this assignment, a good friend from my earlier years in Canada, Wally Schlamp, made a car available for me to use. I believe it was an older model Dodge. It served me well, never broke down, and held to the road like a Mack truck. Nightly in various churches during the week, with special meetings in each church over the weekends, meetings were scheduled. In this unexpected development in my ministry, God honoured His Word, and our team felt good about the choice to follow His leading.

As we visited with Saskatchewan churches, several weeks passed. Then we went to Alberta. One of the Albertan churches was Seventh Avenue Full Gospel Church at which several days of meetings were scheduled, beginning on a Sunday morning. Billeting was arranged in the comfortable home of a church elder, Wally Sczebel. He and his wife, Rosanne, had Sunday school responsibilities. They explained that they would be leaving the home early and had arranged for me to be picked up.

Early on that snowy subzero morning I had a stand-up breakfast and eagerly awaited my transportation. The doorbell rang, and a young lady announced, "I'm Shirley Peskett, and I have come to take you to church." I was lost in an ocean of memories—first from Bible College, then on that fateful Sunday in the UK when I received the call about speaking at a convention because of a tragic accident where their speaker (her husband, Louis) had died.

"Yes, yes," I stuttered to Shirley, and in that fleeting second, I had traveled around the world and computed a million thoughts. Here in front of me for the first time was the smiling lady who weeks earlier had lost her husband and the father of their two boys. *What do I say? How should I respond?* I thought. Somehow I greeted her and then attempted to sympathize, and we were on our way. As we got into the car, Shirley introduced the boys: Alden, nine years old, tall, mature for his age, and with a striking resemblance to his father; and Bill, six, personable, with a blonde crew cut and full of chatter, but with features more like his mother.

Bill's first words to me, as a total stranger, were, "Who was the first person to get to the moon?" I pleaded ignorance, and a rapid fire answer shot from the back seat, "Lady drivers—they can hit anything!" In a panic, the older brother tried to get control of the runaway conversation and tried to settle down his brother and get him to act more politely to me, the new preacher. But it was to no avail.

The morning service moved smoothly; then came my turn to preach the message. As I was preaching, I became preoccupied and was reliving the events of the past months that brought me to this moment. The significance of that phone call, the indecision like Jonah about where to go, and now the extended preaching schedule instead of a prompt return home filled my mind. As the message progressed, these thoughts demanded answers. My emotions were disturbing my train of thought as I noticed, halfway down the left side of the church, Shirley with her two young boys. She continued her work with Alberta Youth for Christ. During the course of ministry, Alberta Youth for Christ invited me to Edmonton, and after the morning service at Shirley's church, I was invited to her home for Sunday lunch.

After we left the church, I heard more jokes from Bill. Within a few minutes, we arrived at their comfortable home. Shirley's mother, a gentle, warm, and regal lady, was there and greeted me. As the ladies prepared the meal, the boys and I visited in the front room. Soon we were called for lunch.

After the blessing was given and the food was being passed, Bill asked me, "When's your birthday?"

To this I replied, "March!"

Not satisfied with the answer, he asked another question: "What date in March?"

His mother and grandma tried to change the subject, but without success. Eventually, as Shirley was serving other dishes, I answered with the date. Silence reined; everything stopped. *What did I say?* I asked myself.

In a flash, before anyone could speak, Bill exclaimed, "That's my dad's birthday!" Conversation resumed, the enjoyable repast continued, and things were back on track. But the coincidence of birthdays had not escaped Bill's attention. He continued by asking, "Are you going to marry my mother?"

Fortunately for Shirley and me, she was in the kitchen and didn't hear that mind-blowing question. Alden's only reaction was, "B-I-L-L!" The afternoon passed pleasantly, and we all left the house to return to church for the evening service. Now I had another opportunity to attempt to preach in a more lucid manner.

God was blessing the people and re-igniting my own spirit for evangelism and teaching. I could sense a fresh anointing for ministry was being released in me. Memories of the years of evangelism in the UK as an associate evangelist to John Wesley White, a Canadian from Pangman and then an associate of Billy Graham, flashed before me. JWW, as he was affectionately known, and who was initially instrumental in my coming to Full Gospel Bible Institute as a student in 1955, persuaded me that the Institute, now Eston College, was the right place for me.

The ten-day preaching spot was now months behind me, and pressure was building from home and business to return soon. What began as a cordial telephone call from my father about how things were and when I would return changed abruptly when he heard me say there were several weeks left of ministry. Again he pointedly asked how quickly I would return to the business. My answer was being framed to say I would pray about it and get back to him soon. Then I heard his *business* voice say, "Are you coming back to run this business, or are you going to fool around with ministry?"

My intended response evaporated as I heard other words fall from my lips into the mouthpiece of the phone. Once I spoke them, they were gone, never to be retrieved. "I'm going to fool around with ministry!"

His response came with equal rapidity, "This business is for you; I don't need more than I have. If that's your answer, the factories will be closed now," and that was just what he did. The factories are long since dilapidated; the roaring business declined with the blending of automation and computer technology, and after a few short years became nonexistent. But my ministry continued and still flourishes. God's ways are not our ways; His ways are best.

The scheduled ministry continued uninterrupted through a Canadian winter, while I, as a British driver, unfamiliar with snowy conditions other than to face an overnight snowfall that would be cleared by the following noon, pressed on with the itinerary. Between preaching points I slipped and slid my way in the old Dodge. On one occasion, just outside of Calgary, Alberta, while filling up with fuel, by chance I happened to ask the attendant, "How far is Surrey, British Columbia?" He replied, "About eleven hours in good weather." It was the middle of winter, and the weather was *not* good.

Although it was early morning, it seemed that my British driving skills were no match for the skating-rink roads to get me to the church on time for an eight o'clock service. The hours passed as the Dodge protested, never having before been pushed to its limits. My hands were locked onto the steering wheel in a knuckle white grip. Hours into the driving marathon, I felt a sense of fatigue, and because of the urge to sleep, I kept closing my eyelids. In an attempt to reverse the urge to sleep, although it was freezing outside, I opened the windows on both sides of the car. Taking water from a bottle, I washed my face around my eyes, and it promptly froze and required me to make a sudden pit stop.

Plowing on again as fast as conditions would allow on a perfectly straight stretch where the distance seemed to bring the road to a vanishing point on the horizon, I saw, in the distance, what seemed to be an animal on the side of the road. I got closer, and as the form became clearer, I soon realized that it was the back of a man walking west. *Just what I need, and an answer to a prayer that I hadn't thought to pray about someone who needs a lift in my direction!* were thoughts that suddenly filled my mind. Guiding the vehicle to a halt without losing control, I slid it to a stop about forty metres ahead of him. As he reached the car, I offered him a lift to his destination, perhaps a hundred miles west, for which he appeared grateful.

*He is just who I needed to keep me awake,* I thought as we chatted freely. He was a First Nations person from a local reserve. This new arrangement of driver and passenger seemed to be working. With the engaging conversation, I was wide awake and able to make better time. The miles were clicking past; he was a real asset to me. Then, after perhaps thirty minutes, he suddenly asked me to stop. He opened his door and began to get out. Knowing that his destination was still sixty miles ahead, I thought perhaps I had somehow offended him. "No," he said, "but I sure don't need to get where I'm going nearly as fast as you need to get where you're going." He thanked me, closed the door, and continued walking. Obviously my skiing Dodge had made him feel uncomfortable.

Making great time, perhaps facilitated by the glassy road conditions, the Dodge pulled into the People's Church parking lot in Surrey in the middle of the worship service, allowing me to begin preaching almost immediately.

While on the West Coast, I continued my ministry through Washington and Oregon. It was in Portland, Oregon, where my path crossed with a dear friend, Pastor K. R. Iverson, affectionately known as Brother Dick. We met when he did evangelism in Ireland just before I came to Bible college in Canada. On that occasion,

God really used him in the rural community of Maguiresbridge and Lisnaskea. It was in that rural area that the venue for his ministry was outgrown, and a disused wood-products factory warehouse provided accommodation for large-capacity crowds each night. That was a sovereign move of God, with thousands of lives being impacted and delivered.

During those days, Brother Dick's visa for the UK expired and could not be extended quickly enough for him to continue ministering each evening. He had to leave the country. As we prayed and discussed the crisis, there was a eureka moment. Since the venue was not far from the Ulster/Eire border, it was decided that he would go out of the UK, across the border, and preach to the capacity crowd each night over the sound system by landline telephone. As he prayed over the phone, the altar calls were dramatic, with many converted to Christ and healed.

During our Portland meeting, Brother Dick pastored a large congregation. He invited me to pastor his college and career group, which was the size of a small assembly. Although that was only a part-time ministry, I had the opportunity to work in recreational sales. This was a fun aside from ministry that allowed me to work with people and minister to them while helping them buy their dream vehicles.

While working for this Christian owner, I experienced my next major fork in the road. On a sunny afternoon while walking between the rows of recreational vehicles, I felt a distinct sense of the Holy Spirit's presence. His presence had often touched my spirit in the past, but what surprised me was that this was in a public business location. When one keeps the lines of communication open to God, one should never be surprised to hear from Him, regardless of the location. By the cares of one's life, un-confessed sin, or unresolved conflict, communication lines can block or silence the gentle promptings of the Holy Spirit.

In that special moment of God's touch, my sense was to do something that could not have been further from my mind and that I had no inclination to do. Without customers on the lot at that time, I returned to the administrative building where the owner was at his desk. Chatting generally about business for a moment, I related what I believed to be my Holy Spirit encounter. My boss, Paul Kipers Sr., was a successful business man, a lay pastor/preacher, and sensitive to the leading of the Spirit. I shared with him that I felt a strong impulse to leave Portland for a few days and make a road trip to Vancouver, Canada, although I had absolutely no natural reason to do so and there was no one there I knew to contact. He immediately said, "That sounds like God speaking to you. You should take time off and go now." He continued to encourage me to leave by saying, "Go and listen for His voice; He will reveal each step as you travel."

At his insistence, early the next morning I was on my way back to Canada. Each time I stopped for fuel or to eat, I wondered if that was the place or if those around me were those God wanted me to connect with, but there was nothing, so I kept driving. After about eight hours of driving and as I neared the Canadian border, a name flashed into my mind. It was of a couple who many years earlier had invited me, as a stray Irish student in Bible college with nowhere to go, to come to their home for Christmas. Somehow my recollection was that they had moved to the Vancouver area. I stopped at a roadside pay phone (before cell phone technology), and directory assistance gave me their number, which I called.

The phone rang a couple of times, and there they were: Gordon and Mabel Mitchell, as warm and friendly as I had known them to be. After a moment's chat, they quickly invited me to stay with them. Soon we were visiting together around their kitchen table, catching up on the many years apart. We were lost in happy memories and fellowshipped until midnight, when it was time for us to go to bed. After the three hundred-mile drive, my room, with its comfortable bed, was welcoming, and I soon fell into a deep sleep. Little did I know that before morning my ordered life was about to change again, forever.

Sometime during the early hours of the morning, it happened. I comfortably awoke out of a deep sleep. As I stirred and opened my eyes, the room that was dark was now flooded with the most brilliant, warm, glowing light.

On other occasions when I had a similar experience, God was always there with a revelation, a *rhema*[29] word, a new direction, usually accompanied by a fork in the road or a junction. Now wide awake and sitting up in bed, I waited for whatever was to come. My spirit was relaxed, at peace, knowing this was probably the reason for the prompting I had experienced on the sales lot in Portland, to go to Vancouver, British Columbia. After several minutes of waiting in God's presence, I received from Him a heavy anointing. In the past I had always experienced warmth coming from my head to my neck, shoulders or arms—even, on some occasions, on my whole body—and that resembled warm flowing oil. My mind and spirit were ready and waiting for whatever the Holy Spirit was about to do or say.

In recent years, as I shared about the Holy Spirit's anointing in leadership schools or seminars, it seemed that on occasion, believers became guarded, even to the point of resisting anything of the supernatural, fearing and suspecting confluence with the paranormal or demonic. Such resistance to the Spirit should not be happening and may be, in regard to the supernatural, the result of disobeying or being unable to understand the Scripture and not recognizing error as it creeps into the faith. Insidiously, resisting the anointing of the Spirit can change faith in a believer's life into unbelief. Consequently, some churches dismiss the genuine divine manifestation of the Holy Spirit for fear of the counterfeit. Paul encourages his son in the faith, Timothy, ". . . from childhood you have known the Holy Scriptures, which are able to make you wise for salvation through faith which is in Christ Jesus" (2 Tim. 3:15 NKJV). "Be diligent [work hard, Greek] to present yourself approved to God, a worker who does not need to be ashamed, rightly dividing the word of truth" (2 Tim. 2:15 NKJV).

Many in Christian circles, even Holy Spirit-led groups, have been sceptical of God speaking in supernatural ways and may feel justifiably compromised because of misuse of the supernatural in today's world. With the infiltration of false eastern religious practices, such as yoga (sometimes now called by the oxymoron "Christian yoga"), icons, and images within traditional

Christendom, the genuine anointing and move of God's Spirit is in danger of becoming questioned or being quenched. Let's be challenged by the following: "Buy the truth and do not sell it; get wisdom, discipline and understanding" (Prov. 23:23 NIV).

As the Holy Spirit spoke by Jude, "I found it necessary to write to you exhorting you to contend earnestly for the faith which was once for all delivered to the saints. For certain men have crept in unnoticed, . . . ungodly men, who turn the grace of our God into lewdness and deny the only Lord God and our Lord Jesus Christ" (Jude 3-4 NKJV). The time has come for those who wear the whole armour of God to be "set for the defense of the gospel" and to "let [their] conduct be worthy of the gospel of Christ: . . . with one mind striving together for the faith of the gospel" (Phil. 1:17b AV, 27e NKJV). In a word, dark days may be ahead for the Church of Christ, possibly from an outside so-called religious aggressor, but more probably it may be compromised from within unless we know what we believe and refute insidious diabolical and intrusive lies.

The bedroom was still bathed in a comforting divine light. I enjoyed worshiping in my prayer language: "I will pray with my spirit . . . I will sing with my spirit" (1 Cor. 14:15 NIV). My spirit readied itself for God's visitation. Quietly, new thoughts began to flow into my mind—more correctly, His thoughts. They were not normal ideas. They were nothing my natural mind would conceive. In their processed form, they were concise and unmistakable; then He spoke to my spirit: "Tomorrow you must telephone Shirley and arrange to go and see her. My will is for you and Shirley to be together." That was all. The supernatural light was gone, and I was alone with my inconceivable assignment.

Yes, I remembered Shirley very well. When first arriving in Eston as a student at eighteen years of age, All the other students and I attended the local Full Gospel church in the town. Given the low winter temperatures, sometimes—50 degrees F (-46 degrees Celsius), we hurried to the warm vestibule to stand and thaw out before trying to make a dignified entrance to a very full and silent auditorium. All those years ago when I looked over the heads of those moving into the sanctuary, across the foyer, I saw an attractive young lady standing alone. I said to a friend, "Wow, who is that?"

To this he replied, "Take your eyes off her; that's her husband over there!" He was a handsome giant of a man, having graduated from the college the previous spring. They were visiting the school, coming from Shirley's home family in the nearby town of Kindersley.

What was left of the night was filled with the emotion of this new God assignment. This was my future, my life—forever! As I had breakfast with my hosts, I shared the revelation that I had the previous night. As mature believers, they understood the working of the Holy Spirit and encouraged me to obey Him without question, which also was my intention.

After breakfast, my inquiries for directory assistance gave me Shirley's Edmonton phone number. I was barely able to put my nervous finger into the phone's rotary dial, and after what seemed like an eternity, it rang. At that instant, I almost wished it could record my voice—like voicemail today—or ring forever, without being answered. Immediately, the unthinkable happened. So very early that morning, a man's strong voice answered. I was crushed! "Shirley Peskett, please!"

To this he retorted, in what I perceived in my vulnerable position as a hostile voice, "Who's calling?"

Feebly, I managed to say, "A friend."

It seemed to take forever for Shirley to come to the phone. My mind found a thousand reasons to hang up the receiver. *What was a man doing at her house so early in the morning? She must have remarried,* I guessed. *What about the anointing of the Holy Spirit the night before? Did God and I get it all wrong? Am I making a most foolish mistake?* I asked myself. Unknown to me, Shirley was still in an administrative capacity with Youth for Christ and that morning was having a breakfast committee meeting at her home. While I was lost in thought, I could hear Shirley's cheerful voice. I identified myself and asked to meet her somewhere convenient. She hesitated with several legitimate reasons. As I pressed her a little harder, she reluctantly, agreed. "Okay, where?" she asked.

"Edmonton Airport, tomorrow afternoon," was my reply.

Again, she strongly protested about the distance from the city. "Why not downtown?" she asked.

"Because I'm coming in from Vancouver," I replied. She agreed to meet me coming off the plane the next day.

As I reached the top of the down escalator on the second level, I could see her waiting at the lower-level exit. After I greeted her with a handshake, she handed me her car keys and said, "You drive; I never do when there's a man around." So I did. As we left the parking lot and headed down the endless driveway to the highway, we were silent.

In career selection, psychological profiling identifies personality types. Having adjudicated many tests on students and having been required to do several personally, the results left little doubt that I was a type-A personality. Among other highlights, this is indicative of prompt or impetuous action. Since I was not there for fun or small talk, it was time for business. I briefly described my encounter with the Holy Spirit, of the lighted room and what I believed He had spoken into my spirit.

As she heard exactly what I understood God had said to me, she sat silently. We had still not reached the highway intersection and, after an interminable silence, Shirley began reacting, "Well, He may have spoken to you, but He hasn't said anything to me yet."

So certain was I that God had spoken that it seemed to me there was only one reply. "Shirley," I began, "I know without a doubt that He has asked me to share my life with you, and I will be a single man until you marry me or someone else." Silence reigned again as we drove for hours.

Then we finally stopped for dinner. We discussed every imaginable aspect of the proposition before she dropped me at a hotel and went home. She promised only to pick me up early the next morning for my return flight to Vancouver.

Reams of letters, hours of long-distance phone calls, and a few more visits all resulted in a wedding six months later. Shirley's side of this story would take another book. Now, forty-plus years later, after two more children, ten grandchildren, three great grandchildren, and twenty-six years in overseas missions, that word from God to me was confirmed as His will for us.

In retrospect, the significant first fork in the road, when the call came to speak at the conference in Eston as I was heading to West Africa, was crucial. The second fork in the road, while I was completing a full schedule of ministry for six months, could have been tragically missed when my father asked me, "Are you coming home to run this business, or are you going to fool around with ministry?" The third fork in the road that removed me from my recreational sales lot in Portland, Oregon, and took me to Vancouver, British Columbia, was also a vital link. Then the fourth fork in the road was when God, in a supernaturally lighted room, revealed His desire for my wife and our perfect future together as husband and wife.

This chapter was not written with the primary intention of telling a romantic story, but rather to relate the vital need for the believer, at every turn of the road, to be alert and sensitive to the prompting of the Holy Spirit. He wishes to speak into the lives of those whose hearts are open to His leading and who are walking in obedience to His Word. His word is a lamp unto our feet and a light unto our path (Ps. 119:105). For me to miss any one of these four junctions in the road from God would have had, for me, far-reaching consequences—not only consequences on each of our lives but also with compounding effect on many other lives to infinity. What a tragedy it would have been to have missed His voice and the fork in the road!

# 4

# THE ASSURANCE OF GOD'S MISSIONS CALL

A fork in the road while driving means an instant choice must be made. The correct choice will lead to the desired destination. The consequence of a wrong one will mean a series of corrections, a frustrating delay, or a missed and seldom-to-be-repeated opportunity.

The stories are legendary of wrong driving choices that I insisted were right as my wife, Shirley, tried unsuccessfully from the passenger seat to help me avoid them. Valuable time was lost, endless miles were driven on winding roads as tension rose, and the important appointment or wedding ceremony was missed, only to have further embarrassment by attending just the reception. If we are honest with ourselves, we would acknowledge that it has happened to us more times than we care to admit.

A fun story regarding right direction occurred a lifetime ago in southern Ireland while I was driving a Canadian evangelist in ministry. We became desperately lost, and no amount of correction helped us because always we returned to the same point. The trouble began as we entered a country road with six roads converging featuring a six-fingered signpost in the center clearly pointing direction. Each time we chose our destination from the post, and we promptly returned there minutes later. It was, however, a round signpost in soggy ground that could be turned by every passing school child. On the critical journey of life, reliable directions are imperative; we only pass this way once.

Within a few, miles we met the local postman riding his delivery bike. I stopped beside him, lowered my window and asked for directions. Clearly, he, in a heavy accent, complied, by saying, "Continue directly to the cross, make a right turn, and go straight ahead." As I was thanking him and leaving, my evangelist friend's hand shot across my face to the postman and said, "Sir, if you continue directly to the cross of Christ, make a right turn, and go straight ahead, you will find your way to heaven." To this the postman, without a second's hesitation, responded, "And how would you be telling me how to find my way to heaven when you can't find your way to Cork?"

What was science fiction, the stuff of space travel with imaginary technology, is now everyday technology, including our indispensible cell phones, complete with their global positioning system. How marvellous if only this rocket science could function in application to the crucial directional decisions of our complex lives! But not so! God, however, in His Word has made this technology available to all who look to him in faith, saying, ". . . I will guide you with My eye" (Ps. 32:8b NKJV).

Individual lives and whole nations are impacted by right or wrong choices. The Bible examples are myriad where these were made. By not acting in his leadership capacity and not communicating to Eve God's instruction not to eat of the tree of knowledge of good and evil, Adam permitted Eve to obey Satan (Gen. 2:9). The consequence of this decision caused their immediate eviction from the garden and plunged the human family into alienation from God with the consequence of its sinful DNA.

Moses' parents made a good decision to save him from Pharaoh's wrath by placing him in a basket on the river to be rescued by his daughter, who raised him as her son and groomed him to be a future leader of Egypt.

With all of Moses' learning and knowledge of Egyptian culture, he was still a Hebrew. His wrong choice was made by killing an Egyptian. His guilt caused him to run from what he was aware of and would be his undoing. His act of killing, even before the law was given by God to him later, was socially taboo, even in Egypt. Moses fled for his life and for the next forty wilderness years lived in his own prison (Ex. 2:3-15).

Until Moses was eighty he had traveled on a secondary choice road until a correction was made the day he observed the burning bush that resulted in a life-altering experience. That day God revealed Himself to Moses. Moses observed a miracle, not of seeing a burning bush, which would be a normal happening in wilderness heat, but in observing that it continued to burn without being consumed (Ex. 3:2).

At the time of the burning bush incident, the commission with which God entrusted Moses enabled him to make a correct choice for the third forty-year period of his life. Choosing to obey God and lead the children of Israel out of Egypt's bondage, representing a type of the world and sin, was to be the greatest decision and contribution of his life. For Moses to lead Israel to the edge of the land of promise represented a type God's righteous provision. After Moses' leadership, they would now enter the land under the direction of their new leader, Joshua.

At the end of Moses' life, with the change of leadership to Joshua and the land of promise within sight, it was necessary for God to prevent Moses from entering into the Promised Land, not as a result of his killing of the Egyptian but because of his disobedience in striking the rock the second time, instead of speaking to it.

Similar examples of human suffering, oppression, and tragedy are many, including Joseph, who was sold into bondage. He became a prince in Egypt and saved his Hebrew family in time of famine (Gen. 37-50). Joseph chose to live a life of integrity before God. Ruth, the Moabitess, made the wise choice to remain with her mother-in-law Naomi and gleaned in the field of Boaz, who became her kinsman redeemer. Ruth became the ancestor of our Redeemer, Jesus Christ.

Perhaps the greatest example of wise choices came at the beginning of Christ's ministry, when He selected the twelve men from everyday life to be His disciples. Judas, in the foreknowledge of God, made unwise and wrong choices. The other eleven disciples, plus Matthias, Judas' replacement (Acts 1:23-26), lived and died for Christ.

Jesus' disciples were destined to follow Him, be mentored by Him, and replicate His ministry after His crucifixion. All of Christ's disciples, except the apostle John and Judas, who betrayed Him, would ultimately be martyred for their choice to follow Him. Their unfailing faith in and loyalty to their Master laid the foundation for the militant church. This is the faith and example of loyalty that we are entrusted to pass on to successive generations. To be equally faithful with them, it is necessary for us to make wise and prioritized choices in every aspect of our lives.

Today, in general conversation, it is common to hear someone say, "If plan A doesn't work, then I'll go to plan B." God has no B plan. Christ commissioned His disciples, telling them: "You go into the entire world and preach the gospel to every creature." This is it; we are His only plan to propagate the good news, and He has no B plan. He has no other plan.

All of the foregoing characters with their choices represent forks in the road. A missed turn or a wrong direction would have had endless compounding results, not only in their lives but also in those of succeeding generations.

In my own life, there have been several major forks in the road.

Thankfully, I believe that I have chosen wisely and have navigated them correctly or at worst, with very minor corrections and without major negative consequences.

Surely, most significant is the fork in the road representing our choice of the gift of God in salvation, when presented in His sovereign will. A close second would be our willingness to prepare our lives academically and professionally for the highest and best use of the Master. Choosing a spouse, that special one who is to become one with us, as a life partner is also a crucial fork in the road for a successful future.

Once an unexpected fork in the road almost blindsided me. Although I had spent my entire life in either fulltime or part-time ministry, I was not expecting a directional change on the next signpost. That sign changed my life forever.

The day began as most others as I went through the routine of dressing, having breakfast, and beginning office activities and appointments. Early in the morning, it was time to leave the house for what I expected to be a well-structured day. While backing the car out of the garage and leaving the driveway, I had a thought to go back and get my Bible. As I stepped into my office, I picked up a New Testament and drove contentedly away. Several blocks later, in what seemed like a thunderclap in the silent vehicle, I distinctly heard the voice of the Spirit in my spirit say, "I said Bible!" With some degree of annoyance, I turned around the car, retraced my steps, and did as He had instructed me to do. Then, happily I continued.

The first item of business was to refuel the car. I lived in Canada only a couple of minutes from the American border, where, at that time, fuel was considerably less expensive, so I made my way directly to my usual station. I turned to the right into the station and filled up with gas, which was uneventful. But leaving was a different story.

When I got back into my vehicle, started the engine, and tried to turn left to return to Canada, I was faced with a problem. The steering wheel would not, under any circumstances, turn left. As I accidently turned the wheel a little to the right, it went freely in that direction. *Great!* I thought. *Now I can get back to cross the border and return to Canada.* But not so; now the steering wheel would only turn to the right, not left. In total exasperation, I allowed it to take me right as I was traveling south and farther into the United States.

I drove normally for a few hundred yards until I came to a crossroad. *Shall I go ahead, right, or left?* To my consternation, the steering wheel turned left, which was impossible moments earlier, and I continued on a deserted tourist road at this out of season and uncustomary early morning hour. It was a dull rainy morning as I was being led up a narrow road that would ultimately take me to Mount Baker in Washington. In this unusual experience, I concluded that God had His hand in it.

As I looked for a place to park, I found one and parked the car on the left shoulder and facing downhill. I recall muttering something like this: "God, if you are trying to reach me, can we do it here?"

At 8:30 in the morning and halfway up a deserted mountain road, what am I to do? "Read your Bible," was the thought that prompted me. Remembering that I had returned to replace a New Testament for the Bible, I retrieved it from the backseat. As I grabbed at it, my fingers divided it about halfway.

Sensing that something unusual was about to happen, I settled down to read at the chosen finger-opened passage of Isaiah 41, with my eyes falling first on verse 8. Slowly I read through to verse 18. Something was very different. There was stillness, a peace, and as each word slowly sank in with fresh meaning, tears poured down my cheeks. I was weeping bitterly for no apparent reason. Although my chest was heaving and unusually warm, I felt good.

Each verse I read was well known to me. This was the Bible that I had purchased at age thirteen, when I began as a teenage preacher. It was my friend, well-marked in various colours, each representing a different theme or thought. What was different on this occasion? Every word, it seemed, carried a personal message just for me. The Holy Spirit was anointing every phrase and gently applying each to my spirit in an unusual and personal way as never before. When I carefully and finally finished reading the passage and as best I could in this sacred moment, I applied its content. It became obvious that God was assuring me that I was His chosen servant and friend. He was saying, "I am your God, and I will strengthen you; you will be upheld with My right hand." The presence of God was so real, it seemed as though I could not contain this special visitation.

On many other occasions the Holy Spirit has been very real to me as He imparted some special message or assurance. At other times the message would be for direction or correction in my own life or the application of a point of wisdom for a family situation. Supernatural anointing had often ministered very deeply into my spirit in the past, but nothing equalled this almost unspeakable moment. The gifts of the Spirit had flowed for His glory in my ministry for many years, but this was a deeper, sacred, holy, and divine encounter.

Nothing in my past experience with the rain of His anointing equalled this morning's flood of visitation. My upper body was soaked with perspiration; my head and hair felt like they were bathed in oil. That was a most sacred moment, and something very unusual was happening to me. As I sat behind the steering wheel that earlier wouldn't turn left, now, only minutes later, I hardly had the energy to grasp it. That was a God moment. His witness in my spirit carried a sense of new beginnings, a fresh anointing of ministry.

Still crying like a baby and trembling with a deep sense of His presence, I understood He wanted to convey the message that the gospel I had preached for a lifetime in the West would change in the sense that I would no longer preach it primarily in the West but in third-world and developing countries. He further instructed me that this same gospel would now be preached with a fresh anointing in the power and demonstration of the Spirit, miraculously touching a hurting world (1 Cor. 2:3–5).

After reading the ten verses in Isaiah 41:8–18 once through my teary eyes, I allowed myself to absorb the new direction my life was about to take at this fork in the road. I was now prepared to leave this deserted mountain road and get back to a normal life.

As I started the car and drove away from this now-sacred spot, I looked in disbelief at my watch. It was already five-thirty in the evening. How could this be? Where did nine hours go? I had no concept of the brief passage of time that had absorbed a whole working day that seemed, at most, about fifteen minutes. All my appointments for that day were forgotten. With sincere apologies, I had to reschedule them.

As I arrived home at about the normal time, Shirley met me in the hallway with the searching questions: "What has happened to you? Did you kill someone?"

I asked her, "Why? What's wrong?"

To this she replied, "Look in the mirror!"

As I did so, I saw that my eyelids were swollen out almost flush with my forehead, and beneath my eyes were also swollen. For two days I didn't leave the house until I was presentable. We both attempted to come to grips with this new dimension of ministry, or more accurately, missions.

Missionary involvement is not something I have relished. In fact, I was most happy in my role as a Western evangelist. During Bible college, I almost caused my own expulsion in the first week because, on principle, I wouldn't join a missions' prayer band, knowing full well my call to evangelism did not include missions. I even refused to sing mission hymns, like, "I'll go where you want me to go, dear Lord, over mountain or plain or sea." I refused to sing a lie because, at that time, I had no inclination to the life of a missionary. If Shirley and I thought that we had experienced a heady moment with this divine intervention and re-commissioning, we had better think again. We hadn't seen anything yet.

Several days later, the telephone rang, and we excitedly spoke with a good friend with whom we had lost touch for several years. He was a missionary working in Asia, and before we lost contact with him, we had tried to help with his support. This was a refreshing, high-energy call as we reminisced about many happy memories.

The tempo suddenly changed when he asked if it would be possible to come and visit us, as he felt strongly that God had given him a word for us. We agreed on an evening to meet, and with eager anticipation, we awaited his visit. At the appointed time, he arrived, and after exchanging a few pleasantries, he became quite focused on his reason for coming.

He shared how, a few days earlier, God had impressed upon him a picture of a change in ministry for us. This would mean preaching the same gospel message that I had been preaching in the West, but I would now preach it mostly in third-world and developing countries. The anointing of God would be evidenced in a dramatic way following the gospel ministry, and signs and wonders would accompany the preaching of the gospel and teaching of His Word. The Holy Spirit would also provide signs and wonders when praying for the sick and in exorcizing demons from the demon possessed.

All of this information came through a man we had not seen for many years who was blissfully unaware of my encounter with God up on Mount Baker. He was relating almost a total duplication of what that morning meant to us. This was another God moment. With rapt attention, we listened as he shared how he felt that God used him to bring this message to us, and he invited us to begin this empowered redirection of ministry on his mission field. Shirley and I were experiencing, to some degree, information overload from all that had transpired before he came. Now, with his confirmation of God's word to us, we felt that this must be the end of the revelation.

Quietly, he slipped a Bible from his pocket and began reading the word God from the Scripture that God had laid on his heart. It was from Isaiah 41. If we thought we had heard everything up to that moment, this was more than we could handle. As he prepared to leave, we considered tentative dates for our first mission venture. That six-week trip materialized and filled a complete chapter. Although we have ministered for years and have witnessed God moving in so many sovereign ways, this supernatural intervention meant that we could think or talk of little else.

Within the week of his visit, there was another phone call. This time the man gave his name and asked me if I remembered him. I did. Thirty years earlier, as a missionary from Africa, he had visited our Bible college to challenge the students for missions. Since then, we had never seen or heard from him. He mentioned how difficult it was for him to locate us and that he would like to come and visit us. In a few days we made an arrangement for him to come visit us, and he did so.

In the natural, we had no idea why he had come. In the spiritual, we suspected it might relate to the events of the past week. After some catch-up chatting, he said God had brought us before his spirit and showed him some changes that were about to take place in our ministry. He made reference to several portions of Scripture from Isaiah 41:8-18 that God had used to change our direction in ministry. He spoke of a greater evidence of the power and demonstration of the Spirit following the preaching of the Word and that our work would be mainly in developing countries, preaching the gospel, which is the power of God. As the missionary before him had done, he also opened the ministry door for us in his country of ministry.

Our spirits were euphoric. How should we handle this kind of revelation?

Just days before, the Mount Baker event alone was more than enough to last a lifetime. Then the second word came and confirmed our unforgettable experience, and now a third reconfirmation, almost identical to the initial word, stretched us to new dimensions of God's new fork in the road journey for us. As the Bible says, every word will be established "In the mouth of two or three witnesses" (2 Cor. 13:1 AV).

We busied ourselves in preparation for a new chapter in our lives. Although we did not know what the future held, we did know who holds the future. There were many plans to make and details to arrange. We accepted and believed that this was a God moment. Within the revelation we had received from God and also through the two missionaries, there was a strong sense that He who was calling us out from our present work to this new work would "perform *it*" (Phil. 1:6c AV). God had initiated this remarkable event, and we trusted Him to do it. This fork in the road was a life-changing call to a new dimension of supernatural ministry, something God had promised He would make happen. In preparation for this new adventure, we believed Him implicitly and went ahead with timid baby steps with God as our only source.

PART TWO

# SPRINTING

---

# 5

# THE FIRST ASIAN ROOKIE TRIP

The supernatural repositioning and direction for our ministry required serious adjustment. With God speaking directly into our lives—first personally and then by two trusted ministers—all plans were in place for the initial six-week missionary trip. We believed the tour would help us experience what God had in store for us.

Almost immediately we began to arrange to leave our many areas of commitment in Canada, which was no easy matter. At the time, two of our younger children, Grant, aged sixteen and Shirleen, aged eleven, were still living at home with us, while our older boys, Alden and William, were already married, on their own, and into their professions. On the one hand, my responsibilities were diverse in business and part-time ministry, all of which initially would not allow us to be gone for too long. On the other hand, Shirley, over a number of years, had built a very successful direct sales marketing business that succeeded only as a direct result of her hands-on management approach.

We made arrangements with the missionary who came to our home first to confirm God's earlier revelation to us to fulfill these weeks in various cities in his field.

Over the earlier months, we had begun to save whatever funds possible for this new adventure, together with donations from those who felt led by the Holy Spirit to partner with us.

As the departure date drew closer, many details, still needing to be settled, surfaced in swarms and at intimidating speeds. Sometimes we would stand back and appraise the daunting task, and we felt like throwing up our hands in despair. Were we up to this new challenge? Were we too set in our old training for conventional ministry? Could we make the transition to this new commission in the power and demonstration of the Spirit that God had promised would accompany the preaching of the Word? All of these fears, intimidations, and questions raced through our minds.

Forty-eight hours before our flight, partly packed cases were everywhere. That first trip of six weeks would stretch our already limited budget to the breaking point. How would we cover all travel costs overseas and also make our regular monthly mortgage payments and bills while away?

My district office of the PAOC kindly receipted all donations from friends who helped make our mission's trip possible. Our trusted friend and senior pastor, Calvin Ratz, became my mentor in relation to the repositioning for our new calling. In many ways, he was the catalyst that brought about the change for our long-term ministry. He imparted great wisdom as a result of his own earlier years on mission fields. His insights were invaluable for the many turns and detours of the road that lay ahead of us.

Shirleen, our youngest child and only girl, would accompany us and celebrated her twelfth birthday while attending Faith Academy, a boarding school in Manila, Philippines. Grant, who was still in high school, would remain at home. He was mature for his age and had a strong personal faith in Christ. We felt sad leaving him at home but confident that he would adequately be able to cope in our absence. Since God was initiating all of this, we felt confident that He would provide the needed grace for every eventuality, including us being overseas with Grant being at home alone. In this venture, God was with us and blessed us and our family.

We had often traveled overseas before, but this was different. Departure day was a blur. We sat on, strapped, and locked our suitcases and then dumped them in cars and whisked to the Vancouver Airport. In early 1986, check-in and security at the airport went quickly and smoothly. The total flight time to the Philippines via Hong Kong, with stopovers, was around fifty hours, including a time zone change of sixteen hours. We arrived as three zombies to find the country in turmoil after the unseating of President Ferdinand Marcos by the efforts of the People Power Revolution just days earlier.

After we cleared through the massive crowds at the Manila Airport and then the greater area city traffic in late afternoon, we immediately began an all-night drive to our destination. As I recall, our vehicle was overcrowded and underpowered. The cultural shock in a fatigued condition that we were experiencing was compounded by the annoying grating sound from the wheels of our vehicle. An inspection at a pit stop in the middle of the night revealed a "gatered" tire—a tire sliced through from tread to rim. It was pulled apart and sprung around an existing canvas tread tire on the wheel and then was gatered or laced through from side to side to hold it "safely" in place for highway driving.

We arrived at our destination just after dawn, and then we were brought to our accommodation and told to have a couple of hours of rest before the morning session. It appeared to us like an economy motel, and by the time we made it liveable, it was time for us to leave for ministry.

Although I had ministered most of my life up to this point, this was my first cross-cultural missions experience. On numerous occasions, I pastored for brief periods, but I knew that evangelism was my primary calling. Also, I had taught elective courses in church, and for three or six months at a time, I had been on teaching assignments.

On this occasion, as we drove from the motel to the venue, the national leader casually mentioned that my first assignment would be to teach pastors. Thinking he meant for one hour or so, I said, "Fine, not a problem."

As we arrived and were entering the building, an atmosphere of expectancy was evident. Several hundred pastors were seated or still milling around when my host supplied the rest of the details. "You will teach the first four hours until noon, breaking for one hour for lunch, and a further four hours until five o'clock. Then we will eat quickly and we have an evangelistic rally daily for the next four days."

If disappearing had been an option for me, I would have selected it. Yes, on occasion, I had taught—but hundreds of pastors for eight hours daily and for four days, I had not. In my wildest dreams, this would have been utterly impossible.

I had preaching and teaching material with me, but it was not adequate for such a marathon. At the most, perhaps stretched to the limit, possibly I could manage ninety minutes. My flesh wanted to die, scream, or run away. But in my spirit, I felt strangely calm. It was as though everything was under control. But I knew better. Given my teaching material, it appeared to me an impossible assignment. At that moment, I wished for a loaves and fish multiplication. How I could use the twelve baskets full of bread and fish that were in excess, if they could only be exchanged for the notes that I needed now!

The commotion subsided. The pastors filed into the seats, the worship leaders began, and the pastors' expressions of worship exceeded anything I had ever previously experienced. The anointing was so rich, the Holy Spirit seemed to have instant access to this body of believers, and they had an instant and abandoned response to Him. Literally, we all seemed lost in the anointing of the Holy Spirit that flowed from their worship. There were musical instrumentalists and vocalists leading the worship, but it seemed as though they had faded or blended with the pastor's voice as that of a heavenly choir. My spirit was lost in the moment; this had a depth and richness of worship that, up to then, I had never experienced. Although in the past God had allowed me to have priceless experiences in the Spirit, this was something into which I had to press deeper. "Please God," my spirit silently prayed, "let us have this rich and deep abandon with You in worship in the West!"

As the leader walked to the podium, what seemed like only minutes was actually over an hour. After he gave a few housekeeping details and briefly introduced me, it was my turn to speak. Except for me, everyone was ready. What would I do with this crowd of leaders, any of whom could fill this assignment better than I, a rookie missionary evangelist, could at that moment?

Through my interpreter, I greeted them with all the warmth I could express under the circumstances. I gave a little of my background to help introduce myself and relate to them for the next thirty-plus hours. As they saw me open the Bible with a single two-sided page of notes, they opened theirs. At that moment, the expression, "My heart was in my mouth" would have fit perfectly. I announced the title of the teaching and read several verses of Scripture.

My introduction had laid the foundation for the structure that I planned to build. Hopefully, with God's help, the national leaders would be led to a deeper understanding of the Holy Spirit in ministering supernaturally to the needs of their people.

About ten minutes into the session, something strange began to happen within my spirit. Since experiencing the fullness of the Spirit earlier in my life, God had led me on a special journey with many signs and wonders, but this was very different.

In the moment before the interpreter finished and I began to speak again, a thought crossed my mind. I had a flashback to the ever-to-be-remembered Mount Baker, Washington, experience. At that time, God called us to third-world and developing countries, and He had assured me that this new focus would be in the power and demonstration of the Holy Spirit. What a very comforting thought that was, given my present predicament! The thought somehow seemed to relax me, but for the life of me, I didn't know why; the impossible mountain of lacking sufficient teaching material still loomed ominously over me.

Then it happened. As my teaching continued to flow, it was as though another voice had taken over from me. The most fluent sentences and most captivating concepts began falling from my lips. The interpreter and I exchanged glances, as neither of us fully comprehended what was happening. Yes, my voice was speaking but not from my mind. The feeling resembled the sensation of hydroplaning, when one drives too fast in heavy rain and the tires lose contact with the road, rising on top of the film of water, and the driver is no longer in control of the vehicle.

This was beyond me; I was no longer in control of this session, in the normal sense of moving into my message. This was God in the supernatural dimension intervening in my life and ministry. It was my initiation as a first-time missionary in the first thirty minutes of ministry, living out His promise of power and demonstration. As one side of my mind enjoyed what was being said in spite of me, the flesh side asked, "What happens if He stops?" The question petrified me. There was no human way that my finite mind could continue to produce such rich eloquence. As a lengthy period passed, my interpreter continued interpreting as I stood there functioning as a conduit for this divine flow of God through my life.

His message was gentle, searching, enriching, loving, warm, and encouraging us to love others as He loves us and to forgive others as He forgave us. He spoke of the joy, the deliverance, and the Holy Spirit's anointing and blessing that would flow in all aspects of ministry as these qualities were implemented in our lives. This was different from the operation of the gift of prophecy or the word of knowledge. By contrast with my past anointing experiences of Holy Spirit, the operation of this supernatural event bore no resemblance to either of those gifts. This was another God moment.

Quietly from one corner of the crowd, a pastor stood and began walking across the floor of the auditorium. He was searching for another pastor. When he found him, they both stood, talking for a moment, and then embraced each other with emotion. One pastor after another did the same thing. I stopped speaking, but the pastors continued criss-crossing the crowd to find one another. For the rest of that day, the Holy Spirit had our attention. Incredible reconciliations, deliverances, and healings followed and flowed. A line for testimonies formed that stretched across the front and down one side of the building. It seemed most of the ministers had received a touch from God. Many received the fullness of the

Spirit, and for the first time for some, the gifts of the Spirit were in operation. It wasn't until almost five o'clock that they began to leave for the rally. Lunch at noon! What lunch?

Since that memorable experience, now over twenty-five years ago, I have experienced numerous similar parallels in the supernatural dimension. My understanding of those sacred God moments is His ongoing confirmation that our mission call is to preach a total gospel, which will result in salvation and deliverance through the power and demonstration of the Holy Spirit.

On one occasion many years later, I had the opportunity to meet and have a lengthy time of fellowship with my former, now very senior, college lecturer, who moved most comfortably in his five-fold ministry. In the course of reminiscing about the college years, we discussed doctrine and various manifestations of the Holy Spirit.

I had not heard others preach on or discuss with one another their similar spiritual experience, and I had not felt free to volunteer mine either. But I had a prompting in my spirit at that time to discuss it with my trusted friend.

In case he would not understand, I led into the subject cautiously. I walked very gently. As I delicately described what was to me a personal and sacred experience, not knowing what his reaction would be, I felt like I was walking on eggs. In total silence and showing no emotion on the subject either way, he listened intently. My heart seemed to pound out of my chest as I disclosed something this personal and possibly controversial, if he were to react negatively.

When I finished sharing my experience, there was a lengthy silence that made me feel uncomfortable. I was in my mid-sixties at the time, but I still felt like a nervous student awaiting a professor's term paper critique, as they used to scowl over their horn-rimmed reading glasses before assigning a grade of B minus.

He began speaking thoughtfully and very deliberately but still not showing a pro or con reaction. He spoke of an omniscient God, who, knowing our needs, has the ability to address those needs and often does so before we recognize it. God addressed the point perfectly when He declared to Isaiah, ". . . before they call, I will answer; and while they are still speaking, I will hear" (Is. 65:24b AV).

Further, my friend spoke of the many supernatural happenings in Scripture that then had no scriptural precedent and were seldom, if ever, identically repeated. An omnipotent God cannot be limited. In any dispensation, He may reveal Himself how, as, and when He chooses, however unusual it may appear. He is still omniscient today and is not limited by our finite understanding. As he continued speaking, he became less guarded, as if he was about to make a serious disclosure. Instead, at this point, he thanked me for sharing this experience with him and said that no one had ever spoken about it to him before. He said that on a couple of occasions this experience had occurred in his ministry, but never before had he spoken to anyone about it until he was in his eighties, and his voice broke with emotion. He considered it a rare and sacred event in his life and felt I was justified in feeling the same way. As I left him that day, I felt something of how Timothy may have felt being assured by the aging apostle Paul.

Seizing the opportunity to share this experience with my friend proved to be in God's timing. Afterward, we went overseas, and on our return a few weeks later, I learned that he had gone to glory.

As I prepared to go to the evening rally following the eventful seminar, I waited outside the building for a vehicle. Resting on a cement slab for a few minutes, I felt a touch on my shoulder from behind. As I turned around, there stood a middle-aged lady. She could not speak English and did not know me but smiled. Where did she come from? Why did she choose me? Her left eye was totally grey with a cataract. She pointed at it, then to me, and with her hands placed together, she requested prayer for it and pointed to heaven. Without standing up, my hand reached toward the offending eye, saying in English, "Be healed in Jesus' name!"

Immediately, she covered her good brown eye, and her face radiated joy as she realized that she could also see through her grey eye, now as brown as the other. She waved her hand joyously toward heaven, chuckled, and was lost in the throng of people who crowded the sidewalk. Was this the second time in my first day of missions with God's assurance that He would evidence obedience to the call with a demonstration of His supernatural power through my life?

My ride arrived. I was whisked away for ten minutes to a fast food outlet, and then we drove quickly and arrived at the small stadium. The missionary who first visited our home and confirmed my Mount Baker encounter, and whose invitation had resulted in our being here, would be the speaker. Still dazed with jet-lag, I was more than happy only to assist him in any way that would be needed.

The stage was filled with musicians and worship leaders. The crowd swelled to capacity and sang and praised God. Then the missionary preached a beautifully concise gospel deliverance message. For those who wished to receive Christ as their Saviour and Lord, the invitation was given to come forward for counselling, prayer, and literature. Those with various other needs were included in that call.

From perhaps four thousand in attendance, about 40 percent responded to the message. Hundreds prayed a salvation prayer and were recorded for follow-up by pastors in their localities. Those who came for other needs were prayed for as a group, first; then, if necessary, individually later. As the event concluded, the crowd exited the stadium. A local pastor asked me to look at the now almost empty field where many hundreds had stood. It was littered with every imaginable medical accessory, including leg braces, crutches, wheelchairs, back braces, etc. God, it seemed, had walked the aisles and healed those who had not come to the front. This was my first day initiation of God's power and demonstration of the Holy Spirit. I was blown away. Could this day be the beginning of living in the supernatural dimension for me?

Each day was packed with similar activities and incredible fellowship. Several ministerial couples from the United States were working on various ministry projects, and as our paths crossed, we developed stronger relationships. After the evangelistic rallies, many evening meals became extended fellowship times and for me, learning times. After our arrival while sitting at a large, round table, immediately after the blessing had been asked, and before any food was passed around, a large seven-inch gecko fell out of the central light fixture unto Shirleen's empty plate. Even without jet lag, that was enough to intimidate any eleven-year-old on her second day in missions.

After I preached one evening and later worked at the altar with the sick and demon-possessed, a man who had received a remarkable healing came to me. He was so thankful and blessed by what God had done for him that he wanted to make an offering. As he pressed the equivalent of thirty cents into my hand, I thanked him but declined. My mentor missionary, observing the incident, asked if I had refused his gift. As I answered in the affirmative, I was severely admonished. "For years," he said, "I have been teaching them to give offerings and to tithe in obedience to the Word, and you undo my work in a single action." I learned another lesson.

In our weeks of ministry, we saw thousands come to faith in Christ and vast numbers healed of many sicknesses. Deliverance came to hundreds who were bound by Satan but now were set free in Jesus' name. "For the preaching of the cross" and "the gospel . . . is the power of God" (1 Cor. 1:18 AV; Rom. 1:16 AV). When the unadulterated gospel is preached, God is bound, by His own Word, to fulfill it. This was God's power in action. These results were not accomplished by preaching a flavour of Pentecost but by preaching His gospel. As I observed God's power in action, it was like I was reliving the book of Acts. Could this be a foretaste of our future in missions? The answer twenty-five years later is a definitive yes!

After the first four days of the pastors' seminar, I was literally changed and had a deeper trust in His leading as I taught. During our stay, I had many more teaching opportunities. Many of them were at a Bible college.

Our time there overlapped with their graduation exercises, at which I was asked to speak. As was the custom there, a number of visiting ministers were asked to pray with and minister to all the students. Several hundred students lined up, and two or three of us moved along, either praying with or ministering in the gifts of the Holy Spirit to each one as the Spirit led us. With our interpreters, this took several hours. Finally, nearing fatigue in the forty-degrees Celsius heat (104 degrees F), I was yet to experience another surprise assignment. Lined against the opposite side of the auditorium were the college's board of governors, staff, and faculty members, who patiently awaited their turn.

Ministering in the gifts of the Spirit is somewhat easier when one has no knowledge of the person receiving ministry. That is not to say that ministering in the gifts of the Spirit is ever easy. It is always a learning experience, as the Holy Spirit moves in various ways with each person. One must be released in one's own spirit to move as He directs and be sensitive to His promptings. Conversely, one must be gentle and at the same time firm in the natural when dealing with the humanness of the individual. This is especially needed when operating in the gift of the word of knowledge.

For example, while my young interpreter and I were ministering down the line of faculty members, I came to an older, senior lecturer. As I waited before him for a few seconds, sensing how the Holy Spirit would lead, I became most uncomfortable in my spirit, which to me was a strong red flag. On this occasion, without seeing any detail, heaviness, darkness, and sadness gripped me. On occasion, I have sometime witnessed a pleasant aroma that seems to envelop the person. This time it was an unpleasant odour, not noticeable to the natural senses but in the Spirit. This task, I began to sense, would be more difficult to handle because of his senior faculty position.

As I began to speak through the interpreter and moved in the positive first, I encouraged him in the Lord, speaking of the significance of his calling and the importance of his ministry channel being pure, through which the Holy Spirit should flow to his students. The interpreter, who has been flowing smoothly with me, suddenly stopped. Knowing that the faculty member spoke no English, he said, "Pastor John, I cannot interpret for you in this instance anymore; I am too young to say what you are going to ask me to say. I must get you a more senior interpreter for this brother to say what needs to be said." Several minutes later, an elderly brother who was capable of interpreting introduced himself.

Without reviewing what had transpired, we began again. Using examples of personal choices, right and wrong, and major crossroads in one's life, he was encouraged to walk the path of purity, righteousness, and moral integrity. He began showing a sign of discomfort. His expression and eye contact changed. We spoke of the human weakness in all of our lives, how that we are still in the flesh. We all have clay feet, we make mistakes, but He remains *faithful* and *forgiving* when there is genuine repentance. He is a God of grace and *mercy*.

As the apostle John assures us, "If we confess our sins, He is faithful and just to forgive us *our* sins and to cleanse us from all unrighteousness" (1 John 1:9 NKJV). The apostle Paul also speaks of God's *faithfulness* to make a way of escape: ". . . but God *is* faithful, who will not allow you to be tempted beyond what you are able, but with the temptation, will also make the way of escape, that you may be able to bear *it*" (1 Cor. 10:13b NKJV). "Therefore, in all things He had to be made like *His* brethren, that He might be a merciful and faithful High Priest in things *pertaining* to God, to make propitiation [atoning sacrifice] for the sins of the people" (Heb. 2:17 NKJV), declared the writer to the Hebrews.

As we proceeded, he became irritated and confrontational. We spoke of God's longsuffering and that He is the Good Shepherd who searches for His sheep that had gone astray and of the Prodigal Father who, regardless of his son's waywardness, searched the horizon daily for his return. All we said to him at the time was to no avail. After we prayed briefly with him, he left, we felt, with a spirit of great heaviness.

Several weeks later, after I left the country, I received a phone call that clarified the issue. A few days after that encounter and the

Holy Spirit's touch, the man tendered his resignation to the college board. Over his many years there, he confessed to his breach of spiritual and professional conduct relating to male students, and as a consequence of his actions, he withdrew from the college.

In my experience, as the Holy Spirit has revealed a person's issues, it is rare when I don't see that person respond positively to such revelation. While God, in His love, tenderly draws the individual closer to Himself for cleansing and forgiveness, as a result, I usually see contrition and reconciliation in that person's life.

Our mission's tour continued on a daily basis. We hardly had a day off in six weeks. It was a challenging and learning experience but with a passion. As we were being thrown into the pool's deep end, so to speak, we had to learn to sink or swim. In retrospect, in my opinion, this was the best way for us to learn.

The rich fellowship of team members and wise mentoring from those who had laboured on the field for years imparted great wisdom and contributed largely to the work God had so far allowed us to do. The times of fellowship in prayer, worship, and ministry in the gifts of the Spirit set a new high in our lives, causing us not to be satisfied with less than His best in these areas.

One of the couples who provided invaluable input to our lives and ministry was Don and Katie Fortune, authors of *Discover Your God-Given Gifts.*[30] Section by section, it clarifies the motivational gifting, enabling one to flow more proficiently in one's proper calling and skill set. It clearly defines how to function at God's highest and best use in one's gifting. For us it is an invaluable tool.

The final days passed quickly. Even on the last evening, before departure, there was a massive open-air rally. Thousands attended, and many hundreds received Christ as Saviour. Hundreds more came for healing and deliverance. As we jumped into a waiting vehicle to catch a plane and return to Canada, our first missions trip to the Philippines was now over.

We experienced notable miracles daily, and the Holy Spirit moved among the people, evoking in us our heartfelt thanks to God for the repositioning of our ministry and an eagerness to fulfill His call upon our lives.

Now that we had returned home, we began to reflect on our six-week time warp. Was it a dream? No, it was not but rather our first real missionary journey. God had walked with us in the supernatural dimension of power and demonstration of the Holy Spirit.

# 6

# TROPICAL ISLAND EASTER MORNING

As it had for millennia, the pre-dawn mist brooded over the South China Sea, which lapped gently on the golden ribbed sand. At such an idyllic location for an Easter morning sunrise service, our underpowered motorbike and sidecar carried four people, plus Shirley and me. On the previous evening, the national leader of the group strongly suggested that we prepare to leave our accommodation by three in the morning. His prompting was because he knew that ahead of us lay an almost indescribably circuitous, bone-bending, two-hour, hazardous journey during the darkness of night.

Already in the early morning the temperature was probably in the twenties Celsius or seventies Fahrenheit as we bumped our way along to the rendezvous of the first service. Suddenly the harrowing experience was over as the sputtering engine fell silent. We braked to a halt almost axel deep on the sandy and powdery beach. We had arrived! Almost as one person, the four agile younger locals leaped off the main bike, while Shirley and I uncurled and tried to pry ourselves from the metal cage appendage that was half our size.

Typically, I am quite a slow learner. My schedule indicated that this Easter weekend was going to be a taxing one. With fifteen meetings to conduct from Friday evening through Sunday, nine of which were on Easter Sunday, this being the first, I naively thought that I was ready for the weekend. But I wasn't prepared for what lay ahead of me that morning.

Straining my eyes to look through the morning haze at a deserted beach, I asked myself, *Why in the world am I standing alone on an empty beach except for those who brought us there?* My next question was, *Why did I have to leave my bed, even as uncomfortable it was, at such an unearthly hour of two in the morning?*

As I lifted my head and looked up I saw a single scarlet hue spill onto the horizon. As the seconds passed, the colour flooded more and more the ocean and sky. Within minutes the sky was painted in the most magnificent fiery golden Easter sunrise hues that I had ever seen.

My concern about being solitary figures on a deserted, sandy beach was unfounded. As I became totally absorbed in the spectacular dawn performance, another phenomenon escaped me. Beyond the beach, as the grassy knoll gave way to a dense group of palm trees, concealed in the pre-dawn haze, a small group of locals was waiting on the beach for the right moment to join us. Slowly four or five people, then three or four families, followed by more and more people, emerged from the palm trees until many hundreds gathered and stood in the breaking sunlight. The silence of the morning yielded to the soft and melodious voices of those gathered there.

Their praises continued at length until the richness of the Holy Spirit's anointing lifted our spirits to a new level of worship. Then, as one voice as though led by an invisible conductor, this group of Christian believers offered up the most moving rendition of "Up from the Grave He Arose," followed by other great Easter hymns and culminated in "How Great Thou Art!" The sense of God's anointed presence was keenly felt. Members of the crowd sang from the depths of their hearts. Not only was my own spirit enveloped by God, but also His touch was evident on hundreds of shining faces in the golden sunrise. As national Christians lifted their hands to the still starry heaven, rivers of tears flowed down their olive cheeks. Seldom, if ever, have I experienced such expressions of heartfelt emotion.

This Easter worship service took us to new levels of God's anointing, a time in which we could be lost in God's presence. The Scripture says, "Enter into his courts with praise" (Ps. 100:4b AV)! This is not a suggestion but a command. Such is the key to higher and richer levels of relationship with Him. The court of worship leads us to the Most Holy Place, the throne room of the Majesty on high. Is it not there that we may experience our deepest and richest, most-sacred moments in the presence of the King of kings?

To be transported by the richness of such an atmosphere of worship from an earthly tropical beach into a rhapsodic heavenly dimension borders on the edge of an out-of-the body experience. In what seemed like minutes, an hour or more must have passed. I had allowed myself to be carried by this rich experience to a dimension that obscured, for the moment, the reason I was there. As quickly and as smoothly as the worship had begun, it ended. Instantly, when I heard the loud speakers, I was reminded of why I was there. I was being called to the platform to deliver an Easter message.

As I faced this beautiful and anointed crowd of people, they stood expectantly waiting for a word from me. With the splendour of this Easter morning and the majestic backdrop of a golden ocean, after such a rich and moving worship time, it somehow made it difficult to make the transition from being one who was receiving from Him to suddenly being called to give to others. Yes, I was ready to minister to them. In this unique moment of time, the message was vivid in my mind and burning in my spirit. It felt like someone should be ministering to me. I felt that I needed time to be alone, to digest, to process, and to assimilate all of the rich and moving thoughts that need to be saved to my spiritual database.

But no, not now, because this anointed crowd demanded my attention and concentration. After I gave a moment of greeting and introduction, I preached an Easter message. On such a day and at this spectacular location, what title did I give to the message? It was, "Because He Lives."

This is the day when millions of Christians around the world pause to celebrate Christ's resurrection from the dead. For the Christian believer, if not for all people, this must be the single greatest event in human history. His resurrection, then, represents to us the peak of an inverted pyramid, above which balances every belief of our Christian faith. If Christ did not rise from the dead, we have no faith, and He would be the greatest imposter.

Often while I minister in major cities around the world, my hosting pastor will try to make time proudly to show outstanding historic sites. In Eastern cities, this may include the tomb or mausoleum of a great leader or founder of a major religion. Typically the sites will be well maintained and perhaps be surrounded by an imposing cast iron fence. Inside the mausoleum there may be another ornately designed and decorated crypt. Within the crypt, there will be a sealed sarcophagus containing a dignitary. Prominently positioned and close by will be the plaque with the significant details of the dignitary's life. The plaque will include his name, date of birth, noteworthy accomplishments, and date of death. In the case of a founder of a great religion, in which millions of devotees put their implicit trust for life, death, and eternity, his decomposed body is still with them. His spirit is gone, his ears do not hear, his eyes do not see, his mind does not comprehend, and his heart has no capacity for compassion. Is such a manmade monument and lifeless corpse enough for one to trust in life and in death?

Nothing elaborate marks the traditional tomb of Christ. Neither is there a preserved body. The rough-hewn tomb is unguarded because the tomb is empty. It needs no security. Jesus Christ ever lives and is seated at the right hand of God the Father to make intercession for us (Rom. 8:34; Mark 16:19; Heb. 7:25). His ear is ever open to our cry, and His arm is strong to save (Is. 59:1). With our hearts we serve Him and trust Him with our lives, our death, and our everlasting destiny. The God who became flesh in Jesus Christ was conceived of the Holy Spirit, born of a virgin, crucified for our sins to reconcile a fallen race to a righteous God, and buried, and now "he is risen, as he said" (Matt. 28:6 AV).

Speaking of the foundation of our Christian faith, the apostle Paul states, ". . . if Christ is not risen, your faith *is* futile [vain, empty, without value]" (1 Cor. 15:17 NKJV) "and we are of all men the most pitiable" (1 Cor. 15:19b NKJV). One of the most-documented events of history is that Jesus rose from the dead, and because He lives, we shall live also.

As I began to unfold that message before an expectant crowd, I enumerated some of the benefits of Christ's resurrection. Through a risen Christ, we can know His peace, His love, His power, His healing, and His cleansing from original and ongoing sin.

Because He lives on Easter morning, and every other morning of our lives, we can know His peace. As Jesus mentored His disciples during their forty-two months of walking with the Master, He made them a promise: "Peace I leave with you, My peace I give to you; not as the world gives do I give to you" (John 14:27 NKJV). The peace that Jesus spoke of is not to be confused with our understanding of humanly contrived peace. Human or natural peace is the result of diligent achievement in the areas of education, career, financial security, happy marriage, healthy children, etc. After spending a lifetime carefully positioning the essential building blocks that should produce human peace, we may feel some degree of satisfaction and achievement. It may all, however, be lost by one unexpected cataclysmic, marital, family, or business disruption. Human peace is elusive and temporary.

Conversely, Christ's peace is not dependent on or forfeited by any level of human achievement or tragedy. His peace that He enjoys with God the Father is divine peace. His heavenly peace is unaffected by any human intervention and interference. The peace that Jesus gives to us, He wants us to appropriate as an integral part of our inheritance by being in the family of God through faith at salvation and which is now ours to possess and enjoy.

Christ's divine peace, however, is a gift that takes time to assimilate. We should learn to give priority to it. For many, our preference for human peace results from a lifetime of catering to the demands of the flesh, through which we develop our own human brand of peace.

The crowd stood in silence in their sun-drenched golden sand sanctuary, seemingly absorbing and digesting my every word. Only the tropical birds in their morning flight seemed to notice the intrusion of this human influx to their usually tranquil surroundings. As the message moved further along to share with them an added quality available to them through the resurrection, it was obvious that this dimension was His love that could be theirs. It touched another chord in their spirits.

In such an atmosphere, ministry was easy. The anointing of the Holy Spirit seemed to emanate from the vibrant and attentive crowd that had only minutes earlier emptied themselves into heavenly rhapsodic worship.

Resulting from the diverse circumstances that prevail in our disturbed global village, it's easy to understand how hostilities build in politics, world government, the threat of terrorism, escalating crime, and the volatile economy. These traumas bring tensions and divisions in communities and families. On every front of media, it seems there is a heart cry for someone to help, to wave a magic wand, as it were, and not just to restore real peace but to redefine true affection and love.

Sadly, in our English language, there is only one word for true affection. That word is love. We use it to describe the artwork on the wall of our home, the family pet at our feet, and the spouse and children for whom we would give our lives. But in Greek it is much clearer. Four separate words are used that help us to differentiate and clarify the use of the word love. C. S Lewis, in his *Four Loves*,[31] differentiates the Greek words: *eros*,[32] representing physical love; *storge*,[33] addressing family love, and *phileo*,[34] speaking of brotherly love. The highest form of love is the fourth Greek word, which is *agape*.[35] This is God's divine love and is used to describe the love of God for a lost world. Agape is God's self-sacrificial love for all human beings. The Scripture teaches that "God is love" (1 John 4:8 AV)—not just that He has the ability to love but that He is love personified. It was this love that necessitated the coming of God in Christ to redeem a sinful creation back to a right relationship with Him.

The apostle John described this world-changing event when he declared by the Holy Spirit's inspiration, "For God so loved the world, that he gave his only begotten Son" (John 3:16 AV). This is the *agape* of God that was perpetuated in the world through the person of His Son, who is without "spot and blameless" (2 Peter 3:14 AV). To pay the price and satisfy the demands of a Holy God, Jesus Christ was the only sinless sacrifice for our sins that was acceptable. Through Christ's love for us demonstrated by His death on Calvary's cross, He has redeemed (bought back) us and placed us by spiritual adoption as sons and daughters of God. By His sacrificial gift, we have been reinstated to our original inheritance through our kinsman redeemer, Jesus Christ (Ruth 4:1-12).

By now it was after six in the morning. The local fishermen were pushing out their small boats to begin their day's work. But they stopped work to take the time to join the morning rally on the beach. Several dozen of them gathered around the periphery of the crowd as I discussed yet another benefit from His resurrection: His power. Because He lives, we can know this resurrection power in our lives to enable us to live in victory over the defeating desires of the flesh. Jesus encouraged His disciples by stating, "Because I live, you will live also" (John 14:19b NKJV). Christ rose to live in resurrection power in "the power of an endless life"; He would now live in and through them (Heb. 7:16 NKJV). He assured them that His new life of power was now theirs also. This word "also" clearly demonstrates Christ's intention to communicate to them that the message of His resurrection life was now theirs and had to be appropriated by them as they fulfilled His commission, empowered to reach and win their generation to faith in Jesus.

This power of which He spoke would assure them that in the moment of their greatest crisis, their deepest need, or when they, like He, would be called upon to lay down their lives for their faith, His power would indeed be adequate to meet such a challenging hour.

As each succeeding thought of the message developed, Christ's provision for them became more meaningful. Many in this crowd, which now had grown to probably two thousand people or more, most of whom had likely never heard a clear gospel presentation before, were hungry to hear more. They responded to the fact that through Christ's resurrection there is also healing—healing from the many scars of life that had compounded over many years. There is healing, by faith, that could be theirs on that day. Finally the answer to their search for the burden of life they had carried for so long had come. It was an end to the years of pain for which they could find no relief. Today it could be theirs. That day they were hearing, many for the first time, that there is another way. There is a way back to God by faith in His finished work on the cross. Then they, too, could be victorious overcomers.

Because Christ lives, they could know His healing. For them to find healing, deliverance, freedom, and the breaking of the yoke of sin's bondage within the reality and truth of a new faith in the Living God, who raised Christ from the dead, was potentially life-changing. This commitment would empower those who confessed their faith in Him to live free from bondage and whatever the problem might be that concerned each one in that sacred Easter assembly. In all of its many facets, they were hearing a message that promoted healing.

In the book of Isaiah, the assurance of healing was heralded. Over seven hundred years before Christ's birth, the prophet Isaiah declared in chapter 53 that, in addition to being wounded for our sins, with His stripes we are healed. Healing for our bodies is in the efficacy of Christ's broken body and lacerated back on the cross. He atoned for our sin through His sacrifice on the cross, shedding His blood and providing cleansing for our sin. Thereby there is total healing for us in Christ's atonement.

Although Isaiah lived before the crucifixion of Christ and his prophecy was for the future, the tense used of this event was prophetically revealed by the Holy Spirit to him as past. To Isaiah, the event was as good as done. As the prophet looked ahead to the cross of Christ, the suffering servant, he declared, "He was wounded," "He was bruised," and

> *The chastisement for our peace was upon Him,*
> *And by His stripes we are healed* (Is. 53:5c NKJV).

Interestingly, in relation to healing being in the atonement, the tense of this verse changes from past to present. The redemptive work was completed and settled in the death and resurrection of Jesus Christ. In practical application, the healing process for every area of the Christian believer's life is an ongoing process. On a daily basis we are being healed (present tense) as we walk by faith in obedience to His Word.

Almost without exception, in every gathering as I share the full gospel of Christ, there are those who, in some form, have a need that His provision of healing in the atonement will address. As I preach healing in Christ's atonement, in almost every service where people respond to this ministry, God heals. In a lifetime of ministry, I have seen God's willingness and power to alleviate human suffering through the work of the Spirit in physical healing. As the power of the Sovereign God has touched them in His own way and in His own time, many have received their healing.

On that Easter morning, I described to the crowd healing testimonies from former events to build faith in the hearts of those who were trusting for their healing. Now it would be their time for their touch from *Jehovah Rophi,* "I *am* the LORD who heals you" (Ex. 15:26 NKJV).

As I approached the end of the message and the service, the crowd seemed to continue to build. Children were playing on the beach, and about a hundred or more were seated on the sand listening attentively. From experience I have learned that, in leading into an appeal for salvation, the most vital point—the gift of salvation—is to be emphasized in its importance and to be clearly explained at the end of the message.

For about ninety minutes, the crowd had stood virtually motionless. On this beautiful Easter morning, they worshiped and praised the Lord. They heard the story of the resurrection and the power that is available to them to live in total victory because of Christ's complete and finished work that fully satisfies the just demands of a Holy God.

They now understood that because Christ lives, they could experientially know His peace, His love, His power, His healing, and now, in this final moment, His cleansing for their sin.

For this group, that same power, if applied to their lives through faith, would enable them to live in victory. As they listened, the message assured them that by coming in faith and simply trusting in the living God and in His shed blood to remove their generational sin of the past, they could walk free from sin through His finished work. We inherited our sin from the disobedience of Adam in the Garden of Eden and consequently received his sinful DNA, which contaminated every human being since that time and separated us from our natural and rightful relationship with God. As His Word declares, "For all have sinned, and come short of the glory of God" (Rom. 3:23 AV). "Behold, I was shapen in inequity; and in sin did my mother conceive me" (Ps. 51:5 AV).

When faith in Christ alone is exercised, the efficacy of His blood and the power of His resurrection provided all the components essential for our salvation. The Scripture declares, "For the wages of sin is death; but the gift of God is eternal life through Jesus Christ our Lord" (Rom. 6:23 AV).

As we accept His gift to us and apply it to a changed lifestyle, it will result in a genuine work of grace, which will be evidenced in our lives.

After I declared to my audience that the penalty for sin is death, everlasting separation from a Holy God, they were now prepared to hear the great news. It is that they have been reinstated to their right relationship with God, which was lost through Adam's sin and now purchased again through redemption (being bought back) by Christ, who died in their place. This is without cost to them; it is "the gift of God." Salvation was for the poorest person present, the little child, and everyone. This is the great and good news of the gospel—the finale.

To conclude the message and this most meaningful Resurrection Easter service, it was fitting that an opportunity be given for those with a need to come to the altar and have time to respond to God's touch on their lives.

The greatest event of all is that even one may find freedom from sin and discover a rich new life in Christ. It is that those with physical, mental, emotional, family, or other needs will also find this moment and this powder sand altar, a place where heaven will touch earth and where the hand of God will touch the heart of man and an everlasting work will be done.

Traditionally, as I made the altar call, those who wished to respond were invited to meet me at the front as I moved from the raised platform to their ground level in front of the platform. This minor move of stepping down to their level made it easier and more inviting and created a warmer atmosphere for their response to God's call. Paul encouraged, ". . . by all means save some" (1 Cor. 9:22d AV).

That morning was different. Almost as though the crowd had a sixth sense, before the call to come forward was made, many began breaking away from the main body of the audience and moved quietly and purposefully to the front beside me. The trickle of penitents grew larger and larger until almost the entire crowd in response moved en masse to the front to the invitation for salvation or personal ministry.

By having a meaningful salvation prayer repeated through one or several interpreters depending on the language or dialects necessary to convey clarity of thought to those seeking the new birth, the most important business of salvation was dealt with first. My practise has been to ensure that each one who responds to the salvation message receives salvation material and completes a registration card for follow-up by the national pastors.

Second, for the next hour or so, time was given for ministry to the sick and for other needs. God works in His own way, and the results are always a blessing to those who have received Him by faith.

What an inspiring Easter service! What a super location! How blessed we all were to see God's hand in His mighty anointing. But I needed to conclude because there were eight more Easter services scheduled for that day!

# 7

# PARAPLEGIC PASTOR HEALED BY FORGIVENESS

The following incident serves to illustrate the power of the spoken word in a lecture setting. Generally we associate a notable miracle with prayer. A typical verse would be, ". . . the prayer of faith shall save the sick, and the Lord shall raise him up" (James 5:15a AV). In a musical analogy, that Scripture could represent one of several notes, when played accurately, that would make a complete chord. Other notes could be holiness, praise, worship, etc. In this instance, the note selected or used by God to move His child to deliverance was forgiveness.

In his sovereignty, God has a unique way of highlighting areas in one's life that require one's attention. Often as a child comes to a parent and asks for something, the parent will readily comply if it is for the child's overall good. On another occasion, when the child asks, the parent may make it conditional: "Yes, you may, when you tidy your room." It would seem that there is a parallel here in how God sometimes answers our prayers.

On many occasions healing, deliverance, or provision come quickly and without effort. Sometimes, however, it would seem that God has a "tidy your room" dimension to the request. As we comply, by modifying our behaviour, adding something we have neglected, or eliminating something that, in His plan for our lives, is superfluous, the request is often granted. Just as every child is different, so our needs and disciplines are varied in how God applies His correction through the Bible.

Many times there may be a prolonged fine-tuning effect until we reach his perfect pitch standard. The dramatic happening related in this lecture serves to illustrate the importance of playing the correct notes to produce a perfect chord.

On most tours, the full spectrum of ministry, in addition to evangelism, includes leadership schools and pastors' seminars. One tour of eight weeks in one country was no exception. As we arrived at the venue on the edge of one of the largest and most productive palm oil plantations in Asia, the pre-seminar volume of sound coming from the worship service sounded more like seven thousand than seven hundred voices.

As we entered the wooden structure that had a corrugated iron roof and long parallel strings of electric light bulbs, it helped to bring the large group of men who were standing with raised hands, lost in praise to God, into sharper focus. For the past week, these pastors had been traveling considerable distances by bus, train, bicycle, motorbike, and many walking, some for days, to arrive there on time for the meetings.

The atmosphere of expectancy was obvious and filled the building. Their worship had a richness and depth that seemed to transform a jungle shed into a veritable holy place. This worship was in contrast to much of the Western style of worship to which many have become accustomed. Yes, there were incredible worship leaders and musicians accompanying them but not leading an audience of mostly observers.

As they worshiped God from their hearts, those saints, with abandon, had created a crescendo of volume and for the most part were virtually oblivious to the incidental music accompanying them. Their praise was not in the words of a chorus another had composed but their own expression of personal praise and prayer in the spirit and with their understanding, singing as one voice to the God, who inhabits the praises of His people. It reflected the sentiment of the Psalmist: "But You *are* holy, Enthroned in the praises of Israel" (Ps. 22:3 NKJV). In encouragement he continues by adding, "Sing praises with understanding" (Ps. 47:7b NKJV). The apostle Paul entreated the Corinthian church by saying, "I will pray with the spirit, and I will also pray with the understanding. I will sing with the spirit, and I will also sing with the understanding" (1 Cor. 14:15 NKJV).

These beautiful Christian believers gave leadership to their small churches throughout their vast country. Although not all highly educated by Western standards, or even possessing what is considered in the West a basic four-year seminary degree, they had learned a great lesson. They had experientially practiced the difference between searching to receive the Holy Spirit's anointing *for* their lives and releasing that anointing in their praise and worship *from* their lives. As the apostle Paul encouraged Timothy, "Therefore I remind you to stir up the gift of God which is in you" (2 Tim. 1:6a NKJV). Could it be that we somehow have neglected this very point—stirring up the gifting that God has equipped us with, which is already within us awaiting our initiative to be released for His glory and the edification of His Body?

Even as we pressed forward through the shoulder-to-shoulder crowd, it was as though the very glory of God in some unseen way was being imparted from them to us. During this short but prolonged walk to the front, it became very obvious that they were not only singing "with understanding" but also "in the spirit." Their voices rose melodiously in their prayer language, blending with those singing with their understanding. That blending produced a divine symphony of sound from which we in the West could well be enriched if we applied it as they did. Perhaps it is not always seeking to *receive* from Him but the *releasing* what we already have to *stir up* our spirits that could be the catalyst, also opening our floodgates of worship.

Although it was just past eight a.m., it was as though everyone had been there for hours. The first teaching session was until noon. An army of local ladies provided lunch, and the afternoon session occupied another four hours. After I reached the front of the building, one of the leaders began to introduce several rows of their most senior pastors. That process took some time, as in addition to a handshake, we greeted one another cheek to cheek on both sides of each face.

Before I went to the platform, there remained one senior pastor for me to meet. He was seated with his wife in the center of the front row, directly in front of the lectern. On either side of him were two well-worn aluminum crutches. This dear saint of God, who was probably in his late sixties, was in fact the pastor to the pastors. They were his ministry family. In addition to his church-planting activities, which had produced many churches of which he was leader over a lifetime, he had established a number of sizable orphanages and children's homes. In the past few years, he had become a paraplegic, not being able to move from the waist down, although he was still very active in ministry. We had a warm and extended time of greeting, made possible by my ever-present interpreter. Finally the welcoming was over, and the teaching day began.

After four hours, which seemed to race by, we were served a sumptuous lunch. Seven hundred pastors and perhaps two hundred of their wives were seated outside at five or six twenty-metre-long (almost twenty-four yards each) tables under what seemed like half a hectare of blue sky tarpaulin supported by dozens of bamboo poles. The fragrance from this jungle paradise and the aroma of exotic Asian foods was beyond my ability to describe.

Then we continued with the last session of the seminar, which seemed to go faster than the first, and the eight hours were almost over. As I was developing the seminar's final point, it led to another significant issue: our willingness for forgiveness to flow from us and without resistance.

Many Scriptures reinforce the necessity of forgiving, such as Ephesians 4:32: "And be kind one to another, tenderhearted, forgiving one another, even as God in Christ forgave you." (NKJV).

Forgiveness is not only something we receive but also something we give. This is not a suggestion but a command.

How did God forgive us? He forgave us totally, completely, and forever. He gave us 100 percent forgiveness for our every sin when we were washed in the blood of Christ. Our sin was not covered, as in the old covenant with the sacrifice of bulls and goats. Instead, our sin was removed; it was taken way. In the new covenant under Jesus Christ, we have John the apostle declaring, "Behold! The Lamb of God who takes away the sin of the world!" (John 1:29 NKJV). He is the Lamb of God who shed His blood once for the remission of our sins. In His divine love and mercy, God forgave us. Paul instructed the Ephesians to forgive even as God in Christ forgave us. That is *divine* forgiveness.

In our new nature as believers, "which is Christ in" us "the hope of glory" (Col. 1:27b NKJV), we have a command to forgive as we have been forgiven.

Our *human* nature seems inadequate to accomplish this. When we try in the flesh, the old nature raises its head, and we often renege. The flesh is weak; hence we are encouraged to forgive "even as" God forgave us. God did not forgive us with imperfect *human* forgiveness but with His adequate and perfect *divine* forgiveness.

As new creatures in Christ Jesus, we "do not walk according to the flesh, but according to the Spirit" (Rom. 8:1b NKJV, 4b). We walk in the power of His resurrection, and we are empowered to forgive others in the strength of our *divine nature*, which is adequate and will succeed. Luke records in his gospel, "Forgive, and you will be forgiven" (Luke 6:37 NKJV). Do we need to belabour the antithesis of this statement?

As the final moments of the seminar began to draw to a close, there were still a few more verses I needed to leave with this great group.

In the middle of the Beatitudes, Jesus taught His disciples to resolve their differences quickly with their brothers. He instructed them to leave their gift at the altar and that their gift or offering would not be acceptable to God until the issue was resolved (Matt. 5:21-26). Also in Matthew's gospel we read, "For if you forgive men their trespasses, your heavenly Father will also forgive you. But if you do not forgive men their trespasses, neither will your Father forgive your trespasses" (Matt. 6:14-15 NKJV).

In his relationship with God, David had learned this lesson of life well when he said: "If I regard iniquity in my heart, the Lord will not hear me" (Ps. 66:18 AV). He is making a significant statement. Whatever "iniquity" lurks un–confessed in a believer's spirit, inhibits, or more strongly, stops the free flow of communication with God. This issue was addressed directly by the apostle James, when, by the inspiration of the Spirit, he declared, "Therefore, to him who knows to do good and does not do *it*, to him it is sin" (James 4:17 NKJV). Our actions, whether overtly or covertly, will fracture our strong relationship of blessing and anointing with God if we fail to follow this principle.

I clearly made the point to the pastors that, as mature believers, we have a command and responsibility to forgive. Period! Were we guilty when we needed forgiveness? Yes! Is the person who has offended us guilty? Yes! Should we have been forgiven by Christ from our guilt? Yes! Should this person be forgiven by us from his or her guilt? Yes! As we have been forgiven, we must forgive others. Someone has rightly said that unforgiveness is like holding a loaded gun at your own head, pulling the trigger, and expecting the other person to drop, or drinking poison and expecting the other person to die. Unforgiveness is being angry at our enemy and taking the poison of anger, which will kill us. On occasion it may be necessary to ask someone who has wronged us for forgiveness, even though he or she should be apologising to us. As believers, our improper response to someone who wrongs us means we also need to ask for his or her forgiveness. Often other people will apologise when they sense the spirit of Christ in our actions toward them. I used many more verses to develop this major closing point fully.

Shortly before the end of the afternoon session, something unusual happened. The senior pastor, who was the spiritual father to the men seated behind him and was sitting between the two aluminum crutches, began to move his hands forward and backward slowly on his thighs. When his wife tried to hold his arm steady so he would not disturb the closing moments, he vigorously declined her gesture.

As I was about to close in prayer, he began to reach for the back of the bench with one hand and push on the seat with the other. Within a few seconds, he was struggling to stand on his feet, which he had not used in years. Timidly and with great effort, this spiritual giant hauled his feeble frame to full stature. His body was weaving to and fro over legs that looked like they were inadequate for the assignment. Slowly he raised one foot for just a second only inches from the floor and then the other. He repeated that sequence many times. Every eye in the room was on their spiritual father. What was this? What was happening? They had not seen him on his feet for many years.

Five minutes later, his feeble legs were lifting his feet higher and faster. Without warning, he began taking feeble baby steps while his family of pastors began to stand and praise God. His baby-like steps lengthened and quickened as he rounded the first corner of a bench and headed down the side of the auditorium. Upon reaching the back of the building and beginning his return up the opposite side, he was moving at a slow trot, which quickly brought him to the front, and then he took several more circuits of the auditorium.

The eight-hour seminar was momentarily forgotten as the audience erupted in praise and worship. They applauded, cried, and hugged each other as they crowded around a man who had been a paraplegic for many years.

What was this about? What had happened? What had been the catalyst to produce such a spontaneous miracle without even a prayer? Would they ever know?

Coincidentally and weeks earlier, as the seminar was being planned, this pastor had also scheduled a dinner at his home after the seminar. When I arrived there, he was already seated in his front room. He immediately began to relate the process that had triggered such a notable miracle.

The story began several years earlier as he considered the sizable work that God had allowed him to develop. Because of the many churches, orphanages, and children's homes that were under his leadership and properties that were in his name, he wanted to be proactive. As he became older, he wanted to train a younger man who would ultimately release him from his heavy load of ministry. After a lengthy screening period, he chose a pastor who was half his age for the position. The plan called for several years of training with the senior man before the reins would be passed to him. The young man was said to be a model trainee and very spiritual. He was thought to operate with integrity, was liked by everyone, and eventually was on the verge of appointment.

Providentially, one day a document came into the senior pastor's hands that seemed to indicate some impropriety by the younger man. Upon investigation, the senior pastor found that during the lengthy training period, the young man had embezzled all of the ministry's properties by making a false conveyance of them into his own name and forging the senior pastor's signature. There were many altercations resulting from that action, which greatly disturbed the senior pastor. A few months later, he became ill, and later he felt that those infirmities resulted in his paraplegic condition.

The senior pastor eventually came to the seminar in which he heard the message of forgiveness, and he sensed the Holy Spirit moving on him. The further the subject developed, the more he felt that he was being led to ask the young man for his forgiveness. By this he meant that he would go to the young man and ask him to forgive him for how he had behaved as a believer and senior pastor in the past turmoil, regardless of the young man's actions.

He not only felt that the Holy Spirit was prompting him to forgive the young man, but also he felt he needed to go and ask for the young man's forgiveness. He planned to do this at a convenient time after the seminar and crusades had concluded.

Moments after committing to this plan of reconciliation, he began to sense slight vibrations and tingling deep in the center of his legs and hips. The sensation increased. It was as though he felt new warmth, and it seemed to him that his blood was flowing quickly in a new way through his arteries. He was then confident to try and support himself in an effort to stand. And stand he did!

For a number of years, our ministry schedule brought us back to his district. When we saw him, he looked younger—not older—by at least ten years. Never did we see him use a wheelchair or any walking device, although he would then probably have been in his eighties.

Any time we fellowshipped in his area, he would recall the miracle moment that changed his life. He spoke of realizing the consequence of the words of his mouth at the time of the conflict and how the attitude of unforgiveness in his heart had injured his spirit. This behaviour had hindered his walk in fellowship with God, which he felt left him open and vulnerable to become paralyzed. He recognized that reversing those issues and reconciling with the brother brought his deliverance. It taught him, he said, to put a watch on his words. Second Peter 3:1 says, "stir up your pure minds by way of remembrance" (AV).

Several years later, while I was traveling between airports in the former paraplegic pastor's country, I heard my name called. As I stopped with surprise and looked around the busy airport, a man was running toward me. He introduced himself as the airport administrator and the son of the former paraplegic pastor. He completed the final chapter in the pastor's story for me.

At an old age, his father had only recently passed away but without any debilitating sickness. His paraplegic condition never reoccurred, and until his death, he never again used even a walking cane.

Together with the multitude of verses that relate to the subject of forgiveness, the lesson of this prince of pastors is one I trust that I will always remember. In concluding this New Testament type of story, two references from the Old Testament would be appropriate: "But the tongue of the wise promotes health" (Prov. 12:18 NKJV) and ". . . good news gives health to the bones" (Prov. 15:30b NIV).

# 8

# SUPERNATURAL EVENTS IN MINISTRY TRAVEL

## God Supplies Water from a Dry Mountain Rock

Our eight-week Asian tour began by teaching at a Bible college for several days. Immediately after this, about twenty-five of the senior students accompanied us for several weeks as part of their ministry internships. We traveled in several vehicles, one of which was a small bus that held most of the students and carried all the baggage, and sometimes a few students, on the roof rack that ran the full length of the not-so-modern bus. Such a mode of transportation is acceptable in many Asian countries, as is the habit of hanging off the outside of vehicles by grasping any metal appendage within reach.

During previous ministry, several of these students had traveled with us and were a tremendous asset to the team. It was not unusual to cover ten or twelve thousand kilometres on such trips as we moved from city to town to village on a three—or four-day preaching and teaching cycle.

As always, ministry would vary. I would take the team to different outreaches, such as to schools, colleges, and universities. On other occasions it would be a factory, a department store, or perhaps a prison. The students always worked hard as they played special musical numbers and gave their personal testimonies. They set up platforms and sound systems, did altar work, prayed for the sick, and monitored the crowds as they helped with preparation of outdoor rallies.

When the tour pushed farther into the jungle, everyone had to be billeted in local huts, including Shirley and me. A separate book could easily be written dealing only with those experiences.

One afternoon as we arrived in a village early to prepare for the evening open-air service, two students were assigned to each hut. One of the better huts was kept for Shirley and me. As we prepared to enter the hut, we were told to wait because it was not yet prepared for us. Happily, we waited a few metres away and chatted with some students. Soon several men approached the hut carrying what looked like a mattress and bed frame. Great! We thought this must be special treatment for the Westerners. We were ecstatic because in that setting usually we slept covered with a plastic sheet with the family on a mud floor.

The men assembled the bed in a corner of the hut, and it looked marvellous to us. This was the first time anything like this had happened in that setting. Then another man arrived and said something in his language to the men who had assembled the bed, and it was promptly disassembled and carried back up the main street of the village.

"What happened to our bed?" we asked a young pastor. Rather sheepishly, he advised us that the last man who came was the owner of the bed who was loaning it to this family for our use. But when he came to survey the scene and saw the size of the two Westerners, he was sure we would break his bed, so he reneged. So we slept where we usually did with the family—on the mud floor.

During that tour, the monsoon season began and made the normal red clay roads into a quagmire. This added many hours to our daily driving time and meant that we had to have earlier starts on the days that greater distances had to be traveled.

On several occasions the red soup we had to navigate bogged

us down, and everyone had to go barefoot with trousers rolled as high as possible to try to set free the convoy.

After a very long day of travel and ministry, I recall having to drive a great distance to our jungle billets. At perhaps eleven-thirty, the inevitable happened. Mud was up to the axel of our bus. We were truly stuck. No amount of pushing or praying moved us that night. Hours dragged by, and finally someone reached a house where there was a tractor. Even the tractor could not move the bus until every man put his shoulder to the bus and pushed as the tractor pulled. Within a couple of kilometres of driving, we were stuck again. Fortunately, we had retained the tractor for such a situation, and this time things went more smoothly. Eventually we arrived at our billets around one-thirty in the morning.

Our accommodation looked fantastic from the outside. It was a quite modern but little house. As we spread around all of our students who needed to be billeted, there was quite a commotion as we awoke everyone in the village that night.

Shirley's and my billet was another story. When it got past midnight, our host assumed that we were not coming. The young married couple who had vacated our bed to sleep on the floor decided to go back to the bed to get a good night's sleep. Upon our arrival, they were awakened and again asked to vacate their bed for us, and they kindly did so. Moments later, and in a state of exhaustion after travel, ministry, and hours of pushing and pulling, we entered a dark room. As we climbed into bed, we realized that the heat from the bodies of the previous couple was coming out of the mattress. The same sheets and hot pillows were used to warm us. After being in bed for a few minutes, I became aware of an unusual odour. As I reached out to my side of the bed, my hand touched a warm motorbike, with its petrol and oil smell. The owner had brought it inside for safety and left it with us. The rest of the night was uneventful. We slept like babies and arose refreshed and ready for another day of whatever God had planned for our team ministry.

Sometimes in circumstances such as those, I find myself reflecting on my youth, early business life, and ministry. At that time, nothing was further from my mind than missionary work. Any heart I had for missions was to pray for those who went or to help with support. To go to a field and have experiences I had heard missionaries share on home assignment was never on my radar. Western evangelism? Yes! Missions? No! But God! With God all things are possible.

Only God, in His sovereign and supernatural way, could ever have persuaded me to become a missionary evangelist. When He called and empowered me, promising that this new assignment of ministry would be in the power and demonstration of the Holy Spirit, my wife and I obeyed and trusted Him every step of the way. Although it has not been easy, it has been a walk of commitment and faith on our part and one of performance and fulfilment on His. Every step has been a supernatural step. God is always there.

While writing about Abraham's faith in the fulfillment of the promised Isaac, the apostle Paul recounted that it was counted to Abraham for righteousness. He said, ". . . what he had promised, he was able also to perform" (Rom. 4:21b AV). So it has been for us during a lifetime of ministry. So it will be for those whose hearts God touches. Those whom He calls, He will enable. Talents and skills will develop; proficiency will increase beyond one's wildest dreams. Nothing and no one can impede the work of the person sold out completely to the call of God. There is no greater honour, thrill, blessing, or anointing than to know one is in the center of God's will. To be aware of the Spirit's prompting in every turn of the ministry road, being propelled and directed only by Him, brings one the most sublime feelings of satisfaction. There is no moment when the one who surrenders and commits his life to ministry will ever be short-changed. God is debtor to no one.

Each day that a ministry schedule unfolds always surprises us, and with a great team of young Bible college workers, it is always exciting.

As we moved to another area of jungle evangelism, we came to a spectacular part of the country overlooking the South China

Sea. The community that was designated for work and would be our base for the next week was located at an elevation of several thousand feet and perched on a crag overlooking a breathtaking ocean and mountainside. We virtually had a 360-degree panoramic view.

It was there that I had one of the most significant God encounters of my life. Several days into the meetings, it was necessary to go from our lofty perch to the ocean village for an assignment. At midmorning, we decided that about twenty of us would go on a pleasant walk down the mountainside. This was not a precipitous or dangerous descent, but it did require agility. We happily walked and stumbled down as everyone fellowshipped and sang. It was quite a heavenly time as we enjoyed one another's company, the presence of God, and the spell-binding views He had created. Within the hour, we arrived at the ocean. All of us busied ourselves in personal evangelism. We used one-on-one encounters, including praying with those who needed a touch from God. In the early afternoon, after several hours of ministry, it was time to go back to our lofty base several thousand feet up the same mountain.

We all began climbing together, but soon the younger members of the team, with their high energies, accelerated their climb. Although I was enjoying the outing, it soon became obvious that my speed was not equal to theirs, and the sun was now generating a temperature in the range of high-thirties Celsius. One young man named Eben remained with me as we walked a little slower than the others. About twenty minutes into the ascent, I became aware of an unusual thirst. At first I thought little of it because the day was hot and we had above-normal exertion. As we looked higher, we could see the speck-size forms of the other team members. As they approached the peak, they looked like tiny mountain goats.

As I climbed further, my mouth became incredibly dry. Minutes later it was as though my tongue was stuck to the roof of my mouth. It was necessary to do something quickly. I called to Eben and told him my plight and that I could go no further without water, which, sadly, neither of us had. As my throat was beginning to close, I knew for the first time in my life I was in serious trouble. Eben said he would run to our base at the top of the mountain and come again with water because there was none on the mountain. He knew that from having grown up in that village. He reckoned the total round trip would take him forty or fifty minutes—time I was not sure I had. He prayed with me and left like a chased rabbit. As I sat down on the shade-less hillside, I covered my head with my shirt and hands. I waited quietly in an attempt to conserve whatever fluid remained, not expecting my life-saving water for what seemed would be a lifetime.

Within ten minutes, he was back, laden with a large Coke bottle full of precious water, and he was in an emotional state. As I emptied the full bottle, my trauma passed. Speech was now possible, and I asked why he was crying.

"Pastor," he sobbed, "I know there is no water on this mountain. Never! While I was running to the top and passing a rocky crag, I heard an unusual sound. As I stopped to investigate, I heard the sound of a waterfall. I looked around the rocks, and there was a heavy flow of water cascading from a cleft in the rock. That has never been there in my lifetime. Pastor, it was God just providing water for you. Also, since all we young people get money for bottles, there is never a bottle wasted. Today at the waterfall this Coke bottle was just lying there at the base. When you recover, we can go there I will show you the waterfall."

Soon we began to climb again, this time at my speed, and within a few minutes, he pointed out the rock, walking me over to the side to see the waterfall. In sheer consternation, he looked at the cleft in the rock from which he had caught the water; there was none. The rock was as dry as it ever had been on the hot mountainside.

"Pastor," he said, "this is the rock. This is the cleft the water gushed from, but now it's gone."

As he stood there in disbelief, I also wondered how this had transpired. While surveying the improbable story, I pointed at his feet. He was standing on a section of saturated earth from which the tailings of water could be traced perhaps fifty feet further down the hillside; it was evidence, beyond a doubt, that a supernatural event had occurred there minutes before. We stood and cried and worshiped together. This was yet another God moment in my life, as He had promised when the missions call came—that we would move in the power and demonstration of the Spirit. Many more such provisions have occurred since and some are related later in the book.

Scriptures flooded my mind for the rest of the climb. I thought of Moses' encounter with wayward Israel when they complained bitterly in the wilderness for lack of water (Ex. 17:1). God instructed him to take his rod and strike the rock and water would come out (v. 5-6). Asaph reviewed this supernatural phenomenon (Ps. 78:15-16) that is also seen in Psalm 105:41. In Numbers 20:8-11, another emergency of thirst occurred. At that time, God instructed Moses to speak to the rock and water would come forth.

At the end of Moses' life, with the change of leadership to Joshua and the land of promise within sight, it was necessary for God to prevent Moses from entering into the Promised Land, not as a result of his killing of the Egyptian but because of his disobedience in striking the rock the second time, instead of speaking to it. As a type, the rock represented our Rock, Jesus Christ, who, as the "last Adam," would be crucified, being struck once, in full and final payment for the sin inflicted on the human family by the "first man Adam" (1 Cor. 15:45b AV). By striking the wilderness rock twice in his disobedience, Moses inadvertently violated the typology by introducing the unthinkable concept that Christ could die more than once for our sins. This would wrongly infer that He may not be the last but a second or subsequent Adam (Heb. 10:10).

Why was God so irate? Since the rock was a type of Jesus Christ, who would be struck only once through His crucifixion, the rock needed only to be struck once and subsequently to be spoken to for the provision of our need of salvation.

When we returned safely to the top of the mountain, my young friend excitedly related the event to the locals, who were sceptical of his account since they also knew there was no water flowing from any rock on the mountain. But he and I knew there was water and that God had honoured His Word.

## Four Lifesaving Interventions in One Evening

We were almost to the end of a lengthy tour, and as always, the pace quickened as more and more bookings were scheduled. At other preaching points, different team members would speak. On this occasion, Shirley and I, together with two others, were scheduled to go from the Southeast Asian mainland to an island on a massive lake. It required several hours of driving, a short ferry ride, and then another lengthy journey to a high-altitude village for a seminar and evening rally.

The plan was that I speak for the seminar at a lower-altitude location. Shirley would continue to the higher mountain location for a ladies' meeting, and then I would join her for the evening rally.

During my seminar, incredible monsoon rains delayed our mountain drive on clay roads that made it almost impossible to pass other vehicles. Because we thought my drive might be aborted, they alerted Shirley that she would probably be preaching instead of me. She quickly prepared a gospel message from a specific text and was ready to preach. I arrived seconds before she was about to begin, and I went immediately to the pulpit. Shirley listened in disbelief as my message began to roll; it was from the same text she had used and addressed very similar salvation points. Either way, God was in control. The deluge continued during the meeting, and after all ministry was over, we piled into one vehicle to head down the mountain, retracing our route to the ferry and then the lengthy drive to our billets for an early-morning departure to another country.

Not so! Because of the road conditions, the empty vehicle would have to go a couple of kilometres to a better road. We would walk there and meet it. One could hardly have visualized a more pathetic group walking through such a downpour in the darkest night imaginable. We were up to the mid-calf in red mud. Men could do that, but to see two ladies do it was another matter.

The problem was that with the rains came all kinds of creepy crawlies. Not the least worry was the small snakes that enjoyed the warm, muddy water. At the end of a hectic day, we thought to ourselves that the hour walk was the last straw.

Although literally soaked to the skin, we were delighted to see our vehicle again and climbed into it with great gusto. The driver was a small man we suspected might have difficulty reaching the pedals. On this very dark evening with lashing rain, we wondered if his very thick glasses were an asset or an impediment to a safe drive down the precipitous mountainside. To our left was a solid rock face rising in steps for many hundreds of feet. To the right of our narrow mud roadway, which was hardly wider than our vehicle, was a precipitous drop of thousands of feet. By any standard, even in broad daylight, this was not a pretty picture.

As I sat in the passenger seat beside the suspect driver, knowing that we had more than an hour's drive and together with being soaking wet, I decided the best option for me was to sleep. Over many years of similar conditions, sleeping has become an easy and welcome escape. So sleep I did!

Suddenly, for no obvious reason, I was awakened from a sound sleep screaming at the top of my voice, "Stop! Stop!" With that command, instinctively my right foot hit the imaginary passenger's side brake. Although our driver understood not one word of English, he could read my body language and hit the brakes with unbelievable intensity. Under those circumstances, we stopped in the shortest distance humanly possible.

Why? Why had we stopped? Why did I wake up shouting, "Stop"?

In my sleep, somehow the Holy Spirit moved on me to awaken, and my act of shouting was like a reflex reaction. The reason? There in front of the vehicle, not six feet away, was a huge mountain slip. Solid shale had been released by the heavy rain. Standing perhaps twenty feet high, it had become its own solid mountain. Had we hit it directly, there is little doubt that we would be here to tell about it.

Now our only option was to back up, which, of itself and given the parameters, was perhaps the more frightening experience. Eventually we found a place to turn around, and we now had to drive in the opposite direction on the only other island coast road, which was a much longer way around. Finally, everyone settled down, and we all agreed that we had enough traumatic experiences for one evening.

An hour or so later, the driver announced to the interpreter that we needed fuel. Where would we get fuel at two o'clock in the morning in the middle of nowhere? The next many miles were spent stopping at houses, waking the occupants, and asking for fuel. Finally at about the fifth stop, a lady referred us to a neighbour who she thought had some, he came to the door and agreed to a price. After getting dressed, he began filling a large dish in preparation for carrying it to the vehicle and pouring it through a funnel into our tank. That was the basic idea, but there was one complication. As he carried a full open dish with both hands, with perhaps ten litres of fuel, we noticed that between the fingers of one of his hands was a lighted cigarette. Did this have the makings of another form of God's protection for that exhausted little ministry team? Even in this potentially dangerous situation, God protected us.

Finally we were on our way. The next stage would be the ferry. Within thirty minutes or so, and still in the dark, we drove along a road, when, for no apparent reason, again I shouted at the driver, "Stop!" Again he stopped, more, I suspect, by reflex than the will to comply with my command. As we drove slowly forward, just ahead and out of the range of our headlights, we were about to approach the deck of a bridge across a river, except that the raging river had inconveniently removed the total deck, leaving only a few toothpick–like support poles. There was no way we could cross here, and we were told there were no other bridges for us to cross the river.

By now it was after four in the morning, and time was running out for our morning flight out of the country. After awaking several more families, we were referred to someone who had a cattle barge and who might ferry us privately over the river.

As we followed directions to his home, presented our need, and agreed to a steep fee in American dollars, we proceeded to his mooring. After we aroused his two helpers, who we later found were high on drugs, they prepared the barge for our departure. Because there was no loading facility, we had to cross the river without our vehicle. The barge was meant only for cattle, which, after many crossings and without having been hosed down, had left their trail on the deck of the barge. There was no gangplank but only a rope ladder. This was not a challenge for the men, but it was a disaster for Shirley, who tried to help an elderly lady up the swinging ladder and over the choppy waters beneath her between the jetty and the barge. On deck, we sat on benches in the open weather, holding umbrellas in front of us to deflect the still-raging storm that had battled us at every turn. Eventually we docked, raced to our rooms, and left for the airport without further drama.

To give glory to God for His care and protection, I have recorded that day's ministry in detail. Had God not overruled, there were many incidences that could have spelled disaster for us. I have also related these experiences in detail with the hope and prayer that they might benefit the new missionary as he becomes established in God's call on his life. Hopefully he will realize that just because God has called one to missions does not necessarily mean that there will not be moments that in the natural could be discouraging. Within any trauma, standing somewhere in the shadow, is an all-sufficient, all-caring, supernatural, and sovereign God.

## A Man Located by God Directing

Over a lifetime of ministry, Shirley and I have never ceased to be amazed at the ways in which the Holy Spirit moves to solve issues that are beyond our capabilities. The incident that follows is one such example.

Several months ago, we were in another country and Shirley was counselling someone on the phone from overseas. The man mentioned a circumstance where he, as a Christian, had been terribly offended and emotionally disturbed by a senior church leader's handling of another man's issues.

On several occasions after that call, Shirley said to me, "We really need to find that person and minister to him." Eventually we visited the country in which the man lived.

One morning as I was leaving our accommodation to attend to several issues, I asked Shirley if she would like to come with me, and perhaps later we would have coffee together. At first she was hesitant to come, but after I gently persisted, she agreed to do so.

As I drove, I took a different route than usual to reach my meeting places and noticed a housing development by a company I recognized. A few minutes later, I dropped off Shirley at a shopping center and continued on my way. At noon, I met Shirley and suggested we have lunch there, but she declined and suggested another place. We came to that coffee shop, and I dropped her off and went to make one more brief call. After I returned there a few minutes later, I found her sitting on a two-seater couch opposite another two-seater with a low coffee table in between. While she was seated there alone, within a few minutes a man came and asked if she would mind if he had lunch opposite her. She agreed, and he left his original table and came over to her. When I came and joined her, he and I began to chat. As his meal arrived, he asked a blessing, to which I responded with, "Amen!"

We began to share about the Lord. After a great time of fellowship, he spoke of his church and how wonderful the fellowship was there but that the church he attended years ago had caused him great difficulty. I asked him if certain personal things had happened to him then. He looked stunned and asked me how I knew this. Then, in greater detail, Shirley began to relate some of the main points that his experience there had caused him hurt, even up to our meeting with him.

As Shirley and I revealed various things to him, his responses began to indicate to us that, in fact, he could be the man who had been identified by the person Shirley had been counselling on the phone and who had been offended by his senior church leader.

Then Shirley asked him if he was a building contractor, to which he responded with shocked silence at first and then said, "Yes!"

Indeed, this was the man Shirley had been sensing in her spirit for months we needed to find, but we had no idea how to do it. But God knew how and did it for us. Later toward the end of the lunch, he looked at me and asked if we had met before, calling me by name. Not personally, but indirectly we had met through his construction development sign as we passed it on our way to my appointments. God took us to where we were able to have extensive ministry with this man for the glory of God. Through this incident, we can clearly see the work of the Holy Spirit in operation, and this is how we should expect Him to work in our lives on a regular basis.

## Angels

On the rare occasion in ministry, usually in an acute emergency or extreme danger, we and others are persuaded that angels have intervened for our protection. The following few of many incidents are related to appraise the reader of God's provision by angels for the believer's care and safety in this dispensation.

By way of a brief explanation as to their ministrations, angels are mentioned 108 times in the Old Testament and 165 times in the New Testament. They are created beings that are enjoined to praise the Lord (Ps. 148:2, 5; Col. 1:16). As created beings, they are in God's control (1 Peter 3:22) and have power (2 Peter 2:11). "Of . . . salvation the prophets have inquired and searched carefully, who prophesied of the grace *that would come* to you . . . To them it was revealed that, not to themselves, but to us they were ministering the things which now have been reported to you through those who have preached the gospel to you by the Holy Spirit sent from heaven—things which angels desire to look into" (1 Peter 1:10, 12 NKJV).

Two-thirds of the angels who retained their first estate are spiritual beings, and among their other duties, they are sent to minister to the saints (Heb. 1:14). The third that fell in rebellion against God with Lucifer are his demons (Matt. 25:41). The book of Daniel tells of a time when Daniel prayed for assistance from God. Daniel's prayer was heard immediately, but help was delayed for twenty-one days (Dan. 10:12-13). War raged in the heavenlies between a fallen angel—now a demon of darkness—called the prince of the kingdom of Persia and the messenger of God. Michael, an angel of light, the chief messenger, and one of the chief princes came to win the conflict and release Daniel's answer (Jude 9; 1 Thess. 4:16).

Angels are significant and were present at creation (Job 38:7), at Sinai (Gal. 3:19), at the birth of Christ (Luke 2:13), and at His temptations (Matt. 4:11). Also, they were at the tomb (Luke 24:23), present on the morning of Christ's resurrection (Matt 28:2), and at His ascension (Acts 1:10). Angels were as significant and active then as they are today.

To illustrate the diversity of application between angels and believers today, consider the example of Balaam and his donkey. When Balaam disobeyed God's instruction to him in Numbers 22, he aroused God's anger. The Angel of the LORD, which Balaam did not see, stood in his way, and his donkey, seeing the angel, refused to pass. Each time the donkey refused to proceed because of seeing the Angel of the LORD standing with a drawn sword, Balaam beat her. Finally, the beast objected by verbally communicating to him in his own language and asking, "What have I done to you that you have struck me these three times?" (Num. 22:28 NKJV). Ignoring what is biologically impossible in the animal kingdom, Balaam engaged in an extended discussion. Finally, God opened his eyes, and he saw what the donkey had seen all the time. The sight of the Angel caused him to repent. The Angel used a four-legged animal to get Balaam's attention, which is similar to what the Lord did for me by using an insect in the story that follows.

## Angel in Sri Lanka

We were behind enemy lines in Sri Lanka during the height of their almost thirty-year recent war conducting several evangelistic festivals. In one such jungle area, the team of national pastors and our Western group stayed in a small village-style accommodation. Ladies were not allowed to accompany us because of the perceived danger. As I returned to my room after the meeting, the pastors advised us that there was a power failure. Not far from my window, the diesel generator loudly confirmed its presence. During the days of staying in the room alone, I noticed the paper-thin door had a very powerful closing mechanism. On more than one occasion while going to speak to a team member, it slammed shut, locking me out.

About midnight, as I prepared for bed, conscious of the danger from the military activities close by, I wondered what to do with my briefcase, which contained all my important documents plus considerable cash to pay all ministry and travel expenses as we moved from place to place.

The bed had a mounted headboard, which meant that it could be pulled away from the wall. I placed my briefcase behind it and pushed the headboard back tightly against the briefcase to the wall. I reasoned that for someone to get the briefcase, they had to get by me first. Moments after getting into bed, the generator stopped, which meant regular power was restored. Because of my busy schedule and the dark room, I quickly slipped into a sound sleep. Within minutes I became aware that my worst enemy, a mosquito, to which I was acutely allergic was buzzing around me like a 747 aircraft. Over and over it droned back and forth by my ears. Trying to catch it in the dark was futile. Finally, with an agitated leap from the bed in the darkness, I sprang to the light switch by the door, determined to take it out. The moment my feet hit the floor, I heard the paper-thin door slam shut as someone quickly left the room.

Like Balaam, I nearly missed the significance of the mosquito. After continuing to look for it before returning to bed, I finally decided there was no mosquito. I believe an angel caused only the sound of the creature I most hated to get me out of bed. I believe the whole exercise was designed to banish the intruder as my feet thundered on the floor. As the intruder heard me, he fled on foot. Was that not God and His angel mosquito security system?

## Angels in Indonesia

We were travelling in the jungles of Irian Jaya, now named the Province of Papua, Indonesia, and coming directly from our base in Wamena. Our Jeep emerged from the dense jungle to a clearing. Contrasting with the verdant green background stood an attractive modern white church. The service had already started. It had a capacity crowd, and the worship was heavenly. The believers drank in every word of the message, and God touched their hearts as He ministered to their needs.

As we drove back to Wamana, our host pastor and his wife shared with me the recent events relating to the attractive white church that seemed stranger than fiction. It all began, they said, when the pastor's wife had a vision of their new church and what was about to take place there. At that time she shared the total vision with her husband that in a certain number of days, two opposing warrior tribes would come together, right beside their new church, to meet and fight to the death with their poisoned arrows and spears merging from their respective villages from opposite sides of their community.

If this were to transpire, the residents of the church community would certainly be the innocent victims. Their church would then likely be razed to the ground. She shared with her husband that at a certain time, just before the day of the massacre, their congregation and any villagers who believed the vision and wanted to escape should accompany them up a distant hillside for safety and remain there, returning only after the conflict.

The pastor and his wife believed in the accuracy of the vision but felt a little foolish telling the villagers and their congregation their plan to escape the bloodshed with nothing more concrete than many would call a silly dream. When the time came, their entire congregation and almost every villager left the area for the hills.

Within a short time, the warring tribes converged on the clearing, and the battle raged. Poisoned arrows and long poisoned spears flew in both directions, and soon warriors from both sides began falling. Some lay dead around the church clearing while others dropped after being poisoned by an arrow or spear tip while trying to retreat to their own villages. The carnage was almost beyond description.

According to the timing of the vision, when it was safe, all of them returned from the hills to the church. When they entered the clearing, dead bodies covered the area. From earlier experience, the pastor knew that there would be total devastation. Every mud or straw hut within sight would be torched, which was the case in the past. But this time their first glimpse of the clearing exposed their new white church standing in all its splendour.

Within days things returned to a semblance of normality and news of the blood-letting began to filter back from both warring villages. The story revealed that as the conflict raged, both warring tribes separately attempted to burn down the church. The problem, the pastor was told, was that they could not approach the church because giant armed warriors were spaced every few feet, totally surrounding the building. They held large, circular shields and brandished massive spears. Other warriors interspersed with them had large and fearsome lighted torches. They reported that it was impossible to penetrate the church's defence system. The vision was true. The congregation returned without loss of life. The church was saved. God strategically placed His fearsome angelic warriors there at the perfect time to protect His house and the meeting place of His worshipers.

## Angel in Hong Kong

For a number of years as missionaries with the Pentecostal Assemblies of Canada, Shirley and I lived in Hong Kong. During the first Iraq war in the early nineties, there was heightened security in many Asian countries, including Hong Kong. One day while walking down a main shopping street in exhausting heat and high humidity, we had a brilliant idea. To reach our destination, rather than walk several blocks and then turn a corner and have to walk some more, we would take a shortcut by cutting diagonally through a shopping arcade and then walking through the reception area of the hotel lobby and out on the other side. In this way we would not only shorten the distance but also enjoy an air-conditioned reprieve from the gruelling heat. What a great plan! Or so we thought.

As we walked through the cooler arcade to reach the hotel entrance, we enjoyed window shopping, which was always a pleasant experience in such an exciting city. As we neared the impressive heavy plate glass entrance doors with their massive circular brass-knobbed handles, something unusual happened. As I reached out with my right hand to open the right-hand door for Shirley and gestured her through, a complete stranger, a distinguished Middle Eastern-looking gentleman, came between us. With his right hand, he lightly gripped my left upper arm while gripping Shirley's right arm with his left hand.

Because I had grown up in Northern Ireland during the prolonged conflict there, we had learned to be protective of our body space. Anyone getting uncomfortably close was suspect and to be avoided for one's own safety. Although that man broke the rules of my body space, we both felt at ease with his actions. He was immaculately dressed and spoke with a rich, cultivated accent. He smiled gently at us with warm brown eyes, and in a strong, firm, but reassuring tone, said, "You really don't want to go in there just now!" Then he slowly and deliberately began turning us away from the doors.

As a protective father holds the hands of his two small children, Shirley and I obediently and quietly walked beside him. I have no recollection of any further discussion with him. After walking us safely to the sidewalk away from the entrance to the arcade, he released our arms, smiled knowingly again, and seemingly dissolved into the crowd. Instantly the lobby of the hotel, where we would have been, erupted with a deafening explosion resulting from a packaged bomb reportedly delivered to the hotel reception. Without doubt, this was another God moment for us.

## Angels in Amsterdam

As we were returning to Canada from overseas ministry, our itinerary scheduled us through Amsterdam with a one-night layover and early-morning departure. After the hotel checkout, we awaited the airport bus, for which we were twenty minutes early. Suddenly a driver approached me, asking if I was going to the airport, to which I nodded in the affirmative. He asked us to hurry with our bags because he was late, and I wondered what was wrong with my thinking. He then said that his was not the bus we were waiting for and to come on his earlier bus.

Our cases were quickly stored in the luggage compartment of the bus, and we carried the normal briefcase and purse, plus an extra package that Shirley had been given, unto an overcrowded bus. Every seat was filled, and bodies were suspended from the handrail, hanging like sides of beef in a traditional butcher shop. I joined the suspended passengers while Shirley perched precariously on a ledge by the front door steps. When we arrived at the airport parking forecourt, the usual push to disembark quickly was in speedy progress. Shirley was in the doorway, so she grabbed her hand baggage and was first to get off the vehicle.

The bus emptied unto the large, already-crowded forecourt. Being on the earlier bus gave us leisurely time to stroll to the check-in and departure gate. Amsterdam's airport is a sprawling terminal requiring long walks between each departure process. About fifteen minutes into the airport, Shirley asked if I had her handbag. In the crowded rush off the bus, she had picked up two bags, one being the extra package, but not the third, which was her handbag.

Shirley waited while I began the five-minute sprint back to the bus. I stepped through the doors onto the massive forecourt, which a half hour before was crowded like matches in a box. It now had a clearing perhaps forty feet wide and seventy feet long (or twelve by twenty-one metres). This clearing gave me a direct line of sight to where we had disembarked, but there was no bus to be seen. The hard-drive of my mind seemed momentarily to crash as the impact of the lost handbag downloaded. Before leaving the hotel after checkout, I had given Shirley my large travel wallet to keep in her handbag for convenience when we checked in at the airport. It contained everything that allowed the ministry on the mission fields to function smoothly. All national pastor contacts, passports, travel documents, and airline tickets, plus cash and travelers' checks, were gone.

While I was trying to recalibrate the consequence of this development, I realized it meant that we would not be flying anywhere. Now we had to try and secure new passports and tickets, to say nothing of all credit cards, identification, and Shirley's other personal and important items, right on the verge of Christmas. What an assignment and challenging predicament!

Before returning to Shirley with this bombshell, I took one more longing look at where the bus, long gone, now containing the lost handbag, had parked. My clear line of vision still allowed me to see that spot. At the exact place we had exited the bus stood two well-dressed bouncer-size men about five feet (or one and a half metres) apart. They were facing the airport doors and me. Looking at them in disbelief, I saw between them on the ground was Shirley's handbag. Because of heightened airport security, I reasoned that the driver may have feared an explosive device in the bag and left it on the forecourt.

As I was deciding on how to approach them, I began walking in their direction. *Shall I ask them for permission to take the bag?* I thought to myself. *Will they require identification, which I no longer possess? Why are they standing beside the bag without examining it or taking it to their security office?* All these questions raced through my mind.

Within a few feet of them, I decided that, since it was our bag, I would just pick it up and return to the airport. They could not have known that we owned the bag and might object to my actions. There was a man on either side of me, and before I had time to say, "Thank you!" and as quickly as I reached to grab the bag, both men vanished from an empty forecourt. I returned the handbag to Shirley, and she confirmed that every single item was there. After completing airport security, we had a comfortable flight and an enjoyable Christmas.

The ministry of angels needs no defence. These and many similar disasters were averted by the intervention of angels. The following Scripture is one of many that assure the receptive believer of God's protection and guidance by His angelic agents. Could these be angels, ministering spirits, to which the writer of the Hebrews refers by asking, "But to which of the angels . . . Are they not all ministering spirits sent forth to minister for those who will inherit salvation?" (Heb. 1:13–14 NKJV).

# 9

# NOTABLE MIRACLES IN INDO-ASIA

## God's Cloud Overshadows Muslims

Power evangelism or supernatural ministry is not, in my understanding, about the skills or techniques of man. Power in ministry is the un-interrupted flow in the human conduit enabling the conveyance of God's power to produce His intended results. As ministers of the gospel, our challenge is to step back and thereby release our control to the Holy Spirit to operate as He wills in and through us.

For me this means, having prepared a message to preach and bringing to the audience every ingredient in the program that will produce what the Spirit intends. To some degree this requires holding tightly the steering wheel, so to speak—being careful to include in the program only that which will benefit and bless the listener. Conversely, the wheel must also be held lightly in respect to the slightest prompting of the Holy Spirit to interject or change the order of a service as He sees best. Such principles are considered normal for those in leadership who seek to allow the Holy Spirit to raise the service to its highest peak of blessing and to bring the most glory to God, which, of course, is our primary reason to live.

In the real estate development world, when speaking of a specific piece of ground, an agent will refer to its use as the highest and best use. By that statement he means that a strategic vacant lot in the center of a major city that is surrounded by fifty-floor high rises should not be purchased at top market value if one only intends to place a single-floor building there. That would not be the highest and best use of the land.

The same is also true in our call to ministry. Finding and flowing with anointing in our appropriate gifting is to operate at our highest and best use. After answering His divine call on our lives, operating at our highest and best use in ministry is perhaps the most important issue. So it is with each crucial service, whether in the so-called developed Western world or the most distant jungle setting.

Every service presents a challenge to the servant of God who is entrusted with breaking the Bread of Life to be clear of the blood of his hearers. He who declares the gospel must declare all of it. The gospel of God in its fullness, not as a community or social gospel only, must be unashamedly declared with the life-changing formula of Calvary. A single hearer leaving a service and passing into a lost eternity without hearing God's way of salvation from the messenger will leave his blood on the messenger's hands. Oh the awesome responsibility that is ours when standing behind the sacred desk!

Some time ago the significance of the Holy Spirit's prompting in a jungle barn setting became abundantly clear to me. While ministering in one of the world's largest Muslim countries, God revealed Himself to me in a most unusual way.

The seriously dilapidated building was packed to over capacity; people were everywhere. A makeshift platform had been improvised from bamboo poles that were tied together and covered with grass-type matting and upon which several of us were seated. The evangelistic service was taking place in that jungle setting as far removed from anything a Westerner could imagine.

The room was lit by kerosene lamps hanging throughout the building from extension wires hooked to roof rafters. Keyboards, the sound system, and the microphones were powered by a very noisy diesel generator behind the platform. It seemed necessary to point the exhaust pipe under the hollow platform, thus allowing the fumes to accumulate there. But unfortunately, they rose through the matting where we were sitting. The fumes were beginning to give us respiratory problems.

The program began with the worship leaders leading an anointed service. After a few minutes, as I observed the packed building, a strange phenomenon presented itself in the far left corner of the building. At about thirty metres (over ninety-eight feet) from the platform, a large, ominous black cloud presented itself. It was perhaps five metres (over sixteen feet) long, three metres (almost ten feet) wide, and about fifty centimetres (about twenty inches) thick. My first reaction was to think that there was another generator at the back of the crowd, but my interpreter assured me that was not the case. As I asked him about the heavy black cloud, he said that he didn't see it.

The worship and special numbers, together with testimonies from people about God's touch on lives from the previous services, led to a beautiful opening for the gospel message. Minutes later my time was spent preparing the crowd with introductory remarks for the message. Then I noticed the cloud was still at the back and hanging over two rows of people about three metres (or about ten feet) above their heads.

As the message progressed, within a few minutes, the cloud appeared to be noticeably lighter in color, although it was still very dark grey. There was an incredible sense of the presence of God in the building, and an unusual quietness hovered over the crowd. In previous similar settings, this has been indicative of a sovereign move of God with His attending blessing of deliverance and healings. In my experience in observing how God moves in a service, there are seldom identical situations or parallels. God works in His own special way, and we, as His servants, should be especially sensitive to His moving. In that way we can gain the most from the service and the best benefit for the seeker.

Twenty minutes later, the cloud was a light grey. As I was bringing the message to a close and preparing for the salvation call to the altar, I noticed the cloud in the same location was now a brilliant, white, fluffy cloud as one observes on a summer day. *What does this mean?* I asked myself as those who needed God to touch their lives began coming forward, even before the altar call was made. Perhaps almost a third of the crowd was on their way to the front when I noticed for the first time that the cloud was moving. It had moved to the right and was over an aisle, coming slowly to the front.

As people continued to come forward from all over the building, the cloud continued to proceed to the front and then moved to the left of the platform. As is the custom in this type of evangelism, the salvation prayer is first. Depending on the country and the situation, there may be as many as two or three languages or dialects being spoken, which means that, on occasion, as many as three or four interpreters may be needed. In such situations, time for the message and the altar work are lengthened.

Although the cloud was quietly resting over the people at my left side, I still received no prompting of the Holy Spirit or explanation for its presence. It just appeared to be a mysterious cloud. Really no explanation was needed; this was just one of the things God did to show us His uniqueness. I led in the salvation prayer for everyone by praying, "Lord Jesus, thank You for Your love . . ." With their respective interpreters everyone seemed to be praying it. That night many hundreds came to give their lives to Jesus Christ. Those who genuinely prayed from their hearts in faith were beginning a new walk with Christ in the power of His resurrection. He would change their lives forever as they walked in obedience to His Word.

An hour or so after the altar work was completed and most of the crowd had gone, a pastor insisted on speaking to us. The story that poured from his lips that was then interpreted for me explained everything about the cloud. He had been working with some of those who had stood at the left side of the platform. This was the story: Under the cloud at the back of the building were about eleven men sitting on two benches. This group had come from another jungle village with the intent of disturbing the service. They related to the young pastor that when they came into the building and sat down, each one was immediately frozen in a sitting position. They were paralyzed and unable to move a muscle. Also, their mouths were locked shut. Throughout the entire service they could neither move nor speak to one another.

When the call came for salvation, with the invitation for people to come forward, immediately their legs and hips became flexible again. They happily stood and walked forward as the cloud accompanied them up the aisle, but their jaws were still locked. As the salvation prayer began, their jaws became unlocked, and they began praying their first free words: "Lord Jesus, thank You for Your love. I receive Your peace . . ." The young assistant pastor who counselled them in their newfound faith was a former Muslim from their village. These eleven Muslims who were intent on hindering the work of God were instead found by the Good Shepherd. The senior pastor released the assistant pastor to return to their village and plant a church to establish these new believers.

What, we may ask, was the significance of the cloud? Was it necessary for preaching? No! Was it necessary for the audience? No! The audience didn't even see it. Was it necessary for the eleven young men? We doubt if they even knew it overshadowed them. Why, then, was the cloud present? Could a logical answer be that God chose on that occasion to present the cloud as part His plan, using His power to lock their jaws and disable their limbs? Although our infinite God often caters to our finite logic, that need not be a prerequisite.

Since I was the only one we know of who saw the cloud, it was surely for my benefit. Once we were also made aware of God's miracle on the men, everything made sense. As I viewed the cloud from the platform with its ominous blackness, this foreboding cloud could represent the nature of the human heart and the condition of the men over whom it hovered. As His Word went forth and His Spirit penetrated their hearts, the lightening of the cloud may have expressed God drawing the men to Himself. It became perfectly white as they were released to respond to His love and forgiveness. This experience taught us that when something unusual occurs, it is most probably indicative of God at work in the service.

Many are the biblical examples of God using the unusual to fulfill His purpose. One example is the apostle Paul's divine arrest on the Damascus road when at noonday, a bright light of the glory of God shone from heaven and blinded him, which shows one of God's methods of accomplishing His purpose (Acts 27:6). Over many years, different supernatural events have occurred during our ministry, always with the purpose of blessing the people and allowing the highest and best use of that service for the glory of God.

## Tsunami Assembly

Over the many years of my ministry, God has moved in the supernatural in response to the ministry of His Word. But the supernatural was not always an instant occurrence, as the event that follows will confirm.

In 2002 while I was appointed on a special assignment for the Pentecostal Assemblies of Canada (PAOC) in Sri Lanka, we witnessed God's hand at work in a unique way. I always enjoyed working with our pastors there. Since 1985, Shirley and I have often ministered in Sri Lanka, and through PAOC ministry there, a few young men called of God found their ministries and began planting small churches. Soon they became known as the Pentecostal Assemblies of Sri Lanka. We have laboured alongside them, encouraged them, and watched them in their growth. Their influence now reaches all over the island.

Some of these national workers were saved in our early evangelistic efforts, and many of them were students when we taught in their Bible college. In most of their ministry, our journey with them has created a very special bond among us. Our activities during the war years, when we worked with them in evangelism in remote areas and behind enemy lines, if recounted, would fill a thrilling book and with fact being stranger than fiction. On occasion we toured with pastor teams to the most remote corners of the island. They doubled as singing and worship groups and intercessory prayer teams, and they fulfilled the vital role of interpreting for me in two languages.

This event began with a phone call from a pastor asking us for an appointment. Later as we fellowshipped, he began to share his burden to extend his little assembly. He told of a small building not much larger than a living room that was almost filled to capacity. He related the story of a neighbouring pastor who had pastored his assembly in the same location for many years, and his church was recognized in the community. This was an important point to note, as it was very sensitive to plant a new church in many areas in the country.

Because the neighbouring pastor and some of the congregation were moving, he was being offered the property as a working assembly to operate in tandem with his church. His purpose in speaking with me was to see if their organization would purchase it. Knowing how difficult the economy was with the war raging, it seemed in the natural like an impossible venture. When he mentioned the sale price, which was substantial, my heart sank, knowing that our budget was stretched to the limit without trying to make an unexpected substantial cash purchase.

Strangely, as we talked and I looked for a tactful way to tell him that it was most unlikely that funds could be allocated at that time, I was aware of something speaking into my spirit. At times like this, one must be ever sensitive to the leading of the Holy Spirit. Although He has moved in this way with me for many years, I sometimes tend to allow my natural business skills to get in His sovereign way, at which time it is possible to miss or frustrate His plan.

Soon I found myself questioning him about the proposed deal. "Is this a firm price, or could there be a lower offer?" I asked. "What about extended terms or owner financing?" We decided that he would speak with the pastor/owner and search for other purchase options.

After several visits to the vendor and to me, it seemed that there was room for negotiation. We fixed the selling price at that time for a future payout and conveyance four years later, with four equal interest-free payments. We agreed upon the terms and miraculously found the first deposit, and he took possession of the property and continued services for both assemblies.

On a prompt of the Holy Spirit, this deal was structured that first day. In the natural, there was no possibility of finding an agreed-upon purchase price, but God had a better idea and knew the miraculous end from the beginning.

As time passed, the pastor traveled the short distance between both preaching points. His own assembly was on level ground about sixty metres or about two hundred feet from the beautiful Indian Ocean, and the new assembly was further inland and at some elevation.

As the weeks passed, both congregations met, and later they made plans to merge as one assembly in the new larger elevated facility. Christmas programs were being planned, and the excitement built as they anticipated their first Christmas as a blended church family in their new miracle property, as transactions of that nature are almost unheard of in that economy.

Christmas Sunday morning came with its attendant excitement for children and parents alike. Both congregations, now one happy family, were safely gathered together for their first Christmas Sunday morning service.

During the service, the tropical island's weather changed abruptly.

Without warning, the tsunami that raged throughout Asia from Banda Ache in Indonesia to Sri Lanka came ashore with devastating force. The normally placid ocean raged ashore, with rogue waves devastating all in its path, including the now-deserted lower oceanside church building.

Some distance away, the full force of the disaster was evidenced by a train full of passengers who were going home for Christmas. The tsunami came with such power that it forced the enormous locomotives and passenger cars off the tracks and threw them aside like matchwood. The horror of that event is indescribable; hundreds of thousands of men, women, and beautiful children lost their lives that Christmas morning.

The unfolding of this miracle took a little longer than those in the altar prayer lines. It began with the young pastor being alert to the Holy Spirit and opening negotiations with the vendor, knowing there was no purchase money for such a large project. He believed God. His several visits with me as we prayed to know God's mind on the matter and then pressed the vendor to think outside of the box and do some innovative (for that culture) financing finally brought the deal together.

As the tsunami took its toll throughout vast chunks of Asia, the members of the congregation, oblivious of the surrounding disaster, joyously celebrated the Saviour's birth. As they left the church that morning, they were alerted to the disaster by the ocean having risen to their hillside building, but it only lapped close to the steps of their new church. None in the church lost their lives. For them this was their tsunami miracle from God.

## Contrasting Methods of God's Dealings in Crusades

Since the approach to this concept of the gospel thrust is based on a supernatural power and demonstration of the Holy Spirit, we have experienced unparalleled anointing during twenty-five years of missions evangelism in almost every part of the world. In a lifetime of ministry that now exceeds fifty-two thousand gospel presentations, with approximately three million individuals praying a salvation prayer, with hundreds of churches planted and tens of thousands of pastors and leaders trained in leadership schools and seminars, I only recall two failed (so-called) events in missions' evangelism, which are related below.

On one occasion, the advance team made and completed detailed plans for an outdoor festival of evangelism in a country experiencing great terrorist activity. After months of planning, the team arrived a few days before the event for prayer and coordination. The sports arena was readied and all equipment in place for that day's first event.

At mid-morning the director of the festival received a legal notice from city hall cancelling the permit for our five-day event. The reason given was that the local religious hierarchy opposed the Christian festival. After months of planning, we had six hours to find a venue and relocate before start time.

For weeks handbills, posters, and banners were in place announcing particulars, including the location. Even if we could find a place, transfer tons of equipment, and reconnect miles of cable, how could we re-inform the public about the new venue?

We found a clear field and negotiated with the owner. We made the switch to the new location, put a fleet of loudspeaker vans on the roads announcing the change, and began on time.

Because the city fathers feared that there would be reprisals from the opposing church, they ordered the police to cover the event.

On the first evening, the police presence outnumbered the audience three to two, with about three hundred policemen. At the altar call, about two hundred police officers came to the front for salvation together with most of the audience. On the second night the crowd swelled to about fifteen hundred with the same police presence. On the third night, about four thousand came, the next night fifty-five hundred, and the last night about seven thousand. This was more than double what the original venue would have held.

During that week, two of the district's chiefs of police made separate visits to my hotel and asked to have whatever had transpired in their constables' lives. I led both of them to faith in Jesus Christ.

At that final meeting, a mother brought from the road outside the field her dying daughter who had just been run over by the back wheels of a bus. The child was totally and completely healed and stood in front of the crowd to testify with the mother. This healing would not have occurred had we not been forced to move to the roadside where the child was injured. God can make the wrath of men to praise him. (This miracle will be more fully related under the section, "Run over by a Bus.")

While doing jungle ministry some years ago, we did an open-air rally on a sandy beach on the Indian Ocean. Beginning in the late afternoon, women and children came from the bamboo hut villages. There were no men. As the sun began to set, their fishing boats began to pull up on the beach as they hauled their catch of the day ashore. Later they came and surrounded the women and children as I preached the gospel. As the altar call was being made for them to respond at the front for salvation, all the men responded first and then the women and children. That evening, almost every man in the villages gave his life to Christ.

Later in the week we moved considerably farther inland for another outdoor rally, which also had been planned for a long time, in a much larger village. After a long wait at the site, I realized there was a problem. Upon investigating, my men told how the village fathers were now refusing to allow us to preach the gospel there. The spirit men and witch doctors there had refused to allow us to begin the meeting. In this case, I felt in my spirit that it would be prudent to wipe the dust off our feet and leave, so we did.

Several months later, the devastating tsunami went through that area. Coming ashore many metres high, right where our beach open-air meeting had been held, it parted to both sides of the fishermen's village, and not one soul was lost to the tragic happening. But it was not so with the inland village. Because of its distance from the ocean, under normal circumstances, this village should have been spared. The village, with its spirit men and witchdoctors who had denied the preaching of the gospel, was destroyed. Not one person survived, we were told. How can a village on the beach survive, but an inland one be annihilated? In what God allows, He is sovereign.

These two meetings that on the surface appeared to fail were, in the plan of God, a display of His judgment and mercy.

# PART THREE

# PERSEVERING

# 10

# IN SEARCH OF UTOPIA

Several weeks into a three-country Asian ministry tour, the team rendezvoused at Singapore International Airport for a pre-dawn Indonesian departure. Nothing could have prepared us for that day that seemed would never end. The less than two-hour flight to the coastal city of Manado had an ETA (estimated time of arrival) of 9:30 a.m. For us, check in and security went smoothly, as did boarding and departure. Once we reached the cruising altitude, a mini-breakfast was being served, and then it happened. For several minutes, severe turbulence shook the plane intermittently, and then a sizable air pocket caused the plane to descend considerably, which brought an abrupt end to our eagerly awaited breakfast service. "Return to your seats and fasten seat belts. We are experiencing some turbulence!" boomed an excited voice over the speakers, not that we needed the announcement to alert us. As our discomfort continued, seasoned passengers recognized that this was more than merely "some turbulence."

About thirty minutes later, a further gallant attempt to serve refreshments was commenced. This time they managed to navigate the food trolley about one-third from the front and within three or four rows of our seats. This would be our breakfast. The aroma of food wafted favourably in my direction, as I was waiting with anticipation. But it was not to be. Although the rough ride resembled someone in a high-speed drive off road and over a ploughed field, it was not as bad. Then, without warning, an air pocket that seemed to cause the plane to descend thousands of feet caused havoc with the food wagons. This meant that the plane disappeared from under their food wagon wheels, and the top of the fuselage dropped toward the tops of the wagons. That moment, which lasted too long, gave me an uneasy sensation.

Again the attendants stowed the wagons, and now a higher-octave voice alerted us to the viciousness of the weather pattern we were experiencing. We were advised that it was monsoon or typhoon season and the pilot was trying to avoid the eye of the storm. In these severe circumstances, I noticed a drop in the conversational volume of the passengers. In a lifetime of air travel, that air pocket was the most violent I had ever encountered. In their mothers' arms, children cried, couples held hands, and others prayed. Those intending to read a book never seemed to turn a page.

About one hour past our original ETA, we were advised that, because of a diversionary route and the unusually severe head winds and as a precautionary measure, we would refuel at another city before continuing to our destination. That decent and landing best resembled the effect of the hurricane waves on a floating ducky with two children bathing. As the plane broke through the thick cloud and approached the almost-hidden runway, except for guide lights, it twisted and skewed in all directions seconds before landing on the tarmac. As the plane landed safely, we clapped and cheered.

A lengthy time passed while we had the unscheduled landing and refuelling before the plane took off again into the same soup. While we all were reliving the earlier or now more-stressful experience, the pilot of the plane fought his way to the desired altitude. As Christian believers, we have the assurance that our lives are in the hollow of God's hand. Since we were on a soul-winning trip, we believed that we were in His will. Personally, I felt assured that the flight would be a safe one and because of our presence on the flight, the other passengers were safe also. I recognize, however, that believers do die on flights. But we have the assurance that, if such happened to us, if we are "absent from" our bodies, we will "be present with the Lord" (2 Cor. 5:8 AV).

By mid-afternoon, it seemed as though we were flying aimlessly in an attempt to dodge the vortex of the ferocious weather patterns that hovered over every square mile or kilometre of the Karimata Strait between Singapore and Borneo as we bounced back and forth for hours over the equator. As the sun set in the late afternoon, an announcement alerted us that arrival at our destination was imminent. As passengers, we greeted this news with uproarious applause. But our applause proved premature because seconds later the attempt to land was aborted because the airstrip lighting for evening landings malfunctioned. A new destination was chosen at a night landing airport still another hour or more away.

One of our valued team members, Beatrice Abbey, was seated about twenty rows behind us on an aisle seat. The center seat was empty, and the window seat was occupied by a middle-aged businessman with a prosthesis for his left arm. They engaged in general conversation for some time, but since Beatrice was more senior and alone, she felt inadequate to answer some questions he had regarding boarding schools in Asia. Remembering that we had researched the boarding school question for our daughter, Shirleen, Beatrice volunteered to exchange seats with me so I could directly answer his questions. She excused herself as she braved the almost-impossible variable incline walk forward as she moved to her new seat. Reluctantly, I did exchange seats with her, but I would have preferred to remain with Shirley on such an uncertain, now all-day flight.

After a few friendly introductory remarks, we began chatting about his son and the father's questions concerning a boarding school. Like me, the father's name was John, and we conversed freely. He shared about his background, which was British, and his profession as a civil engineer moving around the world as his skills were in demand in mega-suspension bridge projects. As the conversation progressed and the plane continued to roll with the prevailing storm, it became obvious from his verbal reaction that the Christian school I could recommend would place his boy at odds with the father's present vocabulary and lifestyle choices. Given the flight discomfort and the delicate subject being discussed, I was experiencing an increasing level of stress.

Silently my spirit prayed for wisdom for how best to handle this additional challenge. As I observed his choice of expletives, it seemed that a son coming home from a Christian atmosphere at term breaks might place him on a collision course with the father. I shared with him about our good feeling for the school in relation to our daughter and her adjustment, he also began to lean in that direction for his son. My reply to his question about whether I thought it would work in his situation was "No!"

This response more than surprised him, and he expressed even more colourful expletives and asked, "Why not?" By now I felt as though I was walking on eggshells as I attempted to paint a realistic picture of contrasting lifestyles. His lifestyle was that of a man of the world, and his son's would be within a cloistered atmosphere within a conservative Christian community, which would be in antithesis to his father. He wanted an explanation for this position, which was not easy for me to communicate.

I began talking about the school and majored on the religious education that might be a contrast with the son's home life during school breaks. I addressed how it risked conflict by putting father and son at variance. Then I began to see other aspects of the situation.

As we talked of his son coming home at Christmastime, I shared about the birth of Christ, the Saviour of the world. When we spoke of Easter, I spoke of the cross of Christ and His resurrection as He finished the work of redemption to offer salvation as a gift fully paid for through His shed blood and in exchange for our sin. We discussed how this scenario would play out given six or eight years in that sheltered and formative influencing environment. How would he react, we wondered, if one day the young man returned home, and announced that he had made a commitment of his life to Christ as his personal Saviour? On the strength of that possibility, and not wanting to create future conflict with the family, we discussed whether it perhaps would not be such a suitable place for his boy. As I recall his reaction these many years later, it seems that he firmly laid his prosthesis on my forearm and then asked, "Why would I not want that for my boy? That's also what I need."

It was at this juncture that he said he had another question. He began, "I need you to explain the meaning of a dream." Earlier in the conversation he had mentioned that, as a child, he had served as a choir or altar boy in an Anglican church. That early involvement helped him to now see me, after this conversation, as a man of the cloth who could interpret his dream. This was to be no ordinary dream but a complex and recurring one.

He related having it early in life and it being replayed at regular intervals since. He held me captivated with its telling, which was no small achievement, given the ongoing trauma that was shattering our supposed two-hour flight that had turned into a daylong ordeal. Adding to the situation, daylight was fading. This meant changing direction again and making an improvised overnight touchdown elsewhere.

The dream continued to unfold as he told of trying to swim from an unhappy or polluted mainland to an island that he perceived to be a utopia where everything would be pleasant and that one would enjoy. But the tides and current were so powerful that it was only possible for him to swim around the perimeter of the island. He was always powerless against the currents to go ashore and was forced back to the undesirable environment from which he was trying to escape. Now, in later life, this repetition had allowed him to memorize the islands along the coastline and purchase every available island map to look for and identify its location. His sole purpose in being on this flight was to visit an island he felt was the one in his lifetime dream. If it was, he would move his family there, to the utopic Island of Sangir. With every confidence that the explanation was forthcoming, he leaned back into his window seat and waited for the answer.

As he related the dream, my own spirit asked God to piece it together and reveal the message that He intended. It seemed right to spiritualize the main points. I began with the land from which he was trying to escape; it was like our natural depraved world. At that point, I explained the total depravity of man, who is lost in sin and born with a sin nature: "There is none righteous, no, not one" and "for all have sinned and fall short of the glory of God" (Rom. 3:10 AV, 23 NKJV).

The island to which he was attracted and which he felt held the answer of life was equated to the place of purity and peace for those who seek God. It was prepared for those who were drawn to and empowered by the Holy Spirit in faith to receive Christ. Christ, God the Son, who became man and who sacrificed Himself in substitutionary death on our behalf made full payment for our sin. He gave us redemption through His shed blood, cleansing us from all unrighteousness and fitting us to be with Him in a place He has prepared for us. The tides and currents driving him back and rending him powerless to escape the pollution of his origin for the new life in Christ was the pull of the old world and the power and influence of Satan endeavouring to thwart the desire and leading of Christ to draw him as a new creature to a divine culture.

Finally, the unplanned delayed flight in which we were all trapped was yet another part of the answer to his dream. The research he had done with island maps and being on that specific flight was his attempt to find peace and purity on his elusive island. The delay and the lady who exchanged seats with me was God's plan to have him find the way from a life of pollution and defeat to an abundant life in Christ by calling on Him in prayer.

With the plane still descending and twisting deliriously, the engineer leaned forward, again placed a hand on my left forearm, and asked me how that change could happen. As I shared different salvation verses with him, it became clear to him that "whosoever shall call upon the name of the Lord shall be saved" (Rom. 10:13 AV) meant just that. Indicating that he was ready, he repeated a simple salvation prayer to receive Christ as his Lord and Saviour. Probably because of the perilous flight we had all endured that day and because my loud preaching voice, even when whispering, carried further than I had expected, several other passengers who had overheard the whole conversation quietly joined in the prayer of salvation.

In retrospect, this was God's delay, since immediately following the prayer, a landing was announced; it was not our original destination. It was a smooth landing. We were all bussed to a hotel for dinner and stayed overnight to attempt it all again the following morning. John, the converted engineer, and I sat together on the bus talking of the decision he had made. The conversation continued over dinner and into the late evening. It was a crash course in a new walk with God. Over breakfast and another bus ride the following morning, we continued to share. This was a God moment. Sometimes I wonder if the main reason for ministry in that part of the world was not primarily for God to reach into that man's life and do an everlasting work. The next morning's flight was beautiful and without event. We talked all the way, and I shared Scriptures that would, if he observed them, change and strengthen his life to walk in victory.

As we left the airport (twenty-six hours later than scheduled) in a bus chartered to drop off passengers at their respective hotels, and just before we got off at our hotel, John asked me another question. "Will you be preaching anywhere when you are here?"

"Yes," I replied.

He asked, "When, and may I come?"

I replied in the affirmative, and as we left the bus, he agreed to meet at our hotel in the evening and attend the meeting with us. Before the scheduled time, my room phone announced that my friend was waiting for me in the lobby.

After another lengthy bus ride and another teaching moment, we arrived at the venue. It was not a church but a large home built, it seemed to me, as a square, leaving a covered quadrangle or conservatory in the ample center of the house. It was there that a substantial number of people gathered for an evening of fellowship and teaching.

As the service opened and worship began, John was seated in the audience, and we were taken to the low-rise stage. As the pastor led worship, there was a rich sense of God's presence. The believers sang as only few others can outside of Wales or Indonesia. Their heavenly singing was lost in the ascending worship, which continued for minutes as believers lifted their hearts in praise and worshiped in their prayer languages. That rich worship and praise of God in the Holy Spirit and without human input is always a sacred moment we would wish to experience more often.

Following that sacred time, the pastor then opened the service for testimonies. One after another, believers stood waiting to testify, each sharing of God's goodness or special touch on their lives and families. I was enjoying every moment, wishing it could continue and pass by my teaching time. Then a thought traumatized me. I went back to the moment on the plane when John and I met and remembered that some of his descriptive expletive words then would be totally out of place in this setting. I honestly panicked, in case he chose to testify. I knew that, as a new believer has to grow in his new birth, it may take time for them to learn to "put off the old man" and "put on the new *man*" (Col. 3:9-10 AV). Assuring myself that it would be most unlikely that he would be confident enough to testify, having only been born again less than twenty-four hours earlier, since that was also his first time in a believer's service and in a foreign country, I decided to relax.

I hardly believed my eyes when, moments later, I saw him standing on his feet. He walked to the platform and stood beside the pastor at the podium. As he spoke, the pastor interpreted. He clearly related the whole event on the plane, our lengthy conversation about salvation, his recurring dream and my interpretation, and concluded with asking Christ into his heart. He testified without a single questionable word. As a result, I was elated. Praise the Lord for another miracle! As Scripture assures us, ". . . if anyone *is* in Christ, *he is* a new creation; old things have passed away; behold, all things have become new" (2 Cor. 5:17 NKJV).

As I left there after an anointed service, it felt like heaven had come down on the audience. The added blessing of the new convert testifying made for a perfect evening. Then we returned to our hotel. Leaving John alone to go to his hotel was not easy for me. In such a short time, so much had been transferred to this new believer as he walked out of my life into a dark Indonesian night. What would become of him? Had that seed of God's Word fallen on good ground? Would we ever know?

Because John's work took him around the world, he didn't leave his address with us. We often thought of that memorable flight and our mini-training encounter and prayed for him. We gave him our address but heard nothing.

Two years had passed before we received a letter in the mail from Asia. It was from John. In part, it read, "You may recall me as the one-armed Englishman whom you converted (led to Christ) in row 29, seat B, on that memorable flight from Singapore to Manado. I appreciate also that you led me back to God. I have a Bible which I read." He continued by giving his credit card number and a substantial four-figure donation "to use towards your ministry to the people." Now thirteen years later, we periodically receive similar donations from him to help us continue to win souls to Jesus Christ. Even as I was writing this chapter, yet another letter came from him promising his usual contribution for our ministry.

In the sovereignty of God, was it just a typhoon? Did God choose to trap a planeload of people for a whole day, shake us around like corks in a bathtub, and terrify everyone, including the cabin crew, to reach this man and those who prayed the salvation prayer around us for the sake of Christ's Kingdom? Was it, you may ask, the emotion of the moment and a prayer forgotten on landing? Heaven will tell the whole story. But after such a long time, there may be more than emotion evidenced here. As I look back thirteen years, this for me was, and still is, a work of God's grace.

# 11

# How God Used a Word of Knowledge

## Delivering a Devious Businessman

What is the Holy Spirit's gift of "the word of knowledge" (1 Cor. 12:8b AV)? Is it for today's church? Is it significant? The purpose of this chapter is to answer these questions. After the crucifixion, the tearing of the veil in the temple from the top to the bottom by the hand of God (Matt. 27:51), and the resurrection of Christ, all of the gifts that were given by the Holy Spirit would follow. The tearing of the veil signified the end of the dispensation of law and the beginning of the dispensation of grace. On the day of Pentecost, each of the apostles were empowered (Acts 2). Later the apostle Paul testified that he was "as one born out of due time" (1 Cor. 15:8b AV). During the dispensation of grace, each apostle lived and ministered, using and seeing the operation of all the gifts of the Holy Spirit as the early church began to grow and flourish.

We are still living in the dispensation of grace. Nothing has changed except that the desire for and understanding of the gifts of the Spirit in some developed countries, unfortunately, appears to be diminishing. Regrettably, in some countries and churches there is a reticence to teach or to practice their use, and a tendency to inhibit their flow in worship in the planning of church services.

Perhaps there is a close parallel to this observation. Over my many years of working in leadership schools, in leading seminars, and in third-world ministry, it has become obvious that there is a close link between the level of spirituality in a local church and that of the senior leadership. Typically to the degree that there is strong spiritual, moral, and ethical senior leadership will be the extent of the promotion and use of these gifts in the lives of the church attendants.

In 1 Corinthians 12, nine gifts of the Holy Spirit appear (12:8-11). In addition, Paul speaks of seven equipping gifts listed in Romans 12:6-8, and he further identifies five ministry gifts in his letter to the Ephesians (Eph. 4:11-12).

When there is a strong senior pastoral leader who endorses the ministry of the gifts of the Spirit and other biblical giftings, one can expect there will be a healthy acceptance of and participation in their use and expression. Where senior leadership lacks or neglects in building and encouraging a healthy biblical model for the use of the gifts in the assembly of believers, there will be a reaction to and reluctance to use them.

Where the ministry gifts have been in operation in a mature assembly, their use will be encouraged by the coming of any new senior pastor of the same mind and who is mature and confident in his own giftings and operates in them. As they become more efficiently operational for the greater good of the congregation, there will be further development in their use. It's sad to say, but also the opposite is true. It is my intention to show how God chooses to use some spiritual gifts in ministry and often in dramatic ways.

Since God's call on my life for missions included the instruction to preach the Word that would be accompanied by the power and demonstration of the Holy Spirit, spiritual gifts have been an integral part of my ministry.

For me spiritual gifts are the equivalent to a full range of tools in a plumber's toolbox. Without the Spirit's anointing on the ministry and the accompanying gifts in operation, it would be similar to the plumber coming to a flooded house without his box of tools. With the Spirit's anointing, ministry in the full spectrum of God's power (a full toolbox) can flow to a hurting world with spectacular results.

It is God's Word that is living and powerful (Heb. 4:12). As I declare the truth and simplicity of His Word, it is the faucet that opens the flow of His power. Preaching the cross is the power of God (1 Cor. 1:18). Without the cross and the resurrection, there is no power. Pentecost was and still is about power. Jesus assured His disciples that when He left them, He would send the Promise of the Father, the Comforter, the Paraclete (*parakletos*, Greek), the "one called alongside." The Holy Spirit, would empower, equip, and enable them for their task of spreading the gospel and planting Christ's church.

The same Greek word carries with it the thought of the Comforter being their intercessor, to pray to the Father for them, and their advocate (defence lawyer) Jesus Christ, to plead their case before the Righteous Judge of all the earth (Gen. 18:25). After the Holy Spirit comes "upon you," you "shall receive power" (Acts 1:8 NKJV). Pentecost is still about power—the power of the Holy Spirit—to change our world. Scripture reminds us that it is "'Not by [natural] might nor by [natural] power, but by [the supernatural power of] My Spirit,' Says the LORD of hosts" (Zech. 4:6 NKJV).

In retrospect, it is beyond my comprehension to conceive of spending more than a quarter of a century in a multi-faceted missions ministry without having the constant assurance that the gifts of the Holy Spirit were always available to me to do in the Spirit what I, in my flesh, could never do successfully without His power. Because of the enormity of the task of missions, in and of ourselves, we are always inadequate. For me to attempt to do missions without a supernatural flow of the gifts to accomplish the task would be unthinkable.

At any of the hundreds of altar services that I've conducted, how humbling it was for me to see Him at work healing a hurting world! Sometimes the after-service requires that I spend hours ministering to needy people who wait in a seemingly endless line. God assured me that He would walk alongside me, and while I prayed with them or during counselling, the gifts of the Spirit would operate transparently as needed and bring His anointing and deliverance to the people.

In one such line, because of the multitude of people, it was only possible for me to touch each one and pray the briefest prayer. After several hundred people had already passed through the line, a mother brought a small girl to me. I touched the mother, but I hardly noticed the child, who was slightly taller than her mother's knees. As they passed by, I realized the child's arms and hands were terribly deformed, and both were twisted grotesquely in a knot up to her shoulders. As I reached to my left to catch up with her, I intended to touch and pray for her. To my amazement, my brief touch on her arm created such a stir it was unnecessary for me to pray. Christ's presence beside her instantly delivered the child, and for the first time in her life, her arms became perfectly normal. Who except the Master can diagnose the human spirit, prescribe, and apply the needed remedy so perfectly and instantly?

Who knows whether the next sovereign move of God across the nations may be placed in the hands of today's young people who will wholly trust God alone? Who will step out of the boat in faith, empowered by the Holy Spirit and equipped with the Word (2 Tim. 3:15) to lead his or her generation to Jesus Christ by the power and demonstration of the Spirit?

To be on the cutting edge and effective in soul winning in Western or developing nations, we must return to the basics, the forthright, uncompromising declaration of the Word of God. To win our world, there must be less people-pleasing preaching and more of declaring the whole gospel.

Biblical doctrine is established from the Word of God, not from the consensus of opinion resulting from cosy home-study discussions, as great as they are, under capable pastoral leadership. With perhaps 150 million believers, the vast majority who met the Master in Holy Spirit-led underground house church Bible studies and meetings, China is a case in point.

Almost thirty years ago, I made my visit to rural China. Then many of its cities were still closed to the Western world. How heart-rending it was to see the price Christians had to pay for their faith. They met in secret and sang our style of hymns silently, miming the words. They had hand-copied chapters from the gospels and epistles, sometimes whole books, and from week to week, they shared them with one another. Because Bibles were difficult to obtain and illegal to own, believers carefully separated each book so that many could learn the Word. Often their secret meeting places were disclosed to the village head man, who in turn would inform the police. As a result, pastors or leaders would be imprisoned, often for lengthy periods and without proper representation or trials. Many Christians are still paying a great price to walk with God. They would tell us, "Persecution is the seed of the church." Can Western lay people and clergy learn lessons from these persecuted Chinese Christians?

There must be a renewed emphasis on the Christian doctrines of the Godhead and on the Word becoming flesh in Jesus Christ. Jesus said, "I am *the* way" (John 14:6b AV), not *a* way (italics mine). Christ's substitutionary death on the cross by shedding His blood for our sin, which we inherited in our DNA from the first Adam, needs clearly to be declared in unapologetic terms. We were conceived and born in sin. We are sinners because we inherited sin, not only because we sin. When we commit sin, we compound our alienation and separation from Him. That sin separated us from a Holy God. In children, His grace and mercy covers them until they reach an age of accountability. The resurrection of Christ is central to our faith. The apostle Paul declared, ". . . if Christ is not risen, then our preaching *is* empty and your faith *is* also empty" (1 Cor. 15:14 NKJV). Jesus Christ was raised and now lives in "the power of an endless life" (Heb. 7:16c AV). Because He lives we shall live also (John 14:19).

Historically, when a move of God births what becomes a denomination with a distinctive doctrinal position, it grows, often rapidly. But in time, as compromise or complacency erodes its strength or distinctiveness, the movement often loses its momentum. Those adherents who held with the original position of their faith raise a new and fervent banner under which they again move forward. In such an instance, God is well able to revive what He has done in the past. He is able to reinvent the vehicle that was capable of conveying His message of power and deliverance to a lost world.

The message of the Word of God has not changed. Culture changes and brings with it a new, and sometimes diminished, respect for the power and demonstration of that Word. Should we be cautioned here to be careful not to compromise the Word in our declaration of the gospel or in the teaching of the Word to facilitate a changing culture? Should we also be careful in the choice of Bible versions we use, which may have been massaged in significant key words, perhaps unintentionally, to dilute the strength or forthrightness of the original text? On more than one occasion while teaching an overseas pastors' leadership school, and while making a significant point from my New King James Version (NKJV), the interpreters will stop and take issue because the thought from my text is totally lost in the reading of their version. If we are not careful, ". . . the word of God" which "*is* living and powerful, and sharper than any two-edged sword" (Heb. 4:12a NKJV) may be diminished.

Those of us who are walking in the distinctive of Pentecost, especially as first-generation Pentecostals who may have paid a high price for what was once seen as the enigma of Pentecost, have the awesome task of carrying the torch high to the next generation. But if we fail to do so, our Pentecostal message and heritage will be in danger of being lost to them.

There are many examples of how God uses the word of knowledge to fulfill His will in a person's life. As I relate the following incident, I still stand in awe as I recall the warmth and gentleness of the Holy Spirit as He made Himself present in a desperate circumstance. In this example, the word of knowledge served to change the life of the person and his family and ultimately affected a substantial part of the city in which he lived.

As I recall this nerve-chilling event, it seemed like that day had begun very early. During the day I was involved in ministry in a city, perhaps at a university, a department store, or a pastors' luncheon. When we arrived back at our hotel in the afternoon, I was looking forward to a couple of hours of rest before the four-hour or more crusade and altar work in the evening.

As I just began to rest, suddenly I was interrupted by a loud and urgent knock on my door. It was my interpreter who occupied the next room. He explained that he had a visitor in his room asking for prayer, and he asked, "Would you please come now?" As I followed him back to his room, I saw a very distinguished middle-aged man sitting on a chair. When I entered, he rose and gave me a respectful bow, which is typical in that culture when meeting an older person. In his own language, he began speaking in a whisper to the interpreter. I assumed that he was detailing his problem that needed prayer.

As I waited for a couple of minutes to hear the reason why he came to the hotel instead of attending the evening service, my spirit became aware that the Holy Spirit was telling of his condition directly. This was the beginning of the operation of the gift of the word of knowledge. Eventually the whispering stopped, and my friend turned to me with an explanation.

Before he began to explain, I said, "We will begin with his throat." Even though he was whispering, that was not all I was sensing in my spirit. In these moments of waiting, God had revealed to me many issues. The gentleman waited for my response through the interpreter. He just expected me to pray briefly and return to my room and he would leave. "Not so fast!" God seemed to indicate to me.

In my experience, the word of knowledge flows in a variety of ways. It may come to me as a verbal message, slowly, line by line, to be repeated by me as I received it. Sometimes it comes to me as a still picture or video that has a sequence of unfolding events, which I then describe to the person. Also, I may receive the word as a colour. On occasion I see red, which may be associated with danger, or grey deepening to black, indicative of tragedy or death, depending on the shade. At times I smell an aroma that may be the signal that unlocks the secret of someone's problems. Usually the moment a person senses the direction in which the Spirit is leading, he or she evidences various emotions affirming the word he or she is receiving, which will usually lead to an early deliverance.

On one occasion, black was the dominant colour while I counselled a brother who did not appear to be sick in any way. He died two days later, and I performed his funeral. The Holy Spirit does not always give a word of knowledge to be fully imparted to the individual at the time. As in this case, the man was not advised of his impending death but only encouraged in his faith and to be ready to be in the presence of His Saviour, whom he affirmed.

Now let's continue with the gentleman who was experiencing difficulty with his throat. He was well-dressed, a high-ranking government official, and began to listen intently to the interpreter, who conveyed to him what was being said quietly. The many things that troubled him had created such turmoil over an extended period that the stress factor had begun to attack him, and if they were not resolved would ultimately destroy his vocal chords. When I asked about other issues that may have brought this condition to a climax, he responded negatively. After several attempts to prompt him for other stresses that might be responsible for his condition, he continued to look surprised, as though the things he was hearing did not resonate with him. It is always best if the person discloses things themselves. It makes it easier on their self-image than if they are confronted with issues of their behaviour or guilt.

Realizing no progress was being made, I began to share God's revelation of him through the interpreter, who looked at me in disbelief and then proceeded. This time there was a significant reaction. He was hearing that the failing of his vocal chords resulted from the stress created by the substantial debt he owed to local businessmen over a very long time. In addition, he was made aware that for several years he had misappropriated government funds from accounts in the finance department to which he had access. I told him that he had two teenage sons, whom he regularly whipped when he discovered their pornographic literature.

By this time he was sobbing bitterly at my feet with his head buried in his hands on the floor. It was then that I told him that his own pornographic addiction to magazines and books, far in excess of his boys', had grown to fill many locked cupboards in his home. I disclosed to him that from his left foot to his thigh, his whole leg was covered with putrid and festering boils. Finally, I said that an additional stress factor was his long-standing extramarital relationship.

By then he was now crouched in a foetal position and sobbing bitterly. After several minutes, I politely asked him to stand up. When he regained his composure, I hugged him and showed him love. I shared with him the love of God and the message of the work of Christ on the cross for him. I presented salvation as a gift from God to him that was fully paid for by the death of Christ. I told him that this gift could be his by faith alone and his sin would be removed; he would become a child of God.

As evidence of a work of grace in his life, he repented and then began making restitution. I counselled him as to how each of these issues must be resolved and told that when they were addressed, his vocal chords would return to normal and his putrid leg would instantly be healed. He prayed a salvation prayer with the interpreter and then, together, we prayed with him before he left.

On our final night in that city, several days later, a message was brought to me on the platform. It was from our distinguished government official, who was in the audience and wanted to speak with me. I met privately with him and the interpreter, and he related to us several new developments in his life.

First, after he fully disclosed to his wife his marital unfaithfulness, and asked her forgiveness, she forgave him, and their marital relationship was restored. He had terminated all contact with the other woman. Secondly, he had confessed his addiction to his sons and apologized to them. Thirdly, for the businessmen to whom he owed money, he fully repaid them.

Finally, he had gone to his superiors, acknowledging his theft from the department and satisfying them with full restitution. They pardoned him and allowed him to remain in his position. The repentance and reconciliation with those involved that I am relating seems inadequate for so many and such major violations. It took almost every day and night for a week for him to correct his misdeeds. I'm not at liberty to give all of the details he related to me.

At the conclusion of the story, and in a strong voice, as he raised his left trouser leg, he asked us to look at his boils. They were gone, and his skin was as clear as that of a newborn child. He then introduced us to his wife and two sons. Finally, his last request was to be permitted to tell his whole testimony in the service. Usually in such a complex situation, I like to wait longer to confirm its genuineness, but on this occasion, it seemed to be fitting for him to share it publically.

At the appropriate time, he was announced and did an admirable job. The crowd, most of whom seemed to know him in his capacity as a city official and some business owners with whom he had just made settlements, registered their delight with loud applause.

Before I left that city during a week that was filled with the evidence of the power of God, I saw so many lives changed. Many people came to faith in Christ, not the least of whom was this man's wife and his two fine young sons. Many significant healings and conversions to Christ were reported in ways that only our sovereign and living God could orchestrate. These results reminded us again that it is "'Not by might nor by power, but by My Spirit,' Says the LORD of hosts" (Zech. 4:6 NKJV).

We heard from those who knew other leaders in the city that this one man's transformation totally affected the community and brought a great sense of conviction on others who were associated with him. The person conveying this news to us said, "In our opinion, this may be the most notable miracle of the week's ministry because it is affecting hearts, and by touching the feelings of those involved, it will be far reaching in the community."

This is only one example of how the Holy Spirit worked His miracles through the gift of the word of knowledge, without which I would likely only have prayed for his sore throat.

Many times we are asked why the gifts of the Holy Spirit are not more often evidenced in the West. A complex answer could be detailed in length, but is beyond the scope of this book. Instead, I will offer a simpler answer.

Paul exhorted the Corinthian believers in the love chapter (1 Cor. 13) to major in love, for without, it he said, "I am nothing" (13:2 AV). He prefaced this statement in the last verse of the previous chapter by encouraging them ". . . earnestly" to "desire the best gifts" (12:31 NKJV).

The simple answer lies hidden in the mists of verse 31, as their use tends to be obscured by postmodern thinking and in our neglect to desire earnestly "the best gifts." If indeed respect for the use of the gifts in the West is diminishing and there is limited opportunity for their ministry, what would be the purpose of earnestly desiring them? The apostle Paul continues after the love chapter by affirming further their use: "Pursue love, and desire spiritual *gifts*" (1 Cor. 14:1a NKJV). We must love one another. We must share His love with the world around us. We must love not only with human love but also with divine love while continuing to desire spiritual gifts. His love is everything and will touch and reach our world when it is released. But it is crucial that we obey the apostle Paul's clear and distinct direction.

Without the frailties or impediments of human love, we should adhere to the divine love found in chapter 13. It takes perpetual practise to let divine love flow freely through us as a natural channel, even though we are new creations in Christ Jesus (2 Cor. 5:17). To be receptive to divine love flowing to us and remain in the right attitude to *release* it to a hurting, impoverished, and lost world around us, wherever our mission field is, demands relentless discipline from us.

This exercise becomes more complex as the natural man seems to interfere with the desire of our spiritual man and may sometimes even try to substitute natural love for divine love.

Natural love is inadequate for the major and demanding endurance tasks intended for our spiritual man's divine love assignments. When we are reaching and sustaining the impoverished masses we are commissioned to reach and love, our human love is utterly ineffective.

This inadequacy became glaringly obvious to me one evening in an outdoor evangelistic meeting, now called a festival of praise to make it more culturally tolerable in Eastern cultures. As I concluded the gospel message and invited those who wished to receive Christ as their Saviour and only living God to come forward for salvation together with many hundreds who also came forward for various other needs in their lives, I left the platform and came down to their level in front of the platform. Very soon I had a crowd surrounding me in a frantic attempt to have me pray for them. The highly spirited Asian jungle crowd pressed in to reach me as one massive body of perspiring flesh with hundreds of heads. Added to this drama was a steaming jungle temperature with high humidity, creating a formula for panic. As I was in the middle of this situation, something happened within my spirit.

As much as I delight in the call to missions and ministry in developing countries and working in such conditions that tax the limits of my physical endurance, on this occasion with His anointing, something snapped in me. I was almost overcome with the heat of bodies as they surrounded me in their eager effort to hug and touch me. I silently screamed out to God: "I have had enough! Get me out of this!" To this He quietly and instantly replied in my spirit, "You feel as you do because you are trying with the wrong kind of love." Although I was totally familiar with the four Greek words for love, I had not differentiated the meanings, especially for this venture, of two of the four Greek words. *Phileo* (brotherly) love is one and needs to be differentiated from *agape* (God or divine) love. In that instant, my ministry was changed forever. Human love will not go the distance. Only divine love flowing through us will go the distance and be sufficient for us to finish the race successfully.

I was still in a vortex and faced with a whirl of activity from which it would be hard for me to escape; suddenly, however, there was no need to do so. Like the flick of a switch, the energy flow of love, switched from human to divine, and the rest of that evangelistic mission's meeting and future years of identical ministry have been, by contrast, easy.

As we seek to honour His Word and obey His instruction that is given by inspiration of the Holy Spirit in the last verse of chapter 12 and the first verse of chapter 14, we are told to continue to "desire" the best gifts; for between both verses, the love chapter is sandwiched. The apostle Paul reiterated the importance of desiring the best gifts immediately before and immediately after the love chapter. Could it be that this emphasis, strategically placed on either side of the love chapter, indicates the significance of the gifts being in operation in the body of believers to enable the body to understand and function fully at the highest capacity of love, *agape*?

Around the world in megacities and far-flung jungles, that desire is still producing gifts and growing substantial congregations. My preaching assignment took me to a church in Africa that did not have a seminary-trained pastor. I was expecting perhaps a congregation of one to a hundred. But as I walked onto the platform, about twenty thousand people awaited my message. Later when I spoke to the leader, he informed me that on the other side of the city he had another church of equal, if not greater, size. He further surprised me by saying that not one of the seven pastors in each church was formally trained for ministry. Each one was a professional in another field, and not all were serving in a full-time capacity. The apostle Paul spoke of it as tent making.

In the worship portion of the service I attended, they had a highly developed gifts in operation ministry that flowed without difficulty and was closely managed, considering the size of the audience. Later, after teaching for several days in their Bible college, it was easy for me to understand their fluency in the gifts. The gifts were given at Pentecost for the benefit of the church of Christ in this dispensation and are intended for its continued growth. Today they are continuing to operate as they were originally intended wherever the Word is fully obeyed.

## Breaking the Bondage of Abuse

While speaking of the gifts in operation in the West, another incident in Western Canada may serve to show how a moment of the supernatural gift of the word of knowledge accomplished what had not been achieved in a young man's lifetime by any human agency.

Some time ago we were enjoying being back in Canada's agreeable climate on a brief respite from tropical temperatures. One evening I had a call from a Pentecostal Assemblies of Canada (PAOC) pastor. It was a cordial, free-wheeling conversation, as we were for many years, and still are, in good fellowship with the PAOC. He discussed his assembly and his wish to have several days of Holy Spirit ministry for his congregation, with me coming as the speaker. We spoke of the details and subjects to be taught and scheduled for several days and a weekend of teaching.

When I arrived, the meetings began with a note of expectation and were very well attended. Various aspects on the subject of the Holy Spirit were taught, developed, and discussed for several evenings, and there was a steady progression in my presentations. The weekend ministry became somewhat more hands on; that gave opportunity for those who wished to move deeper with the Holy Spirit to *release* their own spirits to Him and *receive* from Him.

An interesting observation is that when one is seeking to receive a deeper relationship with the Spirit, it often requires more than just desiring or praying to that end. In many instances there appears to be an additional dimension of release that carries with it the thought of submission or surrender to His leading and will. It is possible, it seems, that we may pray to receive from Him while withholding in some concealed area of our mind or life issues; that segment then becomes an impediment.

A common example would be those who have had a deep desire for many years to receive the baptism in the Spirit with the same evidence as those who received in the book of Acts but have never received the experience. In my altar discussion with them, as they relate to me their discouragement about the delay, it becomes obvious to me that they have a specific format in mind for the event. Sometimes it may almost be a subconscious format. They would like to control the process: when, how, and under what circumstances they would be willing to receive. As they analyze their list of conditions, suddenly the lights go on and they see that release is the operative word. As they ask to receive on His terms without their demands or reservations inhibiting the process, releasing themselves to Him, He answers their prayers.

After teaching in my friend's church on a final evening of ministry, the presence of the Lord was very real in the auditorium. As many people came forward for prayer, I ministered to them. Without any warning, the total atmosphere of the service changed in a remarkable way. Nothing in my past ministry could have prepared me for what God was about to do. The best natural example to describe the scene would be to imagine a powerful commercial vacuum designed to extract every sound from the sanctuary. Total silence reigned!

Everyone looked around in astonishment in an attempt to grasp why we seemed to be in a silent mode—a plastic bubble, perhaps. As I looked to my pastor friend on the platform for help, he raised his shoulders and gestured with a look that said, "Don't ask me!" If silence could be measured on a decibel meter, it would have registered zero. Sensing this was more than natural deafness all of us were experiencing, I turned my thoughts heaven-ward. "God, what is this? What are You saying?" The thought that instantly touched my spirit seemed to say, "This is your burning bush." The event flashed before my mind. I was familiar with Moses' experience in the wilderness as he cared for the flock of Jethro, his father-in-law. To me the parallel was clear.

Moses said about the burning bush, "I will now turn aside and see this great sight." It was not a great sight because a bush was burning, but was a great sight because, "the bush does not burn"

(Ex. 3:3 NKJV). The purpose of the burning bush was not to burn a bush, which was commonplace in desert heat, but for God to get Moses' attention. This silence, then, in our sanctuary was to get my attention. God had something to say to this audience.

The foregoing explanation took only a second of time. God began to speak to my spirit in an unusual way. Different disjointed pieces of information began to come in rapid succession. Some were colours, words, numbers, and times. Individually they made no natural sense. An intelligent sentence could not have been composed from the details. For confidential reasons, the following explanation has been changed from the original message for everyone's privacy.

Still wrapped in our imaginary silent bubble, I shared with the audience what had transpired in my spirit. It went something like this. "The silence we are feeling was for God to get my attention, as He got Moses' attention with the burning bush. He has given me different pieces of information that seem disconnected. I will give them to you as they came to me. There must be a message in them for someone." So it began to flow: "Thursday evening, 9:00 p.m. Blue carpet on the hallway. Phone mounted on hallway wall. Upsetting phone call. The guilt is not yours; you are free of the guilt. Be strong in Me. 6527896578[36]—I will hold your hand."

For a few moments, the silence continued until a young man in his thirties stood to his feet. "This is totally for me," he said. Then he began to share his story.

"Many years ago when I was a child, I was violated. It continued until I was older. He always threatened to tell my family that it was my fault or that he would hurt someone I loved. It stopped many years ago, but the threats continue. In recent years, as I have had some natural, healthy relationships with young women, he will call me and say he will tell if the relationship with her is not terminated. This has occurred several times.

"This week, Thursday at nine p.m., he called again. I answered the phone mounted in my hallway, which has blue carpet. It was another threatening and upsetting phone call demanding that I conclude my dating of this young lady."

He confirmed that the message from God was for him and was just the assurance he needed to get on with his life and ignore any further threats. He sat down, and everyone was blessed with the moving of God's Spirit in the service.

I was delighted that the disjointed statements made sense and ministered to someone. Most of it was relevant, but I thought I missed hearing accurately on the list of numbers. After all, we are still in the flesh and anything that flows in any spiritual gift must reconcile with Scripture or it must be disregarded. A few minutes later, he stood to his feet again, saying, "I forgot to mention that the string of numbers is exactly the caller's phone number." What an example of the Holy Spirit's gift of knowledge in operation in this dispensation!

Almost two years later, I was attending our general conference and met the pastor of that church. We stopped to chat briefly, and he asked if I remembered that event. (I thought to myself, *I would never forget it.*) He continued, "In my church yesterday, that young man and his young lady were married." This is the power of the Holy Spirit at work through a gift of the Spirit, in this case the word of knowledge.

Let's hear the apostle Paul's encouragement again after we have learned to walk in His love chapter outlined in 1 Corinthians 13! Without the fluent operation of the gifts of the Holy Spirit, the body may be deficient in its capacity to function at His intended highest and best use of *agape*, divine love. Hence, by ". . . inspiration of God" (2 Tim. 3:16a AV), it is strategically placed between the double emphases where we are further exhorted to "Follow the way of love and eagerly desire spiritual gifts" (1 Cor. 14:1 NIV) and "eagerly desire the greater gifts" (1 Cor. 12:31 NIV).

## Holy Spirit Revelation on a Demolition Site

Out of many men working on a construction site, one stood out from the rest, not because he was different in any apparent way but because I seemed to be alerted in my spirit about him. Several times that night he came to my mind, and it seemed that the Holy

Spirit was revealing events of his past life, his present condition, and his need to make changes in his life.

The following morning, in a torrential rainstorm, as I was crossing the site I saw the same man already at his work and walking diagonally to his equipment, and his route would intersect with mine. At that moment the Holy Spirit seemed to say, "Stop him and share what you know!"

As our paths crossed, I greeted him and asked if I could have a word with him. I shared what had happened in my spirit regarding him over the last two days, told him of the work of ministry to which God had called me, and asked if he would receive what I felt God had revealed to me about his life. He agreed, and we stood for several minutes in the downpour, soaked, while I supernaturally replayed various events of his life. These events, he knew, were impossible for me to know, since we had just met and had not known each other before those moments.

He became quite moved by this revelation and listened attentively as I presented to him the clear call of Christ by the Holy Spirit on his life, and within minutes he responded to the gospel message by joining me in a salvation prayer.

This is another example of the revelatory gift of knowledge of the Holy Spirit in operation in the supernatural dimension. Could this type of supernatural intervention be part of what is missing in our failure to be open to the direction of and prompting by the Holy Spirit in our day-to-day Christian lives?

# 12

# HEARING AND OBEYING THE HOLY SPIRIT'S PROMPTINGS

Life is an endless learning experience. Certainly ministry is also. Typically I minister several hundred times each year. For some ministers, after a lifetime of pulpit ministry, there is an element of the routine in every event.

But this has not been so for me. Yes, I have undergone similar events and preached messages with parallels, but for the most part, I have experienced an endless variation in many aspects of my ministry. I craft each message to the best of my ability. I handle each counselling session delicately. When I'm preaching or teaching, I make a determined effort to stay within the boundaries of my outlines and biblical texts or the subjects assigned to me for teaching. Even when I deliver a message, I try to be alert to what the Holy Spirit may add to it. But this is not always easy to detect because the Spirit's promptings are gentle, and at first, I could dismiss them as processes of my natural thoughts. As I unfold the details that follow, I will establish the importance of hearing what the Spirit is saying at every moment of the preaching process. Conversely, what a tragedy it would be to miss any additions the Holy Spirit prompts me to add!

During a lengthy ministry tour to one of the most remote jungles on earth and very close to where the most recent undiscovered tribe was found, I held a one-week leadership school. Several hundred pastors and young ministry workers attended it. They had come from some of the most uncharted corners of the country. Some had come by river in dug-out canoes; others had walked for as many as eighty miles or 128 kilometres. Very few could afford train or bus fare, and some came vast distances on bicycles. Most had been traveling for close to ten days and had only the clothes in which they traveled. Earlier in the scheduling of this event we had been advised that there could be no date changes because it would be impossible to contact those planning to attend with only one month remaining before school began.

There was to be a large student body attending the event, with a full day's teaching and evangelism in the evenings planned. To lighten my schedule, there were two other teachers teaching two hours in the morning and two hours in the afternoon, followed by the crusade at night.

The significance of the promptings of the Holy Spirit in our daily lives or during teaching or preaching will be the focus of this story. By using the word *prompting* I mean the interjection of the Spirit overriding my current train of natural thought. I need to be careful not to dismiss the Spirit's promptings as a renegade or irrelevant thought. Over many years of enjoying and benefiting from His supernatural input, wisdom, and direction, I must confess, that until I learned this lesson, on many occasions I dismissed the Spirit's prompting as a stray thought. For me the learning process was fairly basic, which I will first develop to some degree before I present the major details that evolved later in the leadership school.

While working with a problem, such as in counselling, my method would have been the same from my years of experience with dealing with very similar issues. At first when I had a thought that had no natural reason to surface, I would dismiss it and continue counselling in normal manner. But little by little, the Holy Spirit would repeat the teaching process until my spirit responded to Him. This process was gradually developed by trial and error. I have come to recognize several indicators that this intervention in my natural thought processes is about to occur.

One indicator involves something I would not be naturally inclined to say or do. It comes to my mind as a thought beyond the natural, one that would not be easy to reconcile with my thought processes at that moment. Often when I feel prompted to do or say something unnatural, I hesitate to do so to avoid possible embarrassment. It will carry with it the sense that if this is done now, I stand to be embarrassed. Conversely, if it is not done, I could feel as though I had failed to obey the Spirit on an issue.

For me to speak into people's lives when I was not familiar with them, sometimes there was a compelling urgency that produced symptoms that confirmed the validity of the prompt. In my experience, my prolonged delay in responding to a prompting of the Spirit will produce in me reactions such as a tightening throat, damp palms, or a nervous sensation in my stomach.

Before I consider the main subject of the promptings of the Holy Spirit at the conclusion of this section, I will use two lesser examples to emphasize further the significance of the Spirit's leading.

One such prompt urged me to call a friend in his office about forty miles or sixty-four kilometres away. After several attempts to reach him, there was no answer. As I put the phone down, it was like a voice spoke audibly to me, saying, "Drive to his office and bring a three-figure amount of money with you." Although this was not a large amount for most people, it was for me. I looked in my wallet and discovered that I had the exact amount of money that I was instructed to bring, which at the time was almost all we had.

I arrived at his office at just after eight in the morning, and I found my friend standing behind the reception desk of his printing company. His head was resting upon both of his arms. When he raised his head, I saw that his eyes were bloodshot from prolonged crying. My presence startled him. He wondered why I had come. My friend was not a believer, and at first, he did not understand the spiritual significance of my visit. Even so, he agreed to allow me to pray for what was to him an impossible situation. He explained that we were standing in semidarkness because the utilities had been shut off, which explained why he didn't answer his phone. Also, his presses were not running.

As we talked, he said that, had the power not been cut, he could have completed a large order that morning and been paid a sizable amount of money. Now that would be impossible. He answered my question about how much his electric bill was and how much he had in the bank. Unknown to him was that the amount he had in his account together with what the Holy Spirit had impressed me to bring, when added together, was the exact amount needed to restore the power in his plant. Without sharing about my prompting, I asked him to close out his account at the bank, give the withdrawn amount to me, and then I would get his power turned on again.

Not knowing what God had in mind for him, he reluctantly accompanied me to the bank. When it opened, he withdrew his last forty dollars, if I recall correctly, and handed them to me, not knowing that I would also be parting with my last few dollars to help him. When we try to walk by faith and follow the Holy Spirit's leading, it can seem to cost us money. At the hydro office, I presented his bill with his money, plus mine, for the exact amount, for which they issued to me his receipt and then immediately reconnected his power. As we arrived back at his office, he was still crying, this time for joy, because his presses were rolling out the last of his order.

On my return journey home, my thoughts centered upon the beautiful thing God had worked for him, but I was arguing with myself about my substantial financial deficiency in light of my own needs. About halfway home, as I was driving on a rural side road, something happened. I had another prompt! It was as though the Holy Spirit was asking me to make the next turn left. As I slowed down the car in anticipation, the next left was onto a narrow gravel farm road, which opened to a large farmyard with a farmhouse in the distance.

When I arrived, the farmer was working on his equipment. Upon seeing me, he began walking toward my car. My heart was in my mouth. Why was I there? What would I say to a man I had never met and with whom I had no appointment? He greeted me warmly, saying, "I was expecting you." I was speechless. How could this be?

Before I could regain my composure, he invited me to his home for tea. He immediately began to relate his problem and how he thought it could be solved. He desperately needed a service to be provided and felt I had the answer. Although we had never met before and he did not know me, at that moment I was in a position to provide for him the advice and service he needed. About two hours later, his problem and mine were both solved. He was also a believer and had been seeking God to bring someone he could trust with his financial planning. When our meeting was over, and as I was driving away, I did a mental calculation of the commission I had just earned from that transaction with the farmer. It was exactly ten times the amount I had given away in response to the Holy Spirit's prompting earlier that day.

To conclude my printer friend's story, within two weeks a major city newspaper bought his printing business for a substantial amount above its value and gave him a highly paid position in their head office. Sometimes being sensitive to the prompting of the Holy Spirit costs in different ways, and sometimes it pays dividends. God is a debtor to no one.

Perhaps the prompting may be about sharing what the Spirit has revealed about a person. This can be a very delicate issue. There are occasions when the prompting of the Spirit seems to flow in conjunction with some of the nine spiritual ministry gifts. Perhaps the word of knowledge will prepare a person for the message to be delivered. As God uses His gifts to minister to the deeper levels of a person's need, a rich and healing work is effectively and quietly done in minutes that otherwise would take longer with natural methods—if indeed it was ever fully achieved.

I experienced yet another incident when I was walking on the sidewalk in a major Canadian city. It was during a time when I was in part-time ministry and also working in the financial world. On one occasion, while hurrying to a business appointment, dressed appropriately in a business suit, shirt, and tie, a young man accosted me. He wore torn and soiled jeans and a sleeveless t-shirt and had long, dishevelled, and unkempt hair. Either his feet were bare or he wore flip-flops, and he had body piercings in more places than I care to mention. He greeted me with the question, "Do you know Jesus Christ?"

If he had been a drug pusher, I would not have been surprised. His question totally disarmed me. After all, by that time, I had been in ministry for four decades. My response shocked both of us. "Where does he live?" I asked, as though he were looking for a friend in the area. To be perfectly honest, it was very difficult for me to have *him* discuss with me the most important person in my life. At that moment, I was not a good candidate for his witnessing techniques.

He persisted with rapid-fire questions: "If you died tonight, would you go to hell? What does Christ mean to you? Why not give Him a chance?" And he asked many more. Because I was still bewildered by his approach, my response was to lead him on but without disclosing that I was an evangelist. Many minutes, perhaps twenty, passed as he pressed every note on the witnessing keyboard. As he kept up the barrage of questions, suddenly I was aware that I was beginning to process thoughts in my mind. Yes, it was the gentle beginning of a Holy Spirit prompting session. Unknown to him, as he rattled on, I had a new assignment.

Very clearly, the Holy Spirit impressed me to walk with him a few blocks to where my car was parked. He was to be seated in the passenger seat while I sat on the driver's side. Once we were there, I immediately confessed to him that, in fact, I did know Jesus Christ very well and that I had been in ministry for a lifetime. He also heard what had transpired earlier as he witnessed to me and that we were in the car at the Spirit's instruction. I asked him if he had learned to be obedient to the Holy Spirit. We discussed how that can sometimes be a little difficult. He agreed but said that for the most part, he really tried to obey Him. When I asked him if he could trust me to share with him what I felt the Holy Spirit wanted me to say to him, he said yes. I removed my wallet from my back pocket, took every last dollar from it, and offered it to him. At first he tried to refuse, but then he remembered he had agreed to allow me to do this. Then his tears began to flow, and through the sobs, he told me his story.

Within the next couple of hours, by five that evening he had to be back at his apartment with the total payment for his last two months' rent and other incidentals or his landlord would put all his personal belongings onto the front lawn by the street. As he told me his story, he was also counting the money. The story faded into deeper sobs as he tried to say that to the exact dollar, what he now held in his hand was the amount his landlord must have today. We hugged across the car and cried together for joy at how the Holy Spirit had orchestrated such a precious moment. Sometimes I ask myself, "Why is it so hard to release the flesh and the spirit to Him when all He wants to do is bless us more and more?"

Hopefully I have laid the foundation in the previous two examples for understanding the concept of the Holy Spirit's prompting. Now, in a very major way, I will continue with the leadership school event I mentioned earlier as a final example of the subject.

One afternoon while I was teaching on the subject of leadership to several hundred pastors and following my notes carefully to stay on track, it became obvious to me that God wanted to divert me. It is difficult for me to be coherent with an audience while simultaneously the other part of my mind is having a conversation with God. Hearing clearly what He impressed on me was not the issue. The dilemma was how to add His request within the context of the lecture. But He was persistent. "Do it! Do it now!" was the instruction that seemed to hammer in my mind while I was trying to speak intelligently to my audience.

*Where do I include this? How will it fit?* I asked myself. What He asked me to share was so personal and private, as well as totally unrelated to my subject, that it was somewhat confusing to find the best place in my teaching plan to include it.

Not wishing to break from my carefully crafted outline, I decided to add a new branch on my homiletic tree to include this new, urgent message. I took a few minutes to adjust the outline. I could do this without seeming disjointed, and then it all would fit seamlessly. From my vantage point at the pulpit, with the audience at either side of a wide aisle in front of me, my line of vision was clear all the way to the back of this police academy auditorium. The central entrance was large and wide enough to accommodate several columns of police officers to parade abreast. For perhaps ten minutes, I was conscious of an usher walking back and forth outside the doors who was wringing his hands with emotion. He continued to walk while I built the branch to allow an addition to the lecture. Finally, the scene was set as I discussed being strong in the Lord and in the power of His might. I took them to Paul's epistle to the Ephesians, and together we read, "Finally, my brethren, be strong in the Lord, and in the power of His might" (Eph. 6:10 AV). We considered our human frailty in light of wrestling against the power of the enemy.

We studied the major issues of life that we, as believers, can surmount, not in our own strength, but only in His. We spoke of growing strong in Him by developing personal prayer lives and disciplined daily Bible reading. Strength through walking in obedience to His Word will carry us through the most difficult times of testing. I used several Bible examples, including the tragedy of Job's life when he lost everything, including his seven sons and three daughters. After such tragedies, Job could testify, "Though he slay me, yet will I trust in Him" (Job 13:15 AV). Interestingly, God restored to Job double of everything he had lost, except his children. They were replaced in the same number as before, but since the children were everlasting spirits, perhaps together they were also doubled.

Now the new branch of the outline had grown sufficiently to relate what God had instructed me. Even as I began to share, the usher was still pacing back and forth in some kind of dilemma. Reluctantly, I began to relate an event that was personal and too close to my heart to share in public, but because this was God's doing, I had to tell it.

I began talking about my cousin and his wife who were caring for their eldest son who was six years old when he was diagnosed with acute leukemia. The doctors gave him two weeks to live, but the illness was prolonged and took its toll on his parents and extended family. Although the child was loved and prayed for by his parents and many from around the country and various churches, the prognosis was not good. Everything that could be done had been done. He was given every comfort and pleasure his adoring parents could provide. He was their firstborn son. They believed that God could heal their boy but submitted to His sovereign will. Eventually, as he became feeble and the disease took its toll, they trusted in their God of whom they could say,

> *The LORD gave, and the LORD has taken away;*
> *Blessed be the name of the LORD* (Job 1:21c NKJV).

In God's perfect timing, He enfolded their beloved child in His loving arms and bosom to heaven. The boy was healed in God's perfect will with Him in heaven. Jesus said, "Let the little children come to Me, and do not forbid them; for of such is the kingdom of God" (Luke 18:16 NKJV).

Several years later, their second son was in his mid-teens. He was a handsome young man with all the interests of a healthy teenager and had his whole life ahead of him. He had his driver's licence, had many friends, and worked faithfully at his farming job.

One spring day while transporting a load of baled hay to a farm on a tractor trailer, something went terribly wrong. To get to the farm, it was necessary to take a narrow country road. That road led under a low trestle-type railway bridge. The large load on his trailer was covered with a tarpaulin because of the inclement weather, so the tractor driver stopped just short of the bridge and asked the young man to get up and remove it. He climbed on top of the load, folded the tarpaulin into a small package, and pressed it between the bales for safety. Thinking that the young man had gotten off the top of the load, the driver continued through the low bridge opening, but the young man had gotten his foot caught in the bales and was crushed between the top of the load and the underside of the bridge. He was immediately "absent from the body, and . . . present with the Lord" (2 Cor. 5:8 AV).

Several hundred pastors sat in shocked silence. A sense of the Holy Spirit seemed to brood over the group as they contemplated the implications, if that were their situation, of losing a second son. They heard how the parents handled this tragedy with their second boy. They learned, however, that the boy's parents drew upon the strength and comfort of the God, who Himself sacrificed His Son in death so we could have life everlasting.

I spoke of walking into the funeral service with the father, and in a feeble way, I tried to comfort him. He, as a taller man, dropped his arm down on my shoulder, as though to comfort me, saying, his son was "absent from the body, and to be present with the Lord" (2 Cor. 5:8 AV). Then he quickly added that Jesus said, "For where your treasure is, there will your heart be also" (Matt. 6:21 AV).

Just as this story the Holy Spirit had prompted me to work into the lecture was coming to a conclusion, I saw the usher who had been wringing his hands and walking back and forth outside come down the aisle. He walked slowly, looking along each row of men on either side. Eventually he saw the pastor he was looking for and pressed into that row. The usher came to the pastor, bent over, and spoke with him. Both men walked out of the session. They spoke outside the door for several minutes. Finally, they embraced for a long time, and the pastor walked away.

Later I learned the full explanation. When the usher first began wringing his hands outside, it was because he had read a telegram for that pastor, but he could not summon the courage to give it to him. Later he told me that as I began to share about my cousin and his wife's two sons passing into God's presence, he became stronger in his spirit and was able, at the end of the story, to go to the pastor. He mentioned that the pastor had said, "I don't know how I could bear this news if that story had not been told."

He will never know how I almost missed God's prompting. I found great difficulty in finding a way to include a personal family story seamlessly that had no bearing on the lecture. I also had no idea of its significance to one of several hundred pastors who was, at that moment, facing the tragedy of a lifetime.

That pastor had walked perhaps forty miles to the event and now had to walk back those same miles. For every step of the forty miles and for many days of solitude, except for the presence of the Comforter, he would relive the text of the telegram that advised him that his only two young sons had capsized a canoe. Both had drowned and were already buried that same day before sunset.

These stories should help convey the significance of learning to hear and interpret the promptings of the Holy Spirit. It is in this way He seeks to work through us as His servants by supernaturally speaking into the hurting heart at one of the most difficult moments of life. At the same time, He allows us the honour to be channels through which He flows in love and care for His own. God, make me more caring, sensitive, and alert to Your slightest prompting so You may get all the glory!

# 13

# GOD'S UNIQUE PROVISION
# FOR MINISTRY EMERGENCIES

Pulpit ministry or delivering the message is just the tip of the iceberg in ministry. Much more takes place behind the scenes. When one considers overseas evangelistic ministry, behind such ministry is the important factor in funding for an event. The total journey requires a walk of faith.

This chapter will relate the supernatural dimension of God in providing for pressing needs over and above the funding raised by traditionally tried and proven methods. As I have sought to walk by faith in God's work over many years, in my process of learning, I have established basic principles. Namely, in advance of a ministry tour, I must do everything humanly possible to reach my financial goal for a particular mission's tour. Then I trust that God will do what I can't do. His is the supernatural ingredient upon which I depend. In Ephesians, Paul's instruction in relating to a believer's armour of God's protection also applies to the challenge for us to do our part in contributing to the release of the resources for ministry: "and having done all, to stand. Stand therefore . . ." (Eph. 6:13–14 AV). Before I commit myself to an overseas mission's assignment, it is always necessary for me to do everything possible to stand with adequate resources. Then, in His sovereignty, God will provide supernaturally the needed funding, and usually in that order.

Which comes first: the scheduling of a ministry tour or the release of funding to execute it? Do we wait for the budget to be met before scheduling a tour, or do we put together our tour plans and work toward raising the budget? In real life, it is some of both, plus the D (divine) factor.

When I schedule an overseas ministry tour, often it is to several countries over a six—to twelve-week period, and various costs begin to accrue. Advance funding for part of the initial cost of local seminars or crusades in each country is sometimes necessary. Airline tickets have to be booked, which in today's world means immediate payment. Once advance funding has been implemented and travel tickets have been booked, the overseas process is in motion. After the financial commitment has been made, from that moment on, it is really a walk of faith. It is then almost impossible to change one's ministry plans.

Although every human effort is made to reach or exceed the proposed budget before departure, often I experience a substantial shortfall. What do I do in such a situation? To cancel is to lose substantial up-front money advanced to each field, not to mention the disappointment of the various field leaders who have organized seminars with large numbers of pastors committed to attend, or the loss of funds for all of the advertising for many different event locations, including the loss of credibility by not keeping my commitments.

On one such occasion, when it seemed that a postponement would be the prudent action a few days before departure, I called the lead pastor to inform him of my new plans. His response was explosive: "You can't! Dozens of pastors are already walking through the jungle to the event. Some of them will have walked up to sixty miles or almost one hundred kilometres. There is no way to stop them at this stage." He was right; it was too late to change our plans, regardless of our financial situation. This had indeed become a walk of faith. So we went and trusted God for the D factor. He came through supernaturally. After we began the trip, God supernaturally provided financially for our needs.

We must always remember that God's work is, for us, a walk of faith that cannot be undertaken unless we do everything humanly possible first and then rely on the D factor.

On numerous occasions, we found ourselves financially short before going on a major mission's tour. On one occasion, we had done all we knew to do to reach the goal, but we were still almost 50 percent short of our budget and were on the verge of cancelling a major tour the night before our planned departure. But God came through for us financially.

For another tour, we had planned for months in advance. We booked seminars that we expected hundreds of pastors and leaders would attend in various locations in several countries. We arranged for evangelistic festivals, with venues booked weeks in advance, and many were paid for in full. We bought and were issued airline tickets. We packed our suitcases, and we prepared to be away from our home for the next two months. We were to leave the following morning, but with our best human efforts, we were only halfway toward reaching our financial goal. We committed our financial emergency to the Lord. After midnight we went to bed and slept soundly until five in the morning. Regardless of the outcome, we were going. If we had known in advance the how and why of God, would it then have been a walk of faith?

Early that morning, we spent hours on minor details in the home and in-office administration, including sending emails. After breakfast, at around nine o'clock, we began locking up and putting the suitcases in the car. I took one last look around the house and then closed the front door. As the key was in the second lock and as I was activating the deadbolt I heard a phone ringing inside. I quickly unlocked the door and ran for the nearest phone.

Breathlessly, I picked up the receiver and recognized the voice of a donor.

Several months earlier, when discussing this trip with this donor, he said that he would like to contribute toward it and would be in touch before we left. Leading up to our departure, I had sent out a newsletter our donors would have received as a reminder if they still intended to contribute to our overseas tour fund. The caller asked when we expected to leave on the overseas trip, and I explained I had to unlock the door and come back to answer his call. He and his wife were surprised to learn that they had caught us at the very second when we were leaving the house. We agreed to meet them at a local bank within fifteen minutes before we needed to get on the freeway for the airport. As we met them outside the bank, they handed me a check, already in certified funds, for the missing 50 percent of the budgeted amount that we needed. In this way, the budget for our overseas tour was met.

I believe that once people have been made aware of our need by letter or face to face, then I trust God by His Spirit to touch their spirits to release the needed funds. I try not to make further contact with donors so they don't feel pressured to give.

There is no human reason for evangelism, missions, or ministries to be chained by funding constraints. There is no shortage of resources in God's kingdom economy. His economy is not dependent upon the global economy. In God's economy, believers have the privilege to exercise their kingdom position. When we live and walk in covenant or in sacred contract with Him, He releases kingdom provision and favour to underwrite the needs of our ministry to enable the gospel of the kingdom to be declared to the whole world: ". . . then shall the end come" (Matt. 24:14b AV). Over many years of operating in a faith ministry, we have learned that it is not about money being raised but being released. In the hands of believers are the vast resources needed for God's work. It is the believer's responsibility to hear from the Holy Spirit and release the resources needed. The Bible says, "Therefore, to him who knows to do good and does not do *it*, to him it is sin" (James 4:17 NKJV). When this happens, God is then able to trigger the D factor and pour out multiplied blessings to the obedient believer.

In those final moments before the supernatural release of the needed funds, we were given the opportunity to allow the Scripture to penetrate our spirits. It says, "Rest in the Lord, and wait patiently for Him" (Ps. 37:7 NKJV).

God moves in supernatural ways that one never knows when such a move is about to happen. Such was the case on another occasion that will follow. We were back in Canada and attending to Western ministry business to promote our overseas work. One day as I looked at a calendar, I began to realize that a conference we enjoyed attending in the past was soon approaching. Since we were in the country at conference time, we would be able to attend it. The problem was that the location of the conference was a two-day drive each way. In our challenge to budget for overseas tours, would it be wise to spend the time and money for such a trip? But in our spirits we had a settled, good, and right feeling that we would be attending it.

As the weeks went by, the day for registration drew nearer. Still we were undecided about going. In the natural it seemed we should let this one pass. Because we had attended faithfully over many years, an absence from this particular conference would not be a problem. We asked ourselves, "Is this a good thing to do at this time? How will it help missions? Do we need to expend energy for such a lengthy drive?" To all of these questions from a purely human viewpoint the answer would be a resounding no. One of the primary obstacles in our thinking was that, from many past experiences, although it would be uplifting to our spirits and great fellowship and we would be reconnecting with ministry colleagues of a lifetime, it would do nothing to advance our fundraising efforts for upcoming mission's trips. Finally, one morning, it seemed to be exactly the right thing to do. I made the reservations and booked the hotel, and we were ready to go. As a result, again in our spirits we had a settled, good, and right feeling. What brought the change? What made the difference? Why after weeks of indecision did we suddenly feel the freedom to go?

In retrospect, not just about this event but many similar ones, without even being conscious of the Holy Spirit's leading, some of the critical turns I made in life were prompted directly by Him. For example, because of a delay in going to an appointment, I made a contact that I would have missed had there been no delay, and through that contact, I developed a vital link for future ministry.

This delay, the D factor in operation, was God's supernatural intervention in my life and ministry. While mentoring the Philippians, Paul encouraged them when he stated, ". . . for it is God who works in you both to will and to do *His* good pleasure" (Phil. 2:13 NKJV).

Our spring drive through the majestic Canadian Rockies to the ministry conference revealed the presence of an even more majestic Creator. Each snow-capped mountain peak and valley vista was evidence of God's handiwork. The conference met our expectations. We experienced great blessings as we met with old friends, fellowshipped at meal times, and enjoyed God's presence in the worship sessions. In all, it was a great event, but nothing stood out in relation to our mission's financial challenges—or had we missed something?

Weeks earlier we had decided that if we did attend the event, we would visit a lifetime friend for a few days following the conference. After we arrived and were settled in, our friend mentioned that, resulting from their business contacts, some friends of his would come by to visit briefly one afternoon, and it would be nice if we could be available to meet them.

They arrived, and we all enjoyed a pleasant time together. For some time, our new friends questioned us about special miracle moments on the mission field. This, I think, was mostly for the benefit of their pre-teenage boy, to expose him to the supernatural ability of God to work in and change lives by His power.

The next day, our new friends invited all of us to have dinner at their home. They lived in a fine home on a beautiful country estate. As we sat down to dinner together, the family members met with us around a huge table centered in a dining room with a cathedral ceiling. Several of their adult children began asking questions about missions. They were eager to know about God's supernatural works in missions.

Question after question was asked and answered, each taking us down some avenue of God's exciting provision for a desperate need. We testified to them about the physical miracles of lame people who stood up and stepped out of their wheelchairs or discarded crutches that they depended upon for decades. We talked about tumours that disappeared, blind eyes that were opened, and alcoholics and drug addicts who were instantly set free and remained so.

At one overseas missions meeting, even the elements of nature were reversed. It occurred in an open-air sports field crusade located in a hollow by the side of a busy highway. Off the roadside was perhaps a twenty-degree embankment. Several hundred people were attending the event and standing in front of the stage. On the grassy roadside embankment a crowd stood or sat, watching and listening to the program. As the program proceeded, and when it was almost time for me to preach the gospel, ominous clouds began drifting across a sky that was earlier blue. Privately, I wondered if there would be time to do justice to the gospel message before the crowds would be scattered by a vicious monsoon downpour. The altar call and dozens of decisions for Christ—to say nothing of the many who would not then have opportunity to receive their deliverance from their many illnesses—were in jeopardy.

A few minutes into the introduction and the beginning of the message, the first raindrops from a foreboding black sky began to fall on everyone. It would now be impossible to do justice to a clear presentation of the gospel with the downpour of rain. As we watched the event develop, seconds later we became aware that those attending the rally and standing directly in front of the stage seemed oblivious to the weather change. From the roadside and the embankment, those hundreds of spectators, realizing the playing field was their escape from the downpour, stampeded to the playing field.

Thirty minutes later, after a full and clear gospel message presentation, the altar call produced three times the total number of people formally attending in front of the stage. It was obvious to all, including the nationals who witnessed the phenomenon and still speak of it these many years later, that God had orchestrated the rain storm. I related this event and many others to the eager young adults. The sharing of each supernatural event brought praise and glory to God.

As the evening concluded, we returned to our host's home. On our return journey to the west coast a few days later, there was a cell phone call and another one later when we reached home. The outcome of these calls initiated a commitment of missions support from the family we visited for dinner, which to date has resulted in what is the equivalent to support for at least two average overseas missions tours.

How did this incredible provision develop? When did the miracle begin to unfold? Simply stated, in the persistent nudging of the Holy Spirit upon us not to miss the conference and the morning when we sensed, "Yes, we must!" brought us to the decision. That was the God moment, the D factor. This illustrates the constant vigilance we need to use so we do not miss the promptings of the Holy Spirit at every stage of our lives and in every conversation. We should constantly be alert to the slightest nudge of the Holy Spirit, regardless of how it may conflict with our natural inclinations, so we can be open to His best directive for what is ultimately His work. How honoured we are just to be His labourers, His servants!

Ideally, funding for our missions projects is complete, or almost so, before our departure. In this instance, it was complete. Not often do we launch a tour feeling comfortable that it was fully funded. We knew our itinerary and the schedule of evangelism, seminars, jungle church plants, and humanitarian projects. It was a trip with which we were comfortable and excited to be going on, with the knowledge that all of our planned ministries had their funding in place.

We could not, however, know the turns in the road that lay ahead, even though, from past years' experiences, we had been around many of them and have had unforeseen circumstances raise their annoying heads.

Our first stop of the tour in Asia was to avoid the city and urban area to go deep into the jungle. The object of this assignment was to minister with a national leader who wished to do evangelism in many rural areas with four or five gospel thrusts each day. Some of these ventures would hopefully lead to new church plants. Many of them began early in the morning, and moving from village to village, finally we finished late at night. Before continuing our mission, we managed to get some sleep for a few hours before going back on the road, sometimes before dawn, only to repeat the routine for another day.

As the itinerary moved according to schedule, we prepared for the finale, which was to be a four-day leadership school for pastors and workers.

Before leaving on that trip, we had known the number of leaders who would attend, and we budgeted accordingly for 160 of them. Although this was not an excessive number, the attendant cost of travel, material, accommodations, and food made the cost a formidable amount for our small ministry of several thousand US dollars.

It took a few days for the delegates to arrive and several days to register. They had come from all directions and over many hundreds of miles. Some walked for days and without much sleep. When we arrived for the first session, they were in the venue praising and worshiping God. It sounded like we had just tuned into a heavenly choir. The volume from this small group sounded like a much larger crowd. As we walked toward the building, I remember discussing with a colleague, "This sounds like massive crowd." We were right; it was!

Upon entering the building and scanning the crowd, we felt there were perhaps three or four times as many pastors there than were invited. Together with the many invited pastors were other pastors, who joined them along the way, were not invited. Further, many of the pastors also brought their wives and children. In all, perhaps around seven hundred attended the four-day event. This unexpected outcome of such a large crowd played havoc with our very limited budget. We were prepared to handle an extra 10 to 15 percent, but certainly not around 400 percent! When I spoke with the leader, who had organized the fixed number of attendees, he simply said that in their culture, it's not always possible to stick rigidly to a plan.

As I taught the several sessions each day and finished with a rally each evening, it was impossible to keep the natural thoughts of finances out of my mind as I taught and preached throughout the four days. They were special days that God had really blessed. The Holy Spirit honoured the Word, and lives were changed, bodies were healed, and many supernatural "notable miracles" were received. Every aspect of the leadership school was blessed of God. Not before or since have we had such a divine visitation in every facet of ministry as was evident on that occasion.

God's stamp of approval on that event did not, at the time, address the financial haemorrhage that had developed. Each day finished in victory for the delegates who were oblivious of the accumulating and impending budgetary disaster.

As the delegates ministered to and were encouraged by one another, great rejoicing hovered over the campus. They hugged and prayed for one another and rejoiced in the blessing of God on their lives, as the Word had spoken into their areas of need. While they were enjoying their final dinner together and before lining up to receive their travel expenses before their lengthy return journey home, I had to go alone to a local jungle bank to make emergency arrangements and max out every credit card in my possession. Then I made the return trip to the campus with borrowed money equal to five times what I had brought with me for the event.

At that moment, my thoughts naturally went to the story of the feeding of the five thousand. The little boy's lunch of five cakes and two fish was all he had, and at that moment, that was all I had to meet this need. Also, at that time there was no multiplying of my funds (lunch).

I gave the brown paper bags of money to the leader, who passed it on to the winding line of several hundred workers who eagerly waited for the funds to help cover their costs.

Within minutes, our team packed into a vehicle for the long ride to the airport and the next country on our itinerary, even though the funds allocated for that ministry were already spent.

As the weeks passed, each remaining country was visited with the same divine visitation as the first one. In love, God reached down to meet the needs of those who came to Him in faith. As I was enjoying God's outpouring in each conference or seminar, I had the constant nagging remembrance of my maxed-out credit cards and was concerned about what I would do to clear them when the statements became due.

A few more weeks passed, and the mail started coming into my office. I received phone calls as to how I planned to settle the substantial amounts owed on each card.

My mind raced back to our departure. I remembered how we had the thrill of leaving, on that rare occasion, with adequate funding for the total trip, only to see the total budget disappear on the first country's ministry; such was hard to justify. Now what? From where would the funding of this mountainous deficit come?

On the final day in the first country of ministry, I could have just given the funds we had originally agreed upon and left. That would have given us funding for the rest of the trip and no debt. Had that transpired, the local pastor would have been left without resources for many years, as there would be no possibility of him making up such a huge shortfall.

As pressure mounted from the credit card companies, I found myself negotiating for an extension and believed that somehow a miracle would happen to the finances, as they did in the jungle for blind eyes, lame legs, and yes, even finances for the nationals' family needs.

In desperation one night, with nowhere else to go and no one else to speak to about this dilemma, I lay down on my back on the floor and had a heart-to-heart talk with God as to why this happened and as to how it was to be resolved. I prayed, objected, and cried until my hot tears trickled into my ears. How long this silence continued I have no idea, but I recall asking, "Did I make a mistake? Should I not have paid the multiplied amount?" It seemed like deep down in my spirit, I sensed that I should write to people on our mailing list and fully explain the total situation. I entitled the letter, "Did I make a mistake?" That night I hand wrote a detailed letter and faxed it to my office. The secretary placed it on the accountant's desk, and it would be copied and mailed to our donors.

A little later, as I understand the story from that end, the accountant had a client come to him for an appointment. It seems that the accountant left his desk for a few moments, during which time his client scanned the content of my letter, as he had recognized my signature on the bottom. He instructed the accountant that it wouldn't be necessary to mail the letter because he would take the responsibility to cover each credit card bill as it came in until all were paid in full. He did so. He paid approximately thirty thousand dollars!

A few hours later, I had a call from the accountant saying that he saw no reason to send my letter out to our people. His statement confused me because that was not his decision to make. When I pressed him for an explanation, he related the full story, except for his client's name.

In that instance, funding was not received in advance or at the event, even though some of the team members could have underwritten the deficit. In God's time, after He and I had the heart-to-heart talk, He worked His miracle. How faithful and reliable God is!

# 14

# THE ALWAYS ON TIME GOD

## Effective Fervent Prayer

The cells in the human species are held together by glycoproteins such as laminin. It is one of the cell adhesion molecules inside the cell to keep together the other structures. Could prayer, then, as an analogy, be equally vital to maintain balance in holding together the various aspects of spiritual life? What is known as the Colossian theory is seen in Jesus Christ: "by him all things were created . . . and in him all things hold together" (Col. 1:16-17 NIV).

As Christian believers, when our lives become difficult, we often become more energetic and earnest in prayer. If our devotional disciplines were more systematic and carefully planned, perhaps there would be less emergency prayer calls to God. "Let us go speedily to pray before the LORD, and to seek the Lord of hosts" (Zech. 8:21 AV). The apostle Paul encouraged the Roman believers to continue "steadfastly in prayer" (Rom. 12:12c NKJV). Continue means do not stop; steadfast means making up one's mind with determination and resolve.

Effective, fervent prayer signifies energetic supplication. The meaning of supplication is a simple and earnest request. When the righteous pray, much is accomplished. "The effective, fervent prayer of a righteous man avails much" (James 5:16 NKJV).

Recently, in rural Asian ministry, the full weight of discipline in prayer in another dimension spoke forcibly to me. During our outdoor evangelistic festival of praise, many hundreds sat on the ground or stood around the playing field enjoying the program. As I sometimes do, I waited on the sidelines and moved around the periphery of the crowd to study my audience. This waiting prepares me to begin relating to members of the crowd before they get to meet me officially as a foreigner at the pulpit. My mingling beforehand with the crowd helps in building trust with the audience. During pre-service, they get to see me up close as I smile and shake hands with some of them. It also gives me a preview of the platform with its various events.

For our meeting, there was a sizable stage, perhaps ten metres wide by four metres deep and about a metre high (or about thirty by twelve by three feet). To give protection from wind and rain, there was a metal superstructure surrounding the platform for the full platform party, including all of the musicians and worship team members, and two large sets of sound system and other equipment.

Knowing it was almost time for me to be called to minister, my interpreters and I began making our way closer to the stage. Soon the worship team, musicians, and junior pastors left the stage, and we were ready to begin.

Because of the traces of my British culture and conservative background lingering in my DNA, even though my first-generation Holy Spirit stance means everything to me, I became irritated a few minutes into the gospel message.

As I continued to preach and the interpreters sounded out the meaning, a noisy distraction somewhere around me almost caused me to stop and restore order in the service. As the apostle Paul instructed the Corinthians, "Let all things be done decently and in order" (1 Cor. 14:40 AV). At that moment, according to me, something seemed terribly wrong.

In addition to this concealed roaring and moaning, there was a distracting vibration around my feet, almost like a motor or a small generator vibrating against the frame of the metal stage. If confession is good for the soul, I must confess that this unknown was becoming a major irritant to me.

Then, with what I thought was a brilliant idea, I waited until my next line of thought was given to the first interpreter and spoke quickly to the second. For a few seconds, the second interpreter was waiting to proceed with his lines, and then I quickly asked, "What in the world is the noise and vibration?" With a horrified look, and in the brief time he had left, he said, "Pastor, it's the worship team, the musicians, and the prayer warriors all laying on their backs under your feet interceding for you and for souls while we preach."

Wow! I had egg on my face big time! It was my turn to speak again, and there was not a moment for a facial expression change, but my spirit was crushed with emotion. Simultaneously, I wanted to hide, scream, and repent. No, there was no such escape! As before, everything continued until the altar call, except one thing: my attitude and spirit about the noise. Instantly my spirit was one with theirs. Now it wasn't about noise and vibration; it was about the work of the Holy Spirit. He "helps our weakness; for we do not know how to pray as we should, but the Spirit Himself intercedes for *us* with groanings too deep for words" (Rom. 8:26 NASB), and in many languages and dialects spoken in intercessory prayer from under the platform.

For the rest of the message, because of my attitude change, it was like I was preaching from heaven. Every sound, groan, and vibration on the soles of my feet felt like heaven had come down. They were agonizing and interceding for souls, for the interpreters, and for me. They were praying for safety on the grounds and for power over evil spirits that would, within a few moments, manifest themselves during the altar work. That was intercessory prayer—effective, fervent, and energetic supplications at work.

Early in life, those young people had learned a great lesson. They had learned about interceding, wrestling, agonizing, and bombarding heaven with prayer. They were deeply involved in spiritual warfare. That was prayer in its most combative form.

Their sentiment is reflected in the following Scripture: "The effective, fervent prayer of a righteous man avails much" (James 5:16 NKJV).

Perhaps you are asking, "What was the outcome?" Usually within minutes after the message concluded with the customary altar call for salvation and deliverance, I would step down to the front of the platform where those coming in response to the message would stand. I would come *to wait* for their coming and to pray with them. But it was not so this time. There was *no waiting*, but instead, there was a mass move, as though the whole crowd just stepped a few strides forward. Men, women, children, the sick, and the demon possessed came. It was the same crowd, except they moved forward en masse. Hundreds prayed the salvation prayer, were counselled, and then registered for follow-up and were given beginners' literature for new converts.

In His anointing, a wave of Holy Spirit seemed to waft over the heads in the crowd as people received healings without human intervention. Many people who were demon possessed were set free, and bondages were broken in Jesus' name. Some who were demon possessed came forward for the first time, were freed from their tormenting demons, and received their gift of God by faith in the finished work of Christ alone, which is everlasting life (Rom. 6:23).

As the young intercessors lay on their backs under the platform by my feet, they had served the Kingdom of God well. Did God hear their prayer? Did He answer? Yes, God surely did! Those young people had a common desire and purpose: to pray together in agreement.

On the Day of Pentecost in Acts, we are told that the 120 were in the upper room and "they were all with one accord in one place" (Acts 2:1 AV). Agreement means that as two or more agree together with a common desire or purpose, as in our under-the-platform example, Jesus is there. "For where two or three are gathered together in my name, there I am in the midst of them" (Matt. 18:20 AV).

A parallel thought from Isaiah serves well here when he said,

*With my soul I have desired You . . .*
*by my spirit within me I will seek you early* (Is. 26:9 NKJV).

The song of Isaiah in chapter 26 is one of victory. In verse 3 he declares,

*You will keep him in perfect peace,*
*Whose mind is stayed on You,*
*Because he trusts in You* (NKJV).

Isaiah's soul and the Spirit were in agreement in his prayer and in his commitment to seek and follow the Lord. For the child of God, agreement, then, is a significant foundational thread in the weaving of the prayer fabric. Those young prayer warriors under my feet of that platform understood the urgency, the persistence, and the agreement that was necessary to reach the throne room of God and receive their answer from Him. The greater the prayer emphasis in preaching the gospel to the lost, the wider the floodgates of heaven open with the blessing of God's answer to prayer.

When believers walk in *total obedience* to God's Word, He is able to answer us. That means *learning and understanding* it and obeying *every last detail*. Sometimes when we do what we dislike, it seems, at first, to be to our disadvantage. Developing the habit of learning to obey God's Word is not easy. By *obeying His every command*, He said, "try Me now in this . . . If I will not open for you the windows of heaven And pour out for you *such* blessing That *there will* not *be room* enough to *receive it*" (Mal. 3:10 NKJV). Praying in total obedience is a journey and perhaps our greatest challenge. As an aside, in the journey of prayer, patience will most certainly benefit us. We have heard it said, "Lord teach me patience, right now!"

## Dying Mother and Wife Released

At the conclusion of a five-hour Sunday morning service in an Asian country, the pastor asked me if it would be possible to visit his sister who lived close by. During the ten-minute drive to her home, he explained that for a number of years, she had been battling cancer. He shared with me that for about eighteen months, she had been comatose and was very frail.

As the details unfolded, he spoke of the devotion of her husband who cared for her every need, night and day, in their primitive edge-of-jungle setting. He also spoke of the love and care showered on her by her young adult son and daughter.

In similar circumstances over the years, it has not been unusual for the Holy Spirit to give leadership or direction to my spirit in how to approach a situation. Often there will be a word of faith, building assurance in me that whatever lies ahead is in His hands. There is an accompanying divine presence with a confidence that there will be healing or deliverance. During that short drive, there was no such assurance. A single word, however, kept replaying in my spirit. For the last few kilometres, having turned over in my mind the word "release," we pulled into the driveway of her little home. Release; what did it mean? In what context was it to be used in dealing with the patient?

I had to walk around the various angles of the prism of ministry to sense from which angle the word release reflected. Was this a word for the patient to be spoken into the mind of what everyone believed was a comatose believer, encouraging her to let go into the hand of her God? Was it a word for me to release another dimension of ministry or to operate in another gift of the Spirit for her benefit? Yet again, was this word that raced around my mind intended for the husband or the two mature children? With the overwhelming sorrow and care resulting from the critical condition of a wife and mother, could the Spirit be calling to them to release her to His care?

I was standing silently and alone over a spotlessly clean lady who lay on a bamboo mat spread on a cement floor. She was covered with a crisp white sheet. While searching for God's direction in how to minister to her or in the larger picture, in dealing with her family, quietly, in a silent room, it seemed like the Spirit breathed into me the direction I should take. When I moved across the room to where they now stood and stretched an open hand to them, all four placed their hands into mine. Through the pastor who had brought me to minister to his sister, they heard the interpretation of what the Spirit had laid on my heart.

As sensitively as was possible for me to share, I mentioned her critical condition, her strong faith in Christ as her Saviour and Lord, and her love for them and for Him. I offered to anoint her with oil according to James 5:14, at which time we would be praying for her healing. I pointed out that, in the sovereignty of God, He might heal her or take her to be at peace with Himself. It was at that time that I shared with them the word *release* that God had laid on my spirit. Could it be, we pondered, that God was asking us to explore another dimension of obedience to Him, that of each one—her husband, brother, son, and daughter—needed, in their own way, to release her to Him for His perfect will in her life, whether for perfect healing or for her becoming perfect in His presence? "Absent from the body, and to be present with the Lord," came to my mind (2 Cor. 5:8 AV).

In addition to the silence of the room, there was a comforting sense of the Holy Spirit's presence. As all four hands rested in mine, there was a lengthy and quiet time of meaningful worship. Many silent minutes passed that were punctuated with sobbing and at times, groaning.

That moment brought to my mind the prologue to Matthew Henry's treatment of the Lord's Prayer when he wrote: "So far is God from being wrought upon by the length or language of our prayers, that the most powerful intercessions are those which are made with *groanings that cannot be uttered,* (Rom 8:26). We are not to *prescribe,* but *subscribe* to God."[37]

As the fourth and fifth lines of the Lord's Prayer instruct,

> *Your will be done*
> *On earth, as it is in heaven* (Matt. 6:10b NKJV).

As the Lord taught the disciples how to pray, so the family members prayed this prayer, each in his or her own way.

After I led them in prayer, they indicated separately that they were now prepared to release her to the care of the Master or to receive her back, healed by the Master's hand. As we stood around the diminutive form, almost invisible under the cover except for a face nearly the colour of the sheet, we anointed her with oil, asking God to have His will and do His perfect work in the family.

After encouraging them further to keep their eyes on Jesus, to rest in Him, and to allow His divine peace to be theirs, I quickly drove my vehicle back to the hotel. Less than ten minutes after I walked into the lobby, the receptionist waved me over to take a phone call. The voice on the other end was the pastor and brother of the sick lady. "Pastor," he said, "after you left, we all gathered around her and waited quietly. Five or six minutes later, she took a deep breath and was gone into her Master's arms." Was this a healing, one may ask, in the sense that she rose and walked? No! Was this a healing in an even greater sense? Yes!

Can we find within this situation the catalyst that after years of cancer and eighteen months of being comatose, their loved one was so quickly "absent from the body, and to be present with the Lord" (2 Cor. 5:8 AV)? In this instance, within six minutes of the family finding God's peace in their lives to release her to Him, she was more perfect than she had ever been.

When ministering in the fullness of the power of the resurrection to those who look for and welcome the Healer to do His work, over many years I have observed that there are about four major categories into which the sequence of healing falls. In one category, often one witnesses God's healing power flowing directly and instantly in complete and perfect deliverance. In another category, many times God's healing power is expressed through His hand on that of a human physician, together with medicine, to bring healing.

Also, there have been many occasions when, after praying for a major or critical case, there seems to be no improvement. At this time the patient may, in the natural, leave with discouragement, only to find that in the night, or progressively over a period of days or even weeks, total healing has come from the Lord, the one whose name is *Jehovah Rophi* (I am the Lord who heals you).

It is not that the finite mind will ever write a perfect formula for healing, since the permutations and conditions in Scripture are complex, but in addition to the foregoing, there is another category that needs to be acknowledged. Within the Sovereignty of God, whose divine prerogative it is to implement His perfect will, He may choose not to heal at that time or ever heal. He is Sovereign. In the same way that not all who hear the gospel receive salvation, neither do all who come for healing receive it. This in no way alters the fact that we are instructed to come in faith and to pray in faith, believing for His will to be accomplished

*On earth, as it is in heaven* (Matt. 6:10c NKJV).

When we can trust Him with our lives, praying the prayer He taught His disciples and left as a model prayer for us, then we are submitting fully to Him and will enjoy His divine peace and rest in His perfect will.

## Hong Kong ATM Fiasco

On a several-month ministry tour while traveling from Vancouver in the West, we arrived in HK (Hong Kong), the gateway stop to the rest of Southeast Asia. Shirley and I arrived on a Friday and planned to leave at 5:00 the following Monday morning for the next country on our trip.

On Saturday afternoon about three o'clock, I was shopping for a computer component and decided first to visit an ATM machine for cash. Then I proceeded to several stores in search of a suitable part. Finally after about an hour, I walked a mile shoulder to shoulder with the crowd on packed, broken sidewalks, and half a dozen stores later, I arrived at the desired store. As I reached for my planner to make the purchase, to my horror, it was missing. *But where is it?* I asked myself. With a sputtered explanation to the sales assistant, I was soon running at full gait through the same teeming crowds to the ATM I had used earlier. I wanted the planner to be on that machine shelf but knew many thousands of people had pressed past those using it for the past hour or more, so the chances of it being where I left it were extremely slim.

Trusting and praying, with whatever breath I had left, there I was facing the machine with its empty shelf. Gone! Gone was the planner with contact numbers for leaders on the fields we were to visit, air travel tickets, passports, travelers' checks, US dollars in sizable amounts of cash for ministry costs, credit cards, and so forth.

Feeling in a dizzy frenzy, I tried to remain rational. *What do I do now?* I asked myself. I decided to go into the bank by the ATM. *That is it! That is the thing to do!* I thought. The entrance to the bank was at sidewalk level to a lobby with sets of escalators going up and down to and from the main banking floor. As I approached the entrance, I found that the metal roller door was coming down for the 4:30 p.m. Saturday closing. *What do I do?* I thought. We had an early Monday departure, and if I was unable to locate my lost valuables, we would be trapped. When I saw that the roller door was about three feet or just under a metre from being in the closed position, I decided to take action. Without a thought of what could be horrific consequences, I dropped on my stomach and rolled under the now one-foot or thirty-centimetre opening.

*Now what am I to do? Where am I to go from here?* I asked myself. In Asia, banks lead the way in being heavily guarded by security guards. By now I should be looking into a dozen piercing security guards' eyes or several pointed revolvers in this closed bank entrance in which I was an intruder.

I decided to race up the stationary escalators three steps at a time, and I found myself in an empty and dark bank except for security lights. But I didn't see any security guards on duty. I asked myself, *Am I trapped here until Monday? How do I get out? How do I contact Shirley somewhere on the street below?*

Suddenly and silently, out of the darkness behind me, wearing soft-rubber soled shoes a security guard came walking on the marble floor. In broken English, he barked, "Zee bank be closed— you out!" Using my broken English, which I hoped he would understand better, and using many gestures, which I hoped he would be able to interpret, I explained the circumstances leading to my unwelcome entrance.

He listened while I listed the main contents of the planner, avoiding any mention of cash, which would have increased its vulnerability if flagged. Without a word, he disappeared into another room as silently as he had appeared, leaving me standing alone in the darkness. Ten or fifteen minutes later, he returned. This time he had some questions. "What you name? What wife name?" he asked. In possession of this information, again he left me. I had another endless wait in the stony silence of the blackened bank, and he came back into my vision—with the planner, which contents he asked me to check. Every single piece of documentation was present, including the considerable amount of untouched cash.

How God undertook! How He orchestrated the many miracles involved from the time when the planner was lost until it was found! Early that Monday morning we left Hong Kong as scheduled, complete with all vital documents and cash, long before the bank opened. Praise God! That was how God helped us when I had made what could have been a very costly mistake through my unintended negligence. This was another example of living in the supernatural dimension of God.

## Stranger Than Fiction Miracle Moments

The following are stories of three miracle mission's moments.

## 1. His Supernatural Power

In one evangelistic meeting, just before preaching, I felt led to pray for all Christian young people who were open to God's call on their lives if He directed them to ministry. I expected four or five young people to respond from a mostly unconverted crowd, but instead, about two hundred young believers ran forward to fill the altar area. Not being able to go down to pray individually for so many, I began to pray from the platform with my arms stretched to the far left of the building. I moved my outstretched arms like windshield wipers as I prayed across the crowd. Three-quarters of the way across, I happened to look at the young people, only to find that the first three-quarters, up to where my hands had stopped, were all "slain" or resting in the Holy Spirit. As I continued to pray for the rest, they also fell to the floor under the power of the Spirit. That supernatural demonstration progressed into an incredible evening with many hundreds saved and delivered by His supernatural power.

## 2. A Providential Mistake

We accepted an invitation to do several weeklong outdoor evangelistic meetings in a place where terrorism was prevalent. Each meeting went well, but one had a small problem. Two different printers produced the handbills, one indicating the conclusion of the event a day earlier than the other. The earlier period was the correct one. Each night the crowd almost doubled, and many hundreds were converted, healed, and delivered. On the final evening (of the earlier published date), perhaps six or seven thousand attended the open jungle area. On the last evening, many hundreds (perhaps fifteen hundred) came forward for salvation. God gave us a blessed and safe week of meetings.

The next day (the later published date), after the equipment was cleared and all workers had left the area, a huge explosion ripped apart approximately one quarter of the deserted field at the platform and altar area and could possibly have killed up to two thousand people if the later date had been correct. In this instance, the terrorists used the wrongly dated handbill to plan and plant a landmine and detonate the platform and the altar call area on what they thought was the last day when we would have had a large crowd. The LORD said, ". . . before they call, I will answer; and while they are yet speaking, I will hear" (Is. 65:24b AV).

## 3. Run over by a Bus

In outdoor evangelism, the gospel is preached first, then those who respond for salvation are counselled and prayed with, and their names recorded for follow-up work. Those who need prayer for other needs, such as healing, are then invited to come forward.

On one occasion, as I was coming to the conclusion of the

message and about to begin the altar invitation, I had a strong check in my spirit to change the procedure of the service. It was so strong and would mean not calling people forward for the altar call and praying for the sick but to pray for the sick *first* where they were standing and believing for their healing. After the deliverance prayer, the platform director came to me and said that a lady had asked to testify. After she was cleared to come to the microphone, she told the following story as we understood it through her interpreter.

Earlier in the evening, the woman and her little girl had boarded a small bus to travel from her village to the same town where we were holding meetings. She then discovered it was going in the wrong direction and disembarked. The child stumbled on the bottom step, falling from her grasp under the vehicle and in front of the back wheel, which ran over the child's stomach. She picked up her unconscious daughter and began to run home with her. Along the road, someone advised her that the child would die before she reached home but urged the mother to take the girl to the deliverance meeting being held close by in the jungle clearing. She did so and stood there with her dying daughter stretched limply across both of her arms.

It was at this moment that the Holy Spirit's prompt to me was to leave the salvation prayer and pray for the sick *first* where they stood, which I had never done in that order before. She heard the instruction to place her hand on the part of the body that needed healing and to trust God for an answer. She looked in faith to God and believed for prayer to work. Immediately the child stirred as she lay across her mother's arms, regained consciousness, spoke clearly to her, and walked to the platform holding the mother's hand. After closer examination, the bus tire marks were still visible on the child's clothes and skin. Upon subsequent medical examination, there was no indication of injury, as was documented in written testimony ten days later and is now on file. Her testimony electrified the crowd and brought glory to the living God, who works through those who are living in the supernatural dimension.

PART FOUR

# FULFILLING

# 15

# GOD IN THE UNEXPECTED

## A Hitchhiker's Deliverance

One method of soul winning that many young believers practiced in the 1950s and 1960s was to pick up a hitchhiker on the highway and take him part or all of the way to his destination as they traveled to theirs. This was something that I not only enjoyed doing and felt almost challenged about but also, on many occasions, really sensed the prompting of the Holy Spirit to do, even at times after I had driven past them.

Many times this pressure became so pronounced because on some occasions, I would be absorbed in my own world of thought and did not feel like having a soul-winning session. My delay in obedience to the nudging of the Holy Spirit almost always meant that He won the battle and I would have to turn the car around and drive back a considerable distance to pick up this VIP, in God's opinion.

On one such occasion, while driving home for dinner on a particularly black, miserable, rainy winter evening, a young man, perhaps in his mid-twenties, thumbed a lift. Regrettably, my spirit was not in a witnessing mode after an unusually heavy day in the office. Although I had the urge to pick him up, at first I ignored it and drove another mile or so. Then I began to feel guilty about my disobedience. At the first suitable spot, I turned around the car and retraced my way. I went just past the hitchhiker, turned around the car again and stopping beside him, I asked if he would like a ride. As he made his soaking wet body comfortable on the cloth upholstery of an almost-new car, he asked, "Did you just pass me a few minutes ago and turn back for me?"

I answered, "Yes, my Friend wanted you to have a ride."

"Friend . . . ? What friend?" he questioned as he scanned an otherwise empty car.

I replied, "My invisible Friend!" and we both laughed.

This was going to be no ordinary conversation, as the hitchhiker had an almost indecipherable speech impediment. As we chatted, he began to describe his long-distance trucking lifestyle in partnership with his father. As he stammered his way through their unconscionable fornication and lascivious partnership with women of the night during their brief stops on their long hauls, the stuttered filth seemed to fill a formerly clean car and was becoming too obnoxious to tolerate further. By this time, my original urge to pass him seemed to be the correct one, and my discomfort, and perhaps frustration, was now being silently communicated to the one who, against my will, had initiated this meeting.

As I sped rather erratically through the miserable driving conditions in which I found myself, my anger began to express itself in my driving demeanour. Fortunately, there was a brief break in the intense atmosphere as my passenger momentarily fell silent. My own mind was a blur. Such contamination! Never before had anything like this happened to what should be a precious soul-winning session. My first reaction was to stop the car and tell him this was as far as I could take him. The miles passed as he added more detail to his life story. There was no stopping him as his torrent of filth filled the vehicle.

As I reflected on years of past successes, where perhaps hundreds had come to a profession of faith in Jesus Christ, this moment for me was intolerable. I was helpless. Any past skill I may have had to draw upon from similar previous encounters instantly evaporated. It was beyond my ability in this situation to transition to any meaningful communication. My heart was heavy and my spirit grieved; this was not how things should be happening. I felt that I had desperately failed.

Suddenly, without warning, the anointing of Holy Spirit rose up in me, instantly changing my confused thinking. In a split second, without him realizing my "invisible Friend" was revealing to me His answer for this seemingly hopeless situation, my hand flew from the stressful grip on the steering wheel and landed directly and heavily on his shoulder. In the same instant, I heard my voice demand, "Why do you do that?"

He presumed my question was in response to his blithering as he began to defend his behaviour. I abruptly interrupted him with a more specific question: "Why do you stutter?" He exploded in a torrent of profanity and blasphemy with even less clarity than before. As he regained some degree of self-control, he assured me in no uncertain terms that this malady was incurable and the search for a cure had almost bankrupted his family. "There is no medical help for my problem," he said. "No one can help me now."

At this stage of our conversation and journey together, to say that he was livid would be a gross understatement. This was decidedly not the setting for a friendly soul-winning session. As I recall, as I was plowing through the inclement weather, even nature seemed to be throwing its worst at us outside the vehicle. For a brief moment, a beautiful and much-needed silence reigned. Then I heard myself quietly and with a confidence that was not naturally mine in circumstances similar to this say, "I have a Friend who would cure your condition. Would you like to meet Him?"

In uproarious laughter, he stuttered, and with his next breath and in countless syllables, he asked, "When?"

To this simple question, I replied, "Right now, right here!"

Unknown to him at that moment, my spirit was trying to come to grips with this fast-moving development as I tried to determine why I had painted myself into a corner, so to speak, by saying confidently, "My Friend will cure your condition, right now and right here."

Although the gifts of the Spirit were familiar to me, and during years of ministry, several of them on occasion had operated exactly when needed, this was different. Was the confidence with which I had spoken affirmatively to him, saying my Friend would cure him, actually a *rhema* word? Was this in fact the gift of faith in operation?

Without further hesitation, with my hand still firmly in place on his shoulder, he heard the words, "Father, in Jesus' name I rebuke this stammering spirit and receive your healing power to touch this man at this moment, Amen!"

Then he cynically began a torrent of verbal disbelief in the ability of God to do such a thing for him because of his lifestyle, when he suddenly realized for himself what I had been enjoying for some time, that he was 100 percent speaking fluently. There was not a solitary hesitation in his delivery or enunciation. In His sovereign mercy, God had instantly delivered him.

As the effect of this experience sank in, he sat quietly sobbing. When we were approaching his district, he began to give me directions. Within a few minutes, we parked outside his home as I explained how much the God who healed him loves him. I explained how God the Father came in Jesus Christ to die on the cross for all our sin, including his. That hitchhiker heard, for the first time, that salvation was the gift of God for him to receive freely by the undeserved favour of God's grace. He continued to weep and nod in agreement as the gospel story began to sink in for the first time in his life.

Several hours after the hitchhiker—with a tragic life putrefied by sin—climbed into the car, he first received his healing from stuttering, and then, as he listened intently to the plan of the gospel, through his sobs, softly and without impediment, he asked the Saviour into his life. Then, as a new creature in Christ, he climbed out of the car. For him, that night was the beginning of a new life in Christ. As the apostle Paul declared, "Therefore, if anyone *is* in Christ, *he is* a new creation; old things have passed away; behold, all things have become new" (2 Cor. 5:17 NKJV).

## The Lost Briefcase

While on special assignment in Asia for the Pentecostal Assemblies of Canada, for about two years, Shirley and I had a memorable moment. Functioning as their representative with an administrative portfolio for Sri Lanka, it was necessary at one stage to make an overseas trip for a short period from the capital, Colombo, to St. Petersburg, Russia, for evangelism. (This resulted in a successful church plant in St. Petersburg for the Russian Assemblies of God. I was instrumental in planting the church through the support of the PAOC and financial assistance of Christian Life Assembly in Langley, British Columbia. Since then the church in St. Petersburg planted a daughter church nearby).

Just before our departure date from Sri Lanka and for the period of our absence, many extra details had to be cared for in advance. These would include month-end reports, correspondence, pastors' allowances, accounting and checks payable, and a myriad of minor details. The last few days before departure became a blur with meetings and extra interviews, including the personal side of purchasing airline tickets, packing, and arranging for our house to function smoothly during our absence.

It seemed that we were working day and night up to the last evening before leaving. We had a very early morning on the day that we were to fly out that evening, but we had a last minute to-do list that seemed to keep growing. By mid-morning, it was time to leave the house and attend to several appointments, distribute several signed checks, one or two of which the payees' names were left off to confirm their correct spellings before handing them over later. For safe keeping, as we left the house, we also put our passports, airline tickets, and some cash into the briefcase.

The driver arrived to begin my last day's work in downtown Colombo, the commercial capital of the metropolitan region, with a population of about six million people. We were living in the administrative capital of Kotte, on the outskirts of Colombo.

As we were getting into the backseat of the car, someone arrived to speak with me. The conversation continued for several minutes, and I placed the fairly heavy briefcase on the roof-rack while we chatted. Perhaps ten minutes later, we finished the discussion and hurried away, now late for our first appointment.

We drove as fast as the rural road would allow with potholes, people walking, dogs, cows, tri-shaws, cars, and trucks, and it was a hectic experience. As we joined a secondary road, we were able to make better time and soon were at the first appointment, the bank. As I reached down to my feet for the briefcase that wasn't there, my heart almost stopped. Where was it? On the roof-rack, that's where I left it! I was almost afraid to open the car door and face reality, but sheer will power forced me out to confirm my worst fear: it was gone. But where?

As I remembered all the vital contents of the briefcase, especially the passports and unsigned checks, the consequences of its loss on the day of our departure were unthinkable. We retraced our route back to the bumpy road in the vicinity of our house, which we thought would be the most likely spot for it to slide off the roof; we found nothing. Surprisingly, no one walking there saw or found anything. We left from the house, this time more slowly, and doubled back to the bank again, looking with eagle eyes over every metre of road for the several kilometres.

Shirley remained in the car with the driver, and they had a focused prayer of agreement for this valuable item's return. So long after the loss for it to return intact, would be a supreme miracle. I rather dejectedly made my way into the bank manager's office to apprise him of my dilemma.

The first order of business was to put a stop payment on all checks. Even those with names on them were vulnerable. To escalate the drama, the new loose leaf check book with dozens of unsigned checks was also in the lost briefcase with no replacement checks readily available for issue before our evening departure. He and I discussed the strategy that would provide the most damage control.

At that moment, my driver came into the bank and was shown into the manager's office. "Pastor," he said, "your briefcase has been found. We must go and retrieve it." After I excused myself, we made a hasty retreat from his office. As he drove, I recognized the route and asked where he was heading. "To our Bible college," he replied.

This is the story that unfolded as we made our way toward the vital package. When we left the rural bumpy road and joined the secondary road, our speed increased. That acceleration dislodged the briefcase, and it was jettisoned from the car into the traffic. A beggar lurking in the bush off the highway witnessed the drama and rushed quickly into the road, grabbing the item, and disappeared into the undergrowth with his bounty. Settling down in the privacy of his hideaway, he began to open a briefcase unlike any he had probably ever held. Just as he opened the files and began to examine the contents, he was set upon by two city policemen, who had witnessed the whole drama.

Police procedure, we understood, was to return it to the station. There a search for a contact phone number or address would be made. Then they would write or phone the owner for identification confirmation and ultimately to claim the package. Not only could this take considerable time in that culture, but with such attractive contents, anything could happen in the intervening days.

What did happen was this: after retrieving the briefcase, the two policemen searched through a file and saw a name on a check that they recognized. Knowing where that individual worked, they called him from a payphone. He jumped on his motorbike and met the police by the side of the road.

After returning to his work as the dean of our Bible college with the package, he arrived there at about the same time as we did. As I made a thorough search of the contents, not a single document or check was missing; everything was intact, including the original amount of cash. The natural probability of this conclusion in any country, even including the West, was extremely remote.

The rest of the day went like clockwork, given our two-hour patience and trust test. All checks were "unstopped" at the bank and the originals were issued, including those whose signed checks were awaiting correct name spellings.

Although we do our best in His work, we often still slip up and make mistakes. For me that day, the ramifications of my mistake would have been horrific if it was not for God! He was there in His grace and mercy, overseeing the whole ordeal. The right policemen were in the right place at the right time. Although the procedure was not strictly followed by the book, it saved many days of delay and allowed us to meet our midnight departure time.

I could write, at length, of similar supernatural interventions, but in the plan and will of God, this kind of conclusion, in my mind, is beyond natural explanation. We who have lived through many similar happenings readily acknowledge God's miraculous handiwork.

## Conversion to Christ through Prayer Language

On one of our extended evangelistic tours of Indonesia, an auditorium was filled with rural and village people. The program continued with worship, testimonies, and special musical numbers, and then I preached the gospel message.

After clearly explaining the plan of salvation to the listeners, I invited them to come to the altar and join in a salvation prayer. Then I left the platform and walked down to be at their level and welcomed them into their new life in Jesus Christ. Sentence by sentence, they repeated a prayer that, when prayed in faith, was the beginning of their walk with Christ.

But after the salvation prayer and before ministering to their other needs, I felt strongly in my spirit that I should leave hundreds of people at the altar and walk to the back of the auditorium. Knowing that the Holy Spirit had led me there, I waited and looked for the reason of the diversion. After several moments, I felt free to return to the altar to minister to those who had gathered there. As I was returning, I slowed down, and my attention was directed to a man at my left who was sitting alone on the end of a row of seats. I felt led to place my left hand on his right shoulder. As I did so, he remained motionless, and I was silent. After several seconds had elapsed, to my amazement, I began speaking in tongues, my prayer language. Suddenly the thought crossed my mind, "Most likely this man only speaks a dialect of Indonesian." As foolish as this exercise appeared to me in the

212

natural, I continued. As the Spirit lifted, I removed my hand and walked slowly and silently away.

Seconds later and only twenty feet from him, down the seventy-foot or twenty-one-metre aisle, the same man passed me in a desperate dash to the altar. Wondering if I had offended him, I hurried to the front of the auditorium. When I got there, I saw him engaged in an intense conversation with my interpreter.

Later I discovered that he came to the altar to ask for the salvation prayer, to which the interpreter answered him, "The prayer was prayed with all who came to the front earlier." In desperation he insisted that he "must pray the salvation prayer now!"

Again the interpreter pressed the point, "Why not then, and why the panic?"

He blurted out, "That man who preached came, placed his hand on me, and told me the major points of my past life. He shared with me the love of God and how Christ died for my sin and that salvation is a gift and it can only be had by faith in the living God."

Again the interpreter insisted that from the platform I had preached this message in English, with his interpretation, and that I spoke no other language. The penitent insisted that he understood every word in his own dialect and now wished to surrender his life to Christ.

In summary, I know that I spoke in my prayer language. He knew what he heard, which was his dialect. Was the miracle in his *hearing* or in my *speaking*? God knows how it was made possible. Praise Him!

Both the phenomena of *Glossolalia* and *Xenolalia* were evident in the experience of the missionary evangelist and the Indonesian national. Glossolalia literally means tongue speaking. R. P. Spittler says, "GLOSSOLALIA" is defined as "Usually, but not exclusively, the religious phenomenon of making sounds that constitute, or resemble, a language not known to the speaker."[38] The phenomenon called, "*Xenolalia* . . . describes when the language spoken is identifiable as one among the over 3,000 known to occur on the globe."[39] Ralph W. Harris provides documented accounts of the phenomenon of xenolalia, ranging from Arabic to Zulu.[40]

## A Prodigal's Restoration

Since we had recently returned from a ministry trip to Asia and were adjusting to jetlag, in addition to being on heavy antibiotics, and I did not have to preach that Sunday morning, we decided to miss attending church. Shirley stayed home, and I went for a drive with the intention of having a long walk around part of a local lake.

The first road I took I thought would lead to the lake, but it didn't seem to be the right one, so I turned the car around and took another route. A few miles along the second road, although I knew it would lead me to the lake, I had a check in my spirit to turn around again, which I did. Choosing yet a third road, I continued for several miles, singing, praying, and enjoying the presence of the Lord. Not finding any access to the lake for my solitary walk, I turned the car around again and retraced my route.

After a few miles on the narrow country road, in stormy weather, I could see in the distance an older man walking toward me on the opposite side of the road. Before reaching him, I stopped my car and waited for him to come alongside of it. When he arrived, I greeted him and asked if he was from the area. Because we were being drenched with a torrential downpour, we chatted for several minutes about him and people he knew, some of whom were my relatives. He mentioned that some of them attended a little Gospel Hall in the district. When asked if he had ever attended that Gospel Hall, he said, "Yes, when I was a young man and was saved once."

To this point in the conversation, he was not aware that I was a minister. I then asked if that meant he had been born again once; he answered, "Yes!"

Then I asked him, "How many times have you been born naturally?"

To this question he answered, "Once!"

We laughed together as he understood my point. Then I asked, "Was it a genuine spiritual birth?"

He agreed that it was. Now it was only necessary for him, as a prodigal, to ask for forgiveness, return to and be restored by God the Father, and renew his fellowship with the family of God.

I asked if I could pray with him to come back to his first love. As he put his rain-soaked hand through my open car window into mine, he agreed, and we prayed together to that end. Because he was having quite serious health and heart concerns, he decided that this was a good thing to do. He then described the condition by name, and it was exactly the condition I had experienced almost two years before. As I shared this information with him, we held hands again, and this time we prayed for his physical well-being.

After the circumstances that caused Shirley and me to miss church and in all of my driving, I turned the car around and changed roads. I stopped to talk with a stranger in a drenching downpour and had a general conversation with him that developed into a prodigal, coming home. Just before leaving, he said, "This has been good," and we agreed that it had been a God moment. Before he left the car I told him my name was Abraham. He said his was also Abraham. As we talked further, we discovered that his grandfather and mine were brothers.

We then discovered that it was all about reaching a second cousin for Christ. How thrilling, and what a rich blessing! Praise the Lord!

# 16

# THE GOOD NEWS TO PRISONERS

Since a substantial segment of our missionary evangelism has been outside of the conventional church, prison ministry has played a significant role. I will relate a few prison ministry experiences from among many that I could tell.

The Psalmist declared, "The LORD gives freedom to the prisoners" (Ps. 146:7c NKJV). Although prisoners are confined for the duration of their sentence, satisfying the legal term of restitution, within the spirit of the convict, there can be freedom, a loosing, and a setting free within his confinement. Jesus said, ". . . if the Son makes you free, you shall be free indeed." (John 8:36 NKJV).

## Roadside Prisoners Converted to Christ

One afternoon during a six-week trek in a tropical Asian country, the incredible heat forced us to stop our non–air-conditioned vehicle at a roadside stall. This stop was in the hope of finding some pure, filtered bottled water. We parked a distance from the stall, spilled our steaming bodies out of our van, which was filled to over-capacity, and panted our way to a hopeful oasis. As our team approached the stall, it became apparent that there was an unusual commotion, with the presence of high-security police.

Beyond the stall there were several government vehicles, including several police vans and cars. The occupants of these vehicles were all grouped around the stall, as well as ourselves. All of us were seeking to quench our thirst. Since we were the only Caucasians there, we stood out from the crowd and became a focus of attention. Typically, nationals are curious about visitors and we, as such, were no exception.

During our attempt to communicate with a vendor and purchase whatever (sealed and safe) liquid he had for sale, the police superintendent approached us and asked of our business there. Since we were foreigners in his country and in a very rural, jungle-like territory, we felt some obligation to answer his initial question, which led to several more questions that were more probing. With each question and answer, he delved deeper into the real purpose for our being in that area. During what was tantamount to an interrogation, we noticed that many of the other police officers were each chained to other prisoners. Indeed some prisoners, in turn, were chained to other prisoners by hand and foot. In all, there were about twenty prisoners. As it transpired, they were being transported as career criminals and as such, warranted a prison with tighter security.

As we purchased the vital liquids, we continually questioned ourselves about how to handle the police superintendent's questioning. "What do we do next? How do we do it? When and where do we lecture? What do we say?" As the intensity of the police superintendent's interest in our work in his country continued to grow, it became obvious that we were either attracting greater attention than we would prefer and might, ourselves, be the focus of this superintendent's attention or we were having an impromptu roadside encounter similar to that of Philip and the Ethiopian eunuch (Acts 8:26-35). On that occasion and within God's sovereignty, the Holy Spirit directed and transported Philip to the exact location of the eunuch's chariot (vehicle of transportation) to present to him the gospel message.

As I shared with the police officer, he indicated his sympathetic interest sufficiently so that we felt more comfortable to disclose that we did humanitarian work and trained young workers in Christian ministry. As I recall, he asked if we preached in churches and whether we preached the gospel. Immediately upon having an affirmative answer from us, in his own language, he spoke to the total group of policemen and prisoners. The result was that everyone surrounded us, and he asked us to share the gospel with his group.

In a simple but life-changing way, I shared the good news of the gospel with the entire group. Every man stood at rapt attention and hung on every word that was spoken. Although the noonday heat was intense, no one moved for perhaps an hour. During the time that the gospel was presented, others came to the stall to buy, staying to listen, and many remained to the conclusion of the presentation.

Then I offered to pray with them and invited anyone who was willing to accept Jesus Christ as his Saviour to raise his hand. Never will I forget the sight and sound of the next moment. Almost every man, policeman and prisoner alike, raised his hands in a chorus of clanging metal restraints. Some may comment here that perhaps since the men were handcuffed to the person next to them, they had no alternative, even if they wished not to raise their hands. But in reality, I sensed a solemn spirit brooding over the entire group as the voices of prisoners and policemen blended in a sincere prayer of salvation. Following the salvation prayer, they asked us to pray individually for other needs in the lives of each one, including those who had stopped to buy and stayed until the closing prayer.

If there ever was a God moment, this was one. Had this convoy of prisoners and policemen been an hour earlier or later, traveled on a different day, or taken a different route; had we used an air-conditioned vehicle, not requiring us to stop for refreshment or ourselves been earlier or later; or had we not responded warmly to the police superintendent, would this sacred moment have been missed by us forever? Yes! In God's sovereign plan, He orchestrated this encounter so we could share "the water of life freely" (Rev. 21:6 AV) to flow to the parched souls of convicts, policemen, and members of the public alike. Then, as Christ said, ". . . whoever drinks of the water that I shall give him will never thirst" (John 4:14a NKJV). The national pastors who accompanied us that day were then in a position to follow up all who wished to move to the next step of discipleship to grow in their newfound faith. What a God moment for all of us to experience that day!

## Hundreds of Prisoners Respond to the Good News

During times of intense ministry, tightly scheduled for perhaps eight weeks, we have experienced many different locations and types of ministry. These included youth conferences, lectures at a university, crusades, evangelism, or as in the aforementioned case, sharing the gospel with some men at a remote location.

The driver weaved and screeched his tires through the crowded city streets, until we escaped the diesel pollution and could now see more clearly as the urban landscape gave way to a more scenic rural view. Perhaps an hour passed as we relaxed and fellowshipped on our way to share at a men's meeting. As a result of the scant information we had received for this event, we were not concerned about the nature of the meeting or the message to be shared. My spirit was at peace because God would lead and direct as He had done, over a lifetime of ministry and thousands of events similar to this little upcoming meeting.

Moments later the vehicle slowed, exited the main highway, and proceeded along what seemed like a private road. Suddenly red and white barrier poles brought us to an unscheduled stop. The officer in the booth demanded driver and passenger identification. What happened to my cosy, relaxed men's meeting? We were facing heavy-duty security! After the officer questioned us and thoroughly examined all of our documents, he waved us through the now lifted candy-striped pole barrier. A few hundred metres or yards farther, an imposing sign indicated a vast cordoned acreage to be a high-security penitentiary.

After parking and entering the lobby, we were all thoroughly searched and then escorted through what resembled an endless maze of masonry tunnels. Eventually we surfaced from the tunnels, and I, alone, was ushered into a large room. *What a strange room!* I thought to myself. It was perhaps twenty by twelve metres or about sixty-five by forty feet, with a ceiling that rose almost forever. Three sides were made of masonry, and one long side appeared to be removable, perhaps folding or sliding into a side wall pocket. In about the center of the room facing the folding wall was a solitary chair. I saw no reason not to use it for its intended purpose, so I made myself as comfortable as possible under what appeared to be dubious circumstances. Silence reigned!

In the solitude and semidarkness of the room, the minutes that passed seemed to me like hours. In this forsaken holding pen, the only lights permitted were security lights. Why was I left there? Where was the interpreter? When would the men come? Where would they be seated?

The eerie silence of this three-sided concrete tomb was shattered when somewhere, in the unknown distance, I could hear a low and muffled rattling sound. As the minutes passed, it became slightly louder but still resembled nothing I could identify from my memory. Somewhere beyond, I could hear doors opening, and suddenly the volume increased significantly. Clearly now I could identify a metal-to-metal sound. Was this clanging steel? Was this a metal workshop? What was happening?

Without warning, blinding lights pierced the semidarkness in the room, and instantly the powered folding wall disappeared into its pockets on either side of my "tomb." The folding wall opened and revealed a sizable, brilliantly lighted auditorium with seating for perhaps a thousand to twelve hundred persons. It became obvious from my solitary perch that in fact my location was a platform.

Although the metal sound was becoming louder, it was still distant. Several doors opened simultaneously in the back wall of the auditorium. The metal sound was now louder than ever as several columns of wrist-to-wrist and ankle-to-ankle, chained prisoners filed in line to their seats in sets of about five each. Each set had a guard. For the auditorium to be filled from the front to the back took about fifteen minutes. As the last metal clang silenced, the prisoners were all in place. This was to be my relaxed rural men's meeting—not exactly what I have envisioned.

A very brief program followed, my interpreter was waved in, and we were about to begin. Except for our voices, for the next forty minutes, there was not another perceptible sound in the room.

As we walked to the microphones, my mind had a split-second time travel as I recalled my early ministry in the UK as a teenager. Then, to preach to any crowd, it would have been almost impossible to declare the gospel without perhaps all of the crowd knowing the message almost as well as the preacher, even if some at the time were not saved. Then in North America, several decades later, most people would have some knowledge of the gospel, and only a few people would not be familiar with it.

But this men's meeting was different. In this group of hardened criminals, it would be surprising if any one of them had ever heard a clear gospel presentation from which they could register a definitive commitment to Jesus Christ.

After I was briefly introduced to the group, I gradually built a foundation upon which to build a clear presentation of the gospel. In the British and North American settings, there was at least a foundation, no matter how shallow, upon which to build, but on this occasion there was nothing.

So I began preaching from the elementary foundation of the existence of an eternal God who created the universe, the galaxies, the oceans, and every living creature. I spoke of this God who created man, male and female, and who breathed life, and they and we became living souls. For Adam and Eve, God had prepared a utopia garden called Eden for them to enjoy but commanded them not to eat from the tree of the knowledge of good and evil. But they ate from it in disobedience, and the sinless relationship they had enjoyed with their Creator ended as they were driven out of the garden from God's presence. Their pure relationship with God had been severed.

I shared about God's plan to reconcile man because He loved him. In detail, the prisoners heard how God became flesh in the form of His Son, Jesus Christ. Jesus, who knew no sin, became the sacrifice for man's sin and shed His blood upon a cross to remove sin and present the gift of salvation to man without price, reconcile man to God, and justify man, as though he had never sinned.

I presented the cross where the God-man, Jesus Christ, was lifted between heaven and earth, and with His sinless nature, redeeming love, He reconciled sinful man with a Holy God. The prisoners heard how Jesus was buried and on the third day rose from the dead in the power of an endless life. This power enables all who trust in Him to begin as new creations in Christ Jesus and live new lives, not in their own power but in the power of Christ's resurrection.

As every vital ingredient for the recipe of salvation was added, they were presented with the opportunity to receive His love and to experience the power of His shed blood to remove their sin. By freely receiving the gift of God without works, only by His unmerited favour and great mercy, they could now begin to walk in newness of life.

As the moments sped by, I presented the gospel story to them for the first time. No one had moved; not a sound was heard. Now it was time for me to offer to pray with any who would allow Christ to be his "friend *who* sticks closer than a brother" (Prov. 18:24 NKJV) and Saviour. As I gave this invitation to pray, I suggested that any who wished to join in audible prayer with me for this miracle to begin in their lives today should stand to their feet. For what seemed to me like ever so long but in real time, must only have been a few seconds, absolutely no one moved. Then suddenly, as one man, almost the entire assembly of prisoners stood to their feet. As the interpreter repeated the salvation prayer, slowly, sentence-by-sentence after me and the prisoners with him, their thunderous voices raised as they affirmed their newfound faith in the living God, who loved them and gave Himself for them. Their acceptance of this gospel message and the gift of God that is everlasting life became a fresh aroma permeating the room.

As quickly as the meeting had begun, it was over. While they were still standing after the prayer, it seemed that with a silent signal, the clanging metal, with mechanical precision, reversed itself, and the room emptied as quickly as it had filled—except that when they entered the auditorium, they were lost in sin, but when they left it, they were confessing their faith in a living God. The God who would empower them to live in victory, within or without these masonry walls, was now their God. He whom the Son sets free is free indeed.

## A Single Prisoner Hears the Gospel and Many Believe

With all the activities that crowded my schedule from early morning until late at night, it had been a normal day of ministry in the tropics. In part, this could mean a pre-breakfast prayer meeting with the national leadership of the country we were in. A breakfast meeting might follow for ministry strategy, leading to a business, bank, university, or prison ministry during the day and culminating with an evangelistic open-air or auditorium event in the evening. The day's schedule went smoothly, and the evening found the team preparing for the open-air evangelistic rally.

As we arrived at the site perhaps forty minutes before the scheduled rally, my interpreter and I watched the activities as hundreds of chairs were set up on the large flag-stoned forecourt. The platform was the upper level area or apron outside the imposing double doors of the town's local courthouse. Cascading from it in a semicircular fashion was a lengthy set of cement steps that flowed to the flagstone forecourt. For the next several evenings, our audience was to be seated on this. Beyond were the rest of the town's small buildings that yielded to a beautiful valley unfolding in the distance.

On either side of the platform powerful banks of loudspeakers were placed that were perhaps ten feet high and three feet wide (or about three metres high and a metre wide) and were positioned and then re-positioned. We took this action in order to get a perfect sound balance in all directions and so it would carry the sound for miles down the valley. As it turned out, this action plan would prove to be an important detail for the rally.

As the afternoon sun began to set, the intense heat of the day dropped off and brought with it a welcome relief. The sunset painted the distant valley in the most spectacular golden hues, which in itself would become a virtual stadium.

Musical instruments were all in place and their tuning complete. Before the program began, all of the team members met for a brief time of prayer. As dusk deepened with the setting sun, all the floodlights were on and lit up almost a capacity crowd. Typically in most crusades, those who come early or on time are Christian believers and workers who support the event. They come from the many churches that cooperate with or sponsor the rallies.

After the musical instruments began playing and their sound was carried through those massive banks of speakers to the valley beyond, local people began to listen and then came to stand on the fringes of the crowd. Blended together was a sense of natural excitement and divine anticipation—excitement because the weeks of preparation were past and the first of five eagerly awaited events had begun and anticipation because hundreds of believers prayed and planned for months that God would honour His word and ministry each evening as hundreds would have an opportunity to surrender their lives to Jesus Christ. This was the first such event of its kind in the valley for many years. Christians came with expectancy that God would touch many hearts in salvation and minister to many with various physical and other needs.

As the program began, there were singing trios, choirs, solos, and testimonies of salvation and deliverance from some young believers. All of this led to the preaching of the gospel message.

While I was preparing the audience with some introductory remarks, I noticed that the crowd had swelled to about twelve hundred people. My plan was to preach the good news of the gospel and then invite people to come forward for prayer if they wished to surrender their lives to Christ. By so doing, they would receive His resurrection power to live the rest of their lives in His victory as they would grow in obedience to His Word.

Also, at the time of the altar call, they would be invited to come forward for prayer for other types of needs for themselves or for their families. In this way the audience was fully aware of what would transpire as the message concluded.

Over a lifetime of evangelism and altar call experiences, I am convinced that informing the audience beforehand of what to expect is an important, if not a crucial, approach to take for the smooth operation and outcome of such meetings. It helps prepare them during the message for the decision they may make for Christ and for the public confession of their faith in coming forward later.

How often have preachers and missionary evangelists declared a clear gospel and then, without warning, startled the audience by suddenly calling them forward for salvation? In extreme cases, sometimes people in the audience become irritated by the preacher's increasingly loud voice or body language if members of the audience seem to delay in responding to his invitation to come forward.

Usually as I share the gospel, the audience somehow seems to fade in my mind and I become increasingly focused on a single lost person in the crowd with all his attendant problems. It is to this lost person that I direct the gospel of saving grace. "All we like sheep have all gone astray" (Isa. 53:6 NKJV). I unfold the message, make each important point clear, and carefully explain all of the essential steps to salvation. As I conclude the message, the audience anticipates the next step, that of coming forward to surrender their lives to Christ as their only living God. Without hesitation and from every direction, including the people on the fringes of the crowd, perhaps one hundred or more feet away or about thirty plus metres, in a steady stream they come.

For this current rally, I continued to follow those principles. Those who came forward for salvation were counselled further, and I prayed with them a salvation prayer. They repeated this prayer slowly with the interpreter, sentence by sentence. Each individual received salvation literature and completed a registration card for a follow-up call from a local pastor, ideally within the next seventy-two hours.

Afterward, those who needed prayer for other needs were prayed for as they placed their hands on those parts of their body that needed healing. If their needs were not physical, but were for their families' needs, financial or other, they placed their hands on their hearts. At such a time, there might be several healings or deliverance from other binding issues or habits. The service concluded in praise and worship, and an exhilarated but exhausted team retreated to their accommodations. Long after the conclusion of the rally, when most of the team members were gone, a national pastor brought to me an elderly gentleman who was perhaps seventy-five or older. He had long, silver hair to his shoulders, beautiful brown eyes, and a rich olive complexion. He wore a pure white robe that reached all the way to the dusty ground.

Through the interpreter, I asked what we could do for him. His plain reply was, "Pray that I might have the salvation you spoke of in your message." When I asked why he had not responded with the others perhaps an hour earlier, he replied, "I listened to the program over the sound system from my home away down the valley, and it has taken me this long to walk the six kilometres (or almost three and a quarter miles) to have you pray the salvation prayer with me." So we did, and he returned, by foot, the same way he came.

"Their sound went into all the earth" (Rom. 10:18c AV). In fact, the sound of those properly positioned and powerful banks of speakers had really done their job in carrying the gospel message to this elderly gentleman, who now was a new babe in Christ. As an aside, on occasion we have used shortwave radio out of Germany to cover the ten-forty window and beyond to reach as many as two hundred countries so that "His" sound could be heard by as many people as possible.

An even fuller and more dramatic story of that service began to unfold the next evening when the team returned for the second rally. While we were waiting for the program to begin, I was handed an envelope with a letter in it that was addressed to Jesus Christ.

The powerful speaker system had projected the sound of the rally far past the crowd on the apron over and between the town's low buildings and down the distant valley. Somewhere in the distant verdant hills, a young man sat at his window and heard every word of the previous evening's program. Together with those who prayed the salvation prayer, he joined his voice to make a life-changing decision. His letter clearly explained that, although it was impossible for him to attend the event, he had heard and understood the message. In his letter he wrote that he had sinned but had prayed with me the following for God's forgiveness: "I sincerely repent of the sins that I have committed." The letter continued, "Could you please bring me a Bible so that I may be able to come more to the Lord as I am receiving Him as my Saviour? I'm accepting Christ with my whole heart to be my Saviour and Guide." The letter continued, "Please bring the Bible to my prison cell."

As a result of his dramatic letter of conversion to Christ, the events of the next day were almost unbelievable. As soon as our schedule permitted, we purchased a beautiful Bible and set off to find the prison and our penitent prisoner. He was indeed located far down the valley. My recollection is that the prison more resembled a dilapidated farm building. In the outer hallway leading up to the doors and reception area, a subdued moaning seemed to come from different directions, and an obnoxious odour permeated the building. The national pastor was my interpreter. As we pressed more deeply into the bowels of this so-called prison, I took a deep breath in the hallway of the loathsome air.

It was easy to find the prison warden, who was a massive man, twice my width and weight and six inches taller. He could easily have crushed each of us simultaneously with his arms. In spite of his intimidating stature, to us as ministers, he appeared to be a warm and personable individual. After a few cordial remarks, we asked for the prisoner by name. He responded by taking us deeper into the putrid prison. What an uncomfortable experience we had as we peered into very poor quality and overcrowded cells! The pungent human odour was nauseating. The further we proceeded into the darker recesses of the prison, the harder we tried not to breathe deeply. Finally there was an opening in the wall that securely held a massive cell door.

The warden called the prisoner by name, and immediately,

from this fifteen by fifteen square feet or about five by five metre prison cell, he appeared with his face pressed almost between the wrist-thick bars. Between the bars, he shot out his two arms like daggers, clasped his fingers in a headlock behind my neck, and pulled me face to face between the cell door bars. Eye to eye and nose to nose, he then kissed me repeatedly before I had the time or ability to break his neck hold on me. This was my introduction to a young man who the night before had responded to the Saviour's call on his life. That call had been the work of the Holy Spirit within the sovereign plan of God.

After he unlocked his iron grip, he released both hands from either side of my neck, and we then began to visit, indeed, to fellowship. Although a new babe in Christ, he exuded the spirit and presence one would expect from a person who had had a genuine encounter with the Saviour. We gave him a Bible with his and my name written in it and showed him many meaningful verses that would help him as he began to learn from a Bible that he had never previously held or owned.

After about an hour of delightful fellowship and mentoring, it was time for us to leave him. Our urge to leave was not because we must but because the smell of the prison was repugnant, and without time in fresher air, we could not bear much more. As we mentioned that soon we were planning to leave, he became greatly agitated and quite emotional. By staying a few minutes longer, we helped to calm him, and he asked for us to pray with him before we left.

His prayer request was very specific. "Pray the same prayer you prayed last night."

"The salvation prayer?" I asked.

"Yes! Yes!" was his response through our reliable interpreter.

Was his request for me to repeat that prayer again for additional assurance? Was it to remind him of the pattern of the prayer that he had already recognized as having begun to change his life? Whatever the reason, I began to pray it with him again as the interpreter flowed with me in translation, line upon line. The first line said, "Lord Jesus, thank You for Your love!"

As that line left the interpreter's lips and the new convert began to repeat it, it was not said by his voice alone, but there was a chorus of men's voices. In his cell were at least eleven other prisoners. They all had sat silently on the floor against the back wall of the cell almost in complete darkness and unnoticed by us. But they had heard and understood the repeated words of the plan of salvation. By then they were ready to make their commitment to Jesus Christ as a group. As we tried to compose ourselves and finish this segment of prison ministry, the national pastor and I had difficulty holding back our tears of blessing and joy.

Moments later we said, "Good-bye!" not just to him but then individually to the much-larger group. As we were hugging and weeping with them, which continued for many minutes, my heart was melted and felt torn. It reminded me of the sorrow felt by Christian believers as they said good-bye to the apostle Paul before he went up to Jerusalem (Acts 21:13).

The massive speakers that had carried the gospel the six kilometres to our elderly gentleman in his pure white robe had also, by contrast, penetrated the cavernous, dark, and putrid prison the previous evening. The sound had in fact reached the whole prison. The chorus of voices that joined our prisoner were not only those in his cell but also in several of the surrounding cells within earshot of the salvation prayer. In the immediate vicinity of the prison cell, we estimated that about seventy prayed that prayer of salvation with us.

Eventually, as we were leaving to return to the village, two women arrived at the prisoner's cell door. The young prisoner introduced them to us as, "My mother and my wife, and my infant child," who, as I recall, was born during his incarceration. In our friendly chat with them, they told us of the circumstances that brought such calamity on the family. Because they were in financial trouble, the husband broke into a house and stole a small transistor radio that, at the time, was valued at perhaps ten dollars. The homeowner pressed charges, and the prisoner was sentenced to several years. Because he had the misfortune to steal the radio from the home of the local chief of police, his sentence was not commensurate with the crime.

As he shared with his mother and wife the events of the previous night and what had just transpired at his cell door, his mother asked that we also explain to her and her daughter-in-law the whole story of salvation. We repeated the same procedure as we did earlier, and both ladies made their commitments to Christ by praying the same salvation prayer.

Again we made an attempt to leave and let the son, mother, wife, and infant visit, but it was not to be. As we were about to leave, the pastor who was with me explained that the family wished to leave with us. "Why?" I asked. "They have just come." I began to understand as the interpretation flowed that the women, who were so excited about what had transpired with their son and husband and now themselves, also wanted the man's father to hear.

Then came the big question, "Would we drive them close by to share the gospel with him?"

"Well, yes!"

After all that had happened, we felt we must meet the father. Minutes later, our driver, with the family aboard the vehicle, was taking directions to this "close-by" location. The driver was told to go straight, turn left, go straight, turn right, and on and on. Minutes passed, miles rolled by, and we traveled in what seemed to me to be several circles. Within the hour, we were told to park at the roadside. They said, "The house is now just a short walk from here."

We parked the vehicle and began walking along a country path. The path narrowed to a trail that, after forty minutes, became a one-foot-wide retaining mud path between two lakes of paddy fields. This path, we were told, would take us to the woman's husband. The balancing act required to progress on this tight-rope of clay between two ponds is beyond my ability to communicate to you. Every step was a step of faith. Each foot had to be placed carefully and directly in front of the other. Both the pastor and I were experiencing a sharp learning curve and balancing act to handle what was becoming an endless challenge. Our clay pathway turned first right, then left, and then straight ahead. Several minutes later, we repeated the process.

Privately, I thought about Shirley and my family half a world away and wondered if we could balance and retrace our steps to civilization and the comfort of a plane ride to return to the West. It was well past morning, the sun was high in the clear blue sky, and temperatures had soared toward the high thirties Celsius or over one hundred Fahrenheit.

Since we left the local hotel that morning this mini-missionary journey, although it had at most been ninety minutes so far, it seemed like a lifetime. Surely we must be nearing her husband now. "How much further do we have to go?" I had the interpreter ask her.

"Just a little more," came her quick reply.

Her response made me feel somewhat like a small child nearing Disneyland after a two-day drive. We continued by turning right, then left, and by going straight ahead. Sure enough, after another twenty minutes, there he was in the middle of the paddy field planting rice as he was working from a raft.

Great! Now I expected him to come over to us so we could talk, but no. Conveniently tied at the mud path was a raft, which we were told to use to go out to him, so we prepared to do so.

The raft, about six by four feet (or almost two metres by just over one metre), was a series of bamboo poles lashed together with, I think, coconut rope. Five of us were safely aboard, and his wife plunged a long pole into the muddy base of the lake to propel us to her husband. If anyone had told me that this was a usual activity in a missionary evangelist's life, I would have had trouble believing it. The distance between the two rafts closed rapidly, and we were invited aboard his larger and more luxurious coconut-roped raft with poles. The five of us got off our meagre raft and stepped gingerly onto his more secure one. Now there were not four but nine of us on the husband's raft. No one had mentioned that his three other sons also worked the rice paddy farm with their father. As we were invited to sit down on the raft, they offered us a fresh king coconut to quench our thirst and that would double as a belated lunch.

Without my understanding a word, his wife was talking twice as fast to her husband and sons. The interpreter was busy drinking out of his coconut, and I was in the dark as far as the runaway monologue was concerned. Suddenly there was silence, and my pastor came out from under the coconut that he was holding above and as large as his head to get a better drink and to tell me they wanted to hear the same gospel that changed their son's life in prison the previous night.

Again we told the same story, point by point, clearly and at half the speed of the man's wife. That was the first time the father and his other sons had heard the gospel, the good news that God loved them. They heard how God, in the form of Jesus Christ, came to earth to become a sacrifice for our sin upon the cross. He shed His blood to remove our sin and bring us back into a right relationship with a Holy God. We shared how Christ was buried and rose again from the dead on the third day in the power of an endless life, now ever living in heaven to make intercession for us. Through His death, and resurrection we can now live in His power and victory.

On me, at least, the heat of the afternoon was taking its toll. Sitting in the middle of a rice paddy pond on a flimsy bamboo raft on a scorching hot day was not my idea of boating or sailing, but there was still work to be done.

Perhaps two or more hours passed as they asked questions that took a long time to process through the language barrier. But eventually they began to indicate that it was time to make a decision. The father, mother, daughter-in-law, and three remaining sons bowed their heads on the floating raft and together, asked Christ to become their Saviour and Lord. Nothing could convey the joy and elation that accompanied that family conversion. The shine of heaven already seemed to radiate from their faces.

We changed rafts and hurried back to the mud-rope pathway. It took us ninety minutes to reach our vehicle and then headed directly to the evangelistic event. As I walked back between ponds, I found myself reflecting, thus far, on the events of the day.

As a result of the powerful loudspeakers and during our morning visit, our friend in prison responded to the gospel, as did perhaps eleven in his cell, plus about another seventy in the surrounding cells, along with his mother, wife, father, and brothers. All these together represented perhaps ninety-three new Christian believers, plus the hundreds who came to faith at each night's rally as they came forward for prayer at the altar.

That chain reaction of conversions was not the work of man but the orchestration of the Holy Spirit. He worked with us as His servants who became conduits, allowing Him to flow through us the love and peace of God, together with Christ's cleansing blood, as His free gift to remove man's sin. That enabled them to become new creatures in Christ Jesus and to begin walking in newness of life through the power of Christ's resurrection, which brings to mind the Scripture, ". . . the Lord working with *them*, and confirming the word with signs following" (Mark 16:20 AV).

I had only a small make-shift lunch, no evening meal, no shower, and no time to study or pray about the upcoming evening meeting. We arrived just as the program was beginning. The musical specials quickly proceeded, and soon I was at the microphone preaching the same gospel but from a different context.

Yes, the crowd had grown to perhaps in excess of two thousand and were hanging on every verse that would, in a few minutes, bring them closer the Christ of Calvary. That night, however, I wasn't focused on the crowd. The person who I singled out in my mind and preached to each night was not seated on a comfortable chair on the courthouse apron and enjoying the balmy breeze of a tropical evening but was in a quagmire prison cell six kilometres (about three and three-quarter miles) away, incarcerated in a living hell. In my mind that night, I preached to them, my friends from prison, as though they occupied the front seats along with the other church leaders and community dignitaries. The message concluded, and the altar filled with hundreds of people seeking to find peace with God through our Lord Jesus Christ. Hundreds more came for deliverance from crime, alcohol, and drugs and from marriage and family difficulties.

The prayer lines looped once and possibly twice around the apron. As we seemed to be near the end of the evening rally, the prayer line grew again and again. Finally it ended, and we could go to our rooms. It was eleven o'clock and we needed to eat, but everything was closed. A shower and two sheets would have to do for the night. It was a long day but a totally victorious one.

As I relate these few of many experiences, I trust that they will serve to convey the power of the gospel to reach people in some of the most difficult of life's situations. In each of these cases, most of which were connected to crime, God, in His love, by the Holy Spirit reached into each one's circumstance. Nothing and no one is beyond God's reach or His mercy. Anyone may come to God and by so doing, will learn that His everlasting love and forgiveness are infinite and were reserved in His mind for each one of us since before the foundation of the world.

17

# A CATHEDRAL CABIN

When I was growing up in Northern Ireland, before electricity came to my district, on most nights I read under the covers by flashlight. Of the many adventure stories that then captivated me, two came to mind as this hair-raising mission field experience unfolded.

One story was the well-known *Uncle Tom's Cabin* by H. B. Stowe.[41] The other was *The Lonely Cabin on the Forty Mile* by Dr. Charles S. Price.[42] Both books stretched my young mind to its limit. Who could have known then that a lifetime later Rev. Price and I would have a common bond as missionaries: he was with the Assemblies of God (USA) and I was with its sister organization, the Pentecostal Assemblies of Canada?

Not in my wildest dreams could I have imagined that one day, over six decades later, my own cabin story would be related here. It is included only to show another dimension of ministry. This could be the back story of an out of the public eye ministry, a behind-the-scenes snapshot of a private four-day moment alone with God.

## Mandatory Confinement

Generally itineraries and schedules run smoothly on overseas mission tours, but this one was the exception. The first week of six had gone without difficulty; then came the bombshell. Sunday night after five back-to-back meetings, my host pastor mentioned as we drove from the last service that there had been a major mix up and there would be no ministry until Friday. During the interval, however, he would arrange for my accommodation.

Since we were in a jungle area, village stores were rare. This meant that a few items were displayed on a table outside a bamboo-style hut. Stopping there for a moment without explanation, my pastor returned with a brown bag before we continued to the billet. We left the main mud road, and he turned onto what looked like a two-wheel grassy track with heavy vegetation that closed in on both sides of the vehicle. After driving several kilometres in darkness, he slowed to a stop in front of a small wooden structure. "We're here!" he announced happily. This was my billet, a cabin that was perhaps about four by four metres or about four and a half by four and a half yards.

As I unlocked the door, we moved my baggage into the cabin. It was a single room with a tiny bathroom with a toilet, sink, and splash shower. The splash shower that was provided had a drain in a tiny corner where one could stand and splash cold water in a feeble attempt to wash to be able to live with oneself. I had learned from my past experiences that shower drains, usually without a mesh cover, were channels for local rat families. Rain-supplied water was stored in a small cistern above the roof. If there wasn't an available water supply for the toilet, usually there was a spade provided to be used discretely, like the people of Israel in the wilderness. In my small cabin and mounted high on the wall was a tiny air conditioner that my driver said "works if you don't overload" it. Since there were only two small bulbs in the place, that meant that only the air conditioner could be turned on in the daylight or the lights could be turned on at night. As my driver set a brown paper bag on a low table, he said that he would return for me on Friday morning. With a departing wave of his hand, he was gone into the jungle night.

As I was standing alone in my private world, in my mind I traveled from this jungle retreat to Canada, where Shirley and our extended family were living. I recalled being in Africa, where many meetings had twenty thousand-plus people attending them. In my mind I traveled to Korea, where, in a one-week seminar, I had ministered to five thousand pastors and then to Britain, where eight to ten meetings daily was the norm in my rookie preaching days. There I was, not even knowing my location. There was not another human being within miles or house phone, cell phone, or the Internet. What isolation! But surprisingly, I was at peace with God, myself, and the world.

In my earlier days I would have been frustrated about the mismanagement that caused this down time, but not so now. What peace I was experiencing—just God and I alone!

## Alone with God

After midnight I carefully surveyed the inside of the cabin. First I examined the window for mosquito proofing, doing what Shirley would have done if she were with me. I checked my cot for sheets and cleared out any of the insects that were present. Because my day had started at five a.m., it had been a long one. After I conducted five services, many hundreds surrendered their lives to Jesus Christ and hundreds were healed and delivered, many coming from considerable distances away. Nineteen hours had passed since my day started, and it was time for bed. Having made full use of my en-suite bath, I was now ready to relax with a little Bible reading. Just then I noticed the brown paper bag.

As I sat down with the Bible and took the bag to examine its contents, to my surprise I discovered its three items: one two-litre (just over a quart) bottle of water and two bananas! I smiled to myself as I calculated the four days and twelve meals that this supply represented. I thought of Christ and His forty-day fast and temptation in the form of a face-to-face confrontation with Satan. As I compared Christ's situation with mine, I had nothing to complain about. In comparison with His, my supply looked like a feast. With my pen, I drew three equal circles around the water bottle and divided it into four parts. Each represented a day in seclusion. I drew one line around the middle of each banana to restrict myself to eating half a banana a day.

As I settled into my canvas camp cot, my last conscious thought before falling asleep was a plan to structure my solitary confinement. After several hours of dead-to-the-world sleep, I awoke and became conscious of the humidity that induced a cold sweat. The aircon, as it was known locally, would solve the problem. It ran on command but with an ear-splitting clanging. As I tolerated the noise for several minutes, I became aware of another problem. Immediately after the aircon started, a crow became very annoyed and screamed for the duration of the cooling. Later I discovered that the bird had built its nest directly on top of the outside aircon unit.

Now that I was wide awake, I sensed that it was the right time to implement my four-day seclusion plan. To make right and good use of that time, I decided to read and pray alternately until my pastor-driver returned for me. Following the apostles' example (Acts 6:4) in giving themselves to prayer and the ministry of the Word to be more productive, I decided to do the same. Since my fulltime evangelistic ministry began, I had been challenged to find the proper mix of prayer, devotional, and message preparation time and balance them. During my early ministry years, fresh out of Bible college and in the prime of my youth, I found that it was comparatively easy to carry a heavy itinerary.

## Hearing Is Different from Listening

In those years, God took me to task for having such an undisciplined attitude. It seemed like God was saying to me, "You only open your Bible to prepare a message." In Britain, due to the heavy scheduling of evangelistic meetings, except for preaching, I had little time available for anything else.

I have always differentiated between a message and a sermon. To me a message is born from the Word in the heart, lives in the spirit, is given order in the intellect, and is then preached with the life of the Spirit from the heart of the speaker to the heart of the hearer. A sermon can by-pass the heart when preached from the intellect to the intellect.

Further, I sensed God saying in my spirit, "You read the Word to communicate it to the hearer, but it is crucial to let Me minister to you from your devotional reading in addition to and separate from ministry reading." Lesson learned!

## Take Time to Be Filled

In my early ministry and as a slow learner, it took time for me to grasp an important concept. A young fellow minister reading this story may not have already learned the importance of what God has taught me, that to enrich another's spirit, one's own spirit first must be enriched. The physically or spiritually hungry cannot be nourished from an empty plate or heart. To help make my point, years ago, while buying another home, the only disadvantage of the purchase was a swimming pool, which we didn't need. Because we had small children, we were concerned about having it. Each spring we had the chore of emptying, cleaning, and refilling the pool, which, in my mind and the minds of our eager children, seemed to take forever. Finally it was filled and spilled over the edges, as it was designed to do. As long as the inflow remained constant, there was an equivalent outflow. But with steady family and visitor use, the extra spillage was soon depleted by the lack of inflow. The spiritual parallel is similar.

When one has been in a demanding ministry for an extended period, it becomes obvious to others, if not to oneself, that some rest and relaxation, is needed. A suitable retreat or conference might be the answer. Like the restoring of a pool's outflow, a retreat or conference is a time one can set apart to be with God and where one's spirit can be restored to a level of overflowing.

If structured personal daily Bible reading is neglected for a time, the "pool" of His Spirit may not be able to flow through us as readily to those to whom we minister. This became apparent to me when, after extensive prolonged daily ministry, a retreat opportunity became available. Depending on the level of my depletion, it may have taken hours or a day or so of enjoying the breaking of the Bread of Life and His anointing in worship before there was an overflow. Overflow with me is commensurate with the time needed for my spirit to respond to His Spirit and readily overflow.

Having had the opportunity to attend a Billy Graham School of Evangelism many years ago, Shirley and I enjoyed every moment of that great event. On the third morning, the speaker was feeding the sheep by speaking to about three thousand pastors and their wives. The joy of being ministered to was special. As we sat together and relished every nugget of the message, suddenly, without warning, I had an overflow. At first I experienced a warm, good feeling in my spirit. Then I sensed an indescribable feeling in my chest and throat. As tears began to trickle down my cheeks, my breathing changed; the trickle became a torrent, and I became a reluctant but blessed "out-flowing" spectacle. The anointing lasted for many hours, and as I was lost in His presence, it made my lengthy lunch time an added blessing.

A side benefit of that special time was a healing I had sought for many months in private before the Lord and in Pentecostal meetings. Concealed in the blessing of the anointing of an evangelical event, my healing came silently and was not apparent to me until later. The healing from my disability, which I received thirty years previously, has remained. The Scripture affirms that the anointing breaks the yoke. Isaiah says, ". . . the yoke will be destroyed because of the anointing oil" (Is. 10:27d NKJV).

Between the noisy aircon and the enraged crow, sleep was now a distant memory. As I settled down with the Bible, hours of quiet reading quickly passed. As I was alone with God in the cabin, His Word washed and lifted my spirit to new heights. The little cabin became a cathedral. As I lay on top of the cot, it was time to let my spirit talk with God and be silent enough to hear Him. In this way, I searched my own heart while He was searching it even deeper. "Would not God search this out? For He knows the secrets of the heart" (Ps. 44:21 NKJV).

Although the first night was almost over and His Word had spoken to my spirit, the prayer hours quieted and warmed me. But the in-flowing had not yet reached the needed and expected out-flowing level.

By five o'clock on Monday morning, the sun had dawned. As I looked for the first time through the tiny cabin window, the view almost took away my breath. Through the breaking light, about sixty feet or twenty metres beyond a powdery white beach, the golden sun's rays fell across the South China Sea. One detail my pastor-driver failed to mention upon our evening arrival was this beautiful setting that was now in front of me. This was a rare and unique opportunity for me to be alone with God, and it became a sacred moment. As the hours flew by, my relationship with God improved and deepened in richness and unity.

With God's presence, that little and almost dilapidated cabin began to feel like a cathedral. As a place of prayer, it became "a desert place" (Mark 6:31 AV), "a desert place apart" (Matt. 14:13 AV), and the "closet" (Matt. 6:6 AV) where I could be alone with God. It became the "secret place" (Ps. 81:7 AV) where He answers each of His servants who separate themselves from the throng and move quietly into the awesome splendour of His presence.

It compares with Moses entering the tabernacle of meeting *to speak with God*. From above the mercy seat on the ark of the Testimony, which was between the two cherubim, Moses "heard the voice of One speaking to him" (Num. 7:89 NKJV). This principle holds true today. When we determine to enter the secret place of the Most High with the sincere intention of speaking openly with Him, as Moses did, He will also speak with us. We can have the same confidence. "He shall call upon me, and I will answer him" (Ps. 91:15 AV). Not only is it difficult to express the sacred intimacy that flows at those times, but it also somehow feels like a betrayal or breach of confidence to share it.

## God's Strength Comes to Us by Waiting on Him

We are told that nine-tenths of an iceberg is beneath the surface of the water. Its enormous strength is not in what is slightly visible but in the mass of its hidden power below the water's surface. In this there is a parallel to be learned. Among those of us who commune with God, He desires to develop our hidden power, strength, and private relationship with Him. These are the invisible qualities that are represented by the iceberg below the surface of the water. As with the iceberg, our hidden power is derived from being in the secret place with Him. It is analogous to the concealed nine-tenths of the iceberg. That unseen power can now be evidenced as the visible one-tenth to warn of sin and win unsaved people to Christ. As one reads biographies of great men of God, frequently they assert the need for taking a more substantial proportion of private time with God in sermon preparation and lesser time for presentation.

To God it is not important how much time preachers stand behind a pulpit or before a camera, but it is about how much time they spend in a secret place alone with "The LORD of hosts," "your Redeemer," "the Holy One of Israel," and "the God of the whole earth" (Is. 54:5 NKJV). What an awesome honour to minister to God in such a way!

Is it to God's throne room where we come not primarily to pray, plead, intercede, or request, but to "worship and bow down" to Him (Ps. 95:6 AV)? In Scripture we are encouraged to

> *Enter into His gates with thanksgiving,*
> *And into His courts with praise* (Ps. 100:4 NKJV).

It is therefore fitting to enter His presence not with weighty petitions but with pure praise. Let's praise and worship God for who He is and for what He has done in and for us! Let's extol Him, glorify His name, and give adulation to Israel's sovereign God, "THE LORD OUR RIGHTEOUSNESS" (Jer. 23:6 NKJV; footnote: Hebrew *YHWH Tsidkenu*)! This name, which was applied to Israel, now also applies to us as Gentiles who represent the engrafted wild olive branch (Rom. 11:13-18) who are sons and daughters of God by adoption (Rom. 8:14-16). The apostle Paul developed this position when he assured the Corinthian believers, "But of Him you are in Christ Jesus, who became for us wisdom from God—and righteousness and sanctification and redemption" (1 Cor. 1:30 NKJV).

Think of the throne room as our meeting place with God to praise and worship Him. The entrance to that revered personal place is where our thanksgiving begins to flow. We are raising our adulation to the great God and our Saviour, Jesus Christ. When we enter God's throne room, we should do so first in praise and in worship, giving thanks to Him for our imputed righteousness (Rom. 3:22-24); for our "sanctification" (1 Peter 1:2 AV) that separates us from the "beggarly elements" of the world (Gal. 4:9 AV); for our justification (Rom. 5:18), the process by which God places the righteousness of Christ on sinful man, exchanging the guilt of man and placing it on the sinless Christ and then seating us "in the heavenly *places* in Christ Jesus" (Eph. 2:6c AV).

When we praise Him, we enter His majestic presence. He is "the Word" who "became flesh and dwelt among us" (John 1:14 NKJV). In awe of God's glory and redemptive plan, we bow before Him. We were purchased by "The Lamb of God" (John 1:29 NKJV), who poured out His "precious blood," "the precious blood of Christ," who is "without blemish and without spot" (1 Peter 1:19 NKJV). Jesus also became our kinsman redeemer (Ruth 4:1-22) and our soon-coming King (John 14:3; Titus 2:13).

When coming to God in "prayer and supplication" (Phil. 4:6b NKJV), the apostle Paul instructed the Philippians to come first with a heart of praise and worship, "with thanksgiving," before making their requests known in prayer. As he made his prayer request known to the Colossian assembly, thanksgiving was still on the apostle Paul's mind: "Continue earnestly in prayer . . . with thanksgiving . . . praying also for us" (Col. 4:2-3 NKJV). As we observe these principles, it is important when entering into God's presence to make our requests with "clean hands, and a pure heart" (Ps. 24:4 AV). To extol and praise the sovereign God of our redemption, let's lift "up holy hands, without wrath and doubting" (1 Tim. 2:8b AV), and praise Him from a "pure heart," one that is established in "righteousness, faith, love, peace" (2 Tim. 2:22b NKJV) and with thanksgiving. As God's ministers, this is our mandate.

It needs to be underscored that there is a contrast in giving thanks between the human and divine. We teach our children that when they receive a gift, they are promptly to say, "Thank you!" It is only polite to do so. First the gift comes and then the appreciation. But in the divine order, there is a reverse principle in operation. In the kingdom covenant with our heavenly Father, Jesus said, in speaking of the natural man and the world's system, "Therefore do not be like them. For your Father knows the things you have need of before you ask Him" (Matt. 6:8 NKJV). As God's children, we walk in covenant relationship with Him. Isaiah affirms that "before they call, I will answer; and while they are yet speaking, I will hear" (Is. 65:24 AV). The Psalmist reminds us,

> *He who dwells in secret place of the Most High Shall abide*
> *under the shadow of the Almighty* (Ps. 91:1 NKJV).

Our relationship with the heavenly Father will deepen in proportion to our desire to "dwell" and "abide" in Him and He in us.

Already it was past noon. The sun was high in the sky, and suddenly, from being absorbed in reading, I was aware of heat and humidity. Even though the peeved crow protested profusely, the aircon stayed on. It was time for lunch! Somehow with the early morning start and enjoying my time alone, I forgot to eat breakfast. After breaking the seal on the water bottle, as warm as it was and with no refrigerator, I enjoyed my first drink. The banana was next. I cracked open enough of the skin to free about half of the day's portion. The other half of it I sealed tightly closed to preserve it, as much as possible, for the evening meal.

Time quickly passed, and with the sudden sunset, reading became difficult for me. The aircon was turned off, the lights were turned on, and the crow became silent. The anointing of the next six hours was special as God spoke from His living Word to my spirit. I responded sometimes "with the spirit" and at other times "with the understanding," as the apostle Paul did (1 Cor. 14:15b AV). Then at about midnight, God gave me sleep. "He gives His beloved sleep" (Ps. 127:2d NKJV).

## Take Time to Refresh

With each new day, my body was refreshed and my spirit soared to newer and higher heights. Hours seemed to pass as moments. I lost my hunger, yet I felt physically energized and spiritually empowered.

My continuous waiting upon God without contact with the outside world was pure freedom. With no human disturbance, I experienced uninterrupted communion with God. Because of my busy, filled itineraries, I hadn't had or taken the opportunity to be alone with God for a long period of time, such as this. At this point the over-flow was released with almost the briefest of Bible reading or praise and worship. Since I was in an isolated location and there was no human who passed by on the sandy beach near the cabin during that time, my expression to God was uninhibited. Had it not been for my reliable watch with a day/date window, I would have had difficulty keeping track of time.

By now it was Thursday, and a quarter of a banana and a quarter bottle of water were left. As was my new practice, I started the day with a splash shower. The last time I used the shower, I had forgotten to cover the open drain, so there were rodent visitors during the night while I was sleeping, as was evidenced by their droppings. For a sunrise breakfast, I had a single thin bite of solids and a mouthful of water, which was sufficient. I had mixed emotions about that last day, mostly regret that my fabulous communion with God was suddenly nearing an end. I had cried, laughed, sang, and danced; neither of the latter two reflected any natural ability on my part.

Sometimes while lying on my back on the cot during the day, as the anointing would follow lengthy times of pure silence or praise and worship, His presence would become so tangible it was as though I could touch Him. During those times, as I wept for joy with Him, my emotions were stretched to new and wonderful heights. His visitations with me had refreshed my memories of many great but brief similar moments over a lifetime of my relationship with the Holy Spirit. As a result of my lengthy, unbroken solitary time in His presence, my experience with God raised all my earlier peak experiences to new heights.

In a few seconds, I was reduced to tears as I walked back and forth with my hands raised and my eyes closed on the narrow path between the few pieces of furniture as I sang my own song of praise to Him, sometimes in English and at other times in my prayer language. That was the overflowing experience that accompanied my sacred, private, uninterrupted, and divine encounter with God.

## Sometimes God Wants Us—Alone

For certain personal encounters with God, it is desirable for one to have private times with Him. Regardless of one's closeness to another human being, total openness with God in such setting becomes diminished, if not totally forfeited. This is not to say that close friends who enjoy deep fellowship with one another cannot have meaningful prayer and worship times together. But such experiences are limited to common interests rather than searching personal introspection.

I learned this painful lesson in my earlier years. For some time I had shared with a close brother how God had been meeting with me as I secluded myself with Him in prayer, and perhaps overnight, I allowed Him time to pour out of His rich blessing upon me. I spoke of the anointing, praying in the spirit, and how He revealed Himself to me. One day my friend said, "John, I want to go with you on one of those close encounters." We did so, but it turned out to be a disaster. Yes, we prayed and enjoyed the Lord together on common horizontal issues, but our freedom to communicate with Him on spiritual vertical issues lacked depth. Intimacy with God, to a greater extent, was forfeited. We left our secluded location and drove home. I had learned the lesson of how important is was to meet alone with God.

My trip to be alone with God in a little deserted cabin was by divine appointment. He had set me apart in that cathedral cabin so He could share His thoughts about me. "I know the thoughts that I think toward you, says the LORD, thoughts of peace and not of evil, to give you a future and a hope" (Jer. 29:11 NKJV). He is the Good Shepherd who longs to carry me, His lamb, and refresh me for a few moments in the power of the Holy Spirit's anointing. Then again He released me to the work for which He had commissioned me, saying, "Go your way; behold, I send you out as lambs among wolves" (Luke 10:3 NKJV).

## Darkness before Dawn

On my final day of being alone with God, a sunset in its golden hues painted the cabin room, and in minutes it was dusk. Much to the delight of the complaining crow, I switched the squeaking aircon off and then turned on the lights, followed later by the final night's rest.

As I prepared for sleep, it was now time for me to reflect upon the high points of the great moments I had alone with God. They included a sense of the Holy Spirit's presence and the deep work that had been done in me. It re-tuned my instrument of praise and brought me back to perfect pitch, so to speak. After those four life-changing days, I felt like my spirit and indeed, my mind and body, had been energized. With anticipation I awaited the soon-coming morning. I was ready to get back into my next five weeks of scheduled ministry.

Not for reduced heat but more for protection from the ever-present mosquitoes, I pulled a light sheet over myself. I was soon to fall asleep. Warm, good thoughts filled my spirit. The cabin had become more than a billet. It was a sacred meeting place or holy ground. Though God's presence is always within His child, in these four days, God had lingered with me in a rich and unforgettable way. For me it was a four-day God moment.

On numerous crossroad moments or forks in the road in my life, God has revealed Himself to me in unusual ways. Typically I experience these moments if I need to make a major decision and desperately need His wisdom for direction. At such times I will be stopped in my tracks, perhaps while driving or being awakened from a deep, pleasant sleep with the room flooded in the most brilliant, peaceful light. At these times He will speak into my spirit with direction, for or against it, or in how to resolve a dilemma. I have experienced no set pattern of instruction. It may be His voice speaking to my spirit, perhaps directing me to a Scripture reference to provide me with needed wisdom. Whatever His message, the method of a brilliant light is the same. It has always been an uplifting experience and has come when I least expected it.

Perhaps the most significant brilliant light God moment was when I was awakened from sleep to a flood-lit room with His simple instruction: "I have a special person for you; I want you and Shirley together. Phone her in the morning and begin putting it together." This person was someone slightly known to me but with whom I had no connection. I followed God's instruction to the letter, and Shirley and I are in our forty-fifth year of divine and awesome union and enjoying four children, ten grandchildren, and three great-grandchildren.

Suddenly I was awakened on my cot and bolted upright into a sitting position. It was in the middle of the night. When I looked around the cabin, I could see absolutely nothing. Darkness filled the room, and nothing was visible; it was as though I had been blinded. In the past, I was familiar with positive, brilliant light experiences, but this one was negative, with a seemingly impenetrable darkness that was foreign to me.

Instead of the tiresome tropical heat, the room was now uncomfortably and unpleasantly cold. My body wanted to tremble. The rich sense of God's presence I had enjoyed until I fell asleep was gone. This new experience was a black sensation, eerily resembling countless altercations at the altars while dealing with demoniacs—times when one comes against evil spirits that dement and destroy their hosts until they are exorcised in Jesus' name.

As I sat wide-eyed, trying to penetrate it, the unpleasant black coldness intensified. Nothing in my lifetime of ministry or personal encounters resembled it. As I turned my head to the right side of the cot, there stood the problem. In a distinct form, looming larger and heavier than any human being, stood Satan. Often "Satan . . . transforms himself into an angel of light" (2 Cor. 11:14 NKJV), but not this time. The intensity of his black outline was dimensional, standing out dramatically in vivid contrast from the existing blackness. As I looked up to where his grotesque head was, I recognized his flaming orange red eyes, having seen them a thousand times in decades of demonic deliverance ministry.

As our gaze locked, my urge to tremble ceased. I didn't have a trace of fear, but rather anger or righteous indignation arose in me. This was what the apostle Paul warned the Ephesians about: "For we do not wrestle against flesh and blood, but against principalities, against powers, against the rulers of the darkness of this age, against spiritual *hosts* of wickedness in the heavenly *places*" (Eph. 6:12 NKJV). From the apostle Peter also comes the warning: "Be sober [self-controlled], be vigilant [watchful]; because your adversary the devil, walks about as a roaring lion, seeking whom he may devour. Resist him, steadfast in the faith" (1 Peter 5:8-9 NKJV).

The Holy Spirit was present there in and with me as I quietly said, "It's yourself, Satan. Go in Jesus' name!" Instantly, he and the intense darkness were gone, as though both evaporated, and the light of the room returned to normal.

## Satan May Come in Attractive Disguise

"What was that about?" I asked myself after four supreme days in the cabin in the presence of the Holy Spirit and Jesus Christ, the King of kings. Would it be reasonable after such a divine encounter, where my spirit had been immensely strengthened, that Satan would present himself to me? Was this his opportunity to disrupt, test, or challenge the validity of the divine blessing and power of those life-enriching days? In relation to Job, Satan made an unannounced visit after walking back and forth on the earth: "and Satan came also among them" (Job 2:1 NKJV). The incident I experienced was unprecedented in my life as an attempted attack on me. In contrast with the joy of the Lord I experienced in those days was Satan's dramatic presence and his dismissal through the victorious name of Jesus.

I quickly went back to sleep, and soon it was dawn on the last morning. Shortly after arising, I had a splash shower, dressed quickly, packed my belongings, finished the last piece of banana, and drained my solitary water bottle. While I sat down to wait for an early departure, I began to read Paul's letter to the Ephesians. In concluding his letter to the Ephesians, Paul, while detailing the armour of the believer, gave these instructions: "Finally, my brethren, be strong in the Lord, and in the power of His might" (Eph. 6:10 NKJV). As believers on the front line of spiritual warfare and ministers of the gospel behind the pulpit, should we not be more careful to activate the "be strong" of verse 10, working only in His strength and proclaiming His supernatural, life-changing power to a lost, dying, and hurting world?

Could the cataclysmic events of today be birthing a new world order? Today's world is experiencing economic meltdown and political uncertainty. Record-breaking, unprecedented natural disasters in magnitude, frequency, and diversity are ravishing the globe. Is this the time for the informed believer to wake up spiritually? We are salt and light, catalysts to bring about change in the world. We stand between the Creator, the sovereign God of the universe, and the created, who are "without Christ, having no hope, and without God in the world" (Eph. 2:12 AV). Will we function as catalysts that will stand in the gap? That's a great question. God said, "I sought for a man among them who would . . . stand in the gap before Me on behalf of the land, . . . but I found no one" (Ezek. 22:30 NKJV). Someone once asked, "If not me, who? If not here, where? If not now, when?"

We, the soldiers of Christ, are initiated through His work on the cross, washed in His blood, immortalized by His resurrection, energized by the power of His Holy Spirit, and are provided with and instructed to wear the whole armour of God. We remain here until He comes or calls us home, to "stand fast in one spirit, with one mind striving together for the faith of the gospel" (Phil. 1:27d NKJV).

As unusual and out of character as that melodrama was, it was the only time thus far in my life for such an encounter. It was not Satan's usual modus operandi, as in his method or nature of working. Rather, his appearance is as an angel of light: "For Satan himself transforms himself into an angel of light" (2 Cor. 11:14 NKJV). His attacks will most likely be embodied in more natural, everyday guise.

The apostle Paul, urging us to vigilance, said, "But what I do, I will also continue to do, that I may cut off the opportunity from those who desire an opportunity to be regarded just as we are in the things of which they boast. For such are false apostles, deceitful workers, transforming themselves into apostles of Christ? . . . Therefore *it is* no great thing if his ministers also transform themselves into ministers of righteousness, whose end will be according to their works" (2 Cor. 11:12-13, 15 NKJV).

As believers, on occasion the unexpected attacks of Satan may be well disguised in the form of a close ministry colleague, another believer, or a trusted family member. Generally the greater the emotional closeness to the individual concerned, the more sensitive the issue becomes and the more perceptive our spirits should be in dealing with the issue.

In sharing with or in counselling ministry leadership pastors around the world, it often is the case that the greater the call of God on His servant, the more vulnerable he or she is to Satan's attacks. Also, it is true that the severity of the attack intensifies when Satan's arrows are redirected to the ones closest to and most loved by the leader. This is often harder on the leader than if the attack were personal. This closeness often makes the issue more delicate to handle.

A personal incident will serve to illustrate this point. Shirley and I entered our little hotel after a particularly powerful deliverance rally in an Asian jungle. Hundreds had been healed and many demon-possessed people were delivered. To the left was a bathroom, which I had entered. Shirley proceeded further into the room, and then I heard a massive thud and an injured cry. As I rushed out, I found her lying in a heap in the furthermost corner of the room. She described the attack as being "picked up by an unseen force and thrown across the room." This was Satan's retaliation, in the most vicious way, to hurt the one most close to me, which in turn hurt me even more.

In the grace of forgiveness, the apostle Paul encourages us, saying, ". . . forgive and comfort *him*, lest perhaps such a one be swallowed up with too much sorrow. Therefore I urge you to reaffirm *your* love to him. For to this end I also wrote that I might put you to the test, whether you are obedient in all things. Now whom you forgive anything, I also *forgive*. For if indeed I have forgiven anything, I have forgiven that one for your sakes in the presence of Christ, lest Satan should take advantage of us; for we are not ignorant of his devices" (2 Cor. 2:7-11 NKJV).

Greater tact, wisdom, love (not only human love, but also divine), and forgiveness (not only human forgiveness, but also divine) is needed—often not just once, but ad infinitum, as the old injury may resurface. This is not to say that the act of forgiveness was negated, but since we are new creatures in Christ since conversion and are still in the flesh, we have the propensity to recall and review the past to our detriment. We need to leave past offences under the blood of Christ's forgiveness instead of reopening old wounds to be re-infected. Yes, we forgave, but the enemy of our souls is still at large, still lying, and still accusing Christian believers. Believers who genuinely learn forgiveness are never at the mercy of their assailants but are enriched, free from bondage, and enabled to walk in divine freedom and health.

When believers harbour lengthy negative and destructive anger, and unforgiveness, mental, emotional, and physical deficiencies are often triggered. In so doing, they perhaps inadvertently forfeit the armour of security and protection available to them in Ephesians 6. Believers, who are now vulnerable, give Satan opportunity and greater access to disrupt, pollute, or debilitate them, their families, and their possessions. Often in adversity or when sickness strikes, no amount of counselling, medical care, or medication will alleviate their problems if the issues are caused by neglecting God's instruction manual. When the root causes are dealt with on a spiritual basis, through submission and obedience to His Word, the problems will be resolved.

It is for this reason God's Word instructs us to deal with these issues on a twenty-four hour basis. "'*Be angry, and do not sin*': do not let the sun go down on your wrath, nor give place to the devil . . . Let no corrupt word proceed out of your mouth, but what is good for necessary edification, that it may impart grace to the hearers. And do not grieve the Holy Spirit of God, by whom you were sealed for the day of redemption. Let all bitterness, wrath, anger, clamour [*confused shouting or continual uproar*], and evil speaking be put away from you, with all malice. [*A wish to hurt or make suffer; active ill will; spite*] And be kind one to another, tender-hearted, forgiving one another, even as God in Christ forgave you" (Eph. 4:26-27, 29-32 NKJV).

The caution from those who have embraced and practised the principle of divine forgiveness is that this grace leaves them vulnerable to abuse by those who take advantage of the believer's spiritual maturity. They say and do what they please, knowing they will always have the mature believer's forgiveness. They themselves often remain ignorant of God's Word, which would instruct them in salvation and mature spiritual development to correct the catalogue of failings found in Paul's second letter to Timothy (2 Tim. 3:1-9). Those who haven't learned still continue to be an offence: "ever learning, and never able to come to the knowledge of the truth"(2 Tim. 3:7 AV). This is a prophetic, end-times description of the un-regenerate from which the believer should turn away. This passage should catalogue nothing of a believer's behaviour or stunted spiritual growth that identifies with the carnal, fallen nature.

The work of Christ on the cross becomes to them "A stone of stumbling, and a rock of offence" (1 Peter 2:8a AV; Isa. 8:14 AV). The apostle Peter continues, "They stumble, being disobedient to the word, to which they also were appointed" (1 Peter 2:8b NKJV). In Peter's first letter, he speaks of the word of the Lord that endures forever, with reference to Isaiah 40:8, and then continues, "Now this is the word which by the gospel was preached unto you." (1 Peter 1:25b NKJV). Again Peter exhorts that those professing to walk as spiritually developing believers lay aside the contamination of the fleshly nature. He encourages the ingestion of pure Word nutrition: "Therefore, laying aside all malice, all deceit, hypocrisy, envy, and all evil speaking, as newborn babes, desire the pure milk of the word that you may grow thereby, if indeed you have tasted that the Lord is gracious" (1 Peter 2:1-3 NKJV).

Where there is spiritual birth, there must be evidence of spiritual growth indicated by a voracious desire for the milk and then the meat of the Word. The absence of this desire puts the normality of the birth in question.

Paul's warning to Timothy is also for our instruction (2 Tim. 3:15). His warning was specific: "For men will be lovers of themselves, lovers of money, boasters, proud, blasphemers, disobedient to parents, unthankful, unholy, unloving, unforgiving, slanderers, without self-control, brutal, despisers of good, traitors, headstrong, haughty, lovers of pleasure rather than lovers of God, having a form of godliness but denying its power. And from such people turn away!" (2 Tim. 3:2-5 NKJV).

## Keep a Clean Campsite

Every serious wilderness camper knows that food left exposed at a campsite fire pit will attract predators. In like manner, virtual odour from un-forgiveness, anger, hatred, and stubbornness, left to ferment, eventually will reach Satan's nostrils, attracting the "the devil's schemes" in his many forms and disguises (Eph. 6:11c NIV). The biblical caution to King Saul, which is also applicable to God's people, is worth repeating here: "For rebellion *is as* the sin of witchcraft, and stubbornness *is as* iniquity and idolatry" (1 Sam. 15:23 AV). Victory will reign in our lives when we forgive, forgive, and continue to forgive in Jesus' name.

Satan's days are numbered; his end is in sight. The apostle John, in Revelation, gives a vivid glimpse of the commencement of what will become Satan's ultimate demise. "So the great dragon was cast out, that serpent of old, called the Devil and Satan, who deceives the whole world; he was cast to the earth, and his angels were cast out with him. Then I heard a loud voice saying in heaven, 'Now salvation, and strength, and the kingdom of our God, and the power of His Christ have come, for the accuser of our brethren, who accused them before our God day and night, has been cast down. And they overcame him by the blood of the Lamb and by the word of their testimony'" (Rev. 12:9-11 NKJV).

The mission of Satan is to defeat the kingdom of God. Believers are God's subjects, His children, His sons and daughters; therefore they are prime targets for Satan's "fiery dart" attack. We are not to worry, as the apostle Peter encourages, ". . . casting all your care upon Him, for He cares for you. Be sober, be vigilant; because your adversary the devil walks about like a roaring lion, seeking whom he may devour. Resist him, steadfast in the faith, knowing that the same sufferings are experienced by your brotherhood in the world" (1 Peter 5:7-9 NKJV).

## Signs of the Times

Jesus, speaking of false prophets, warns us by saying, "Beware of false prophets, who come to you in sheep's clothing, but inwardly they are ravenous wolves" (Matt. 7:15 NKJV). John the apostle sounds his clear warning, "Beloved, do not believe every spirit, but test the spirits, whether they are of God; because many false prophets have gone out into the world. By this you know the Spirit of God: Every spirit that confesses that Jesus Christ has come in the flesh is of God, and every spirit that does not confess that Jesus Christ has come in the flesh is not of God. And this is the *spirit* of the Antichrist, which you have heard was coming, and is now already in the world" (1 John 4:1-3 NKJV).

Could this cataclysmic season be birthing the new world order? Global economic meltdown, world banks and financial institutions having failed, and recovery systems and strategies teetering on the edge are causing economic and political mayhem and are now shaking leading world governments like a 9.0 earthquake on the Richter scale. The strongest governments, it appears, are the most vulnerable.

A new world order is fast taking shape. One-world government is not far away. A single world currency is within sight. Record-breaking natural disasters that are unprecedented in magnitude, frequency, and diversity are ravishing the globe. Wars, terrorism, and heinous crimes that were unimaginable in the recent past all point to our redemption drawing near. To describe the present tumult, the media is heralding terms unheard of from them until recently—terms like cataclysmic, end times, and Armageddon.

In addition to the predicament of the world, there are fast-paced changes occurring in the name of Christ today within His church that are also cause for alarm. The dilution and manipulation of the tenets of the Christian faith, in an effort to establish an "interfaith" leading to a one-world religion, is past the embryonic stage. Be vigilant not to permit God's inspired Word to be dissected to accommodate those with ulterior motives who wish to form unacceptable religious alliances (Gal. 1:6-10; Deut. 4:2; 12:32; Prov. 3:5-6).

No longer is the enemy outside the church; it is also inside of it as ravenous wolves masquerading in sheep's clothing, working feverishly to rewrite the very fundamentals of our faith. Will we sleep through this offensive and repulsive onslaught within the religious ranks? Is this the wake-up call of the informed believer? We are the catalysts who stand in the gap to bring about positive change.

The joy of the Lord for those four days culminating with Satan's dramatic presence and victorious dismissal through the name of Jesus brought a heightened sense of God's anointing.

In regard to wearing the full armour of God, Paul enjoins Ephesian Christians as follows: "Finally, my brethren, be strong in the Lord and in the power of His might. Put on the whole armor of God, that you may be able to stand against the wiles of the devil" (Eph. 6:10-11 NKJV).

As believers on the front line of warfare and ministers of the gospel behind the podium, should we not be more careful to activate the "be strong" of verse 10, working only in His strength, proclaiming His supernatural, life-changing power to a lost and hurting world?

We stand between the Creator, the sovereign God of the universe, and the created, who are "without Christ . . . having no hope and without God in the world" (Eph. 2:12 NKJV).

We, the soldiers of Christ, initiated through His work on the cross, washed in His blood, immortalised by His resurrection, and energised by the power of His Holy Spirit are provided with and instructed to wear the whole armour of God. We are garrisoned here until He comes or calls us home to "stand fast in one spirit, with one mind striving together for the faith of the gospel" (Phil. 1:27d NKJV). We and the faith we contend for are successfully defended by wearing the armour of God enumerated in Ephesians 6. Wearing the armour of God is at our own volition. Again in verse 11 we have the active verb, "put on." It is optional. It is totally left to the believer's discretion. Do we choose to comply?

His Word, His shed blood, His name, and prayer and fasting are five crucial pieces of warfare weaponry. With these, the warrior behind enemy lines will do valiantly, emerging victoriously.

My pastor-driver arrived in mid-afternoon with two jungle-cooked chicken wings and said, "In case you might be hungry . . ." As I walked from the cabin to the van, I was filled with a tinge of sadness. To me the humble little cabin was now a cathedral. As we drove away, my eye scanned the silver sand beach upon which, because of God's anointing, I had not thought to set foot.

The incredible Holy Spirit's power accompanied the balance of my ministry in that nation. Thousands of people were spiritually born into God's kingdom, and many were healed and delivered.

The interruption of my itinerary was no mistake; it was by divine appointment. The Holy Spirit and I had four uninterrupted and unforgettable days together in a humble little cabin that had become a sacred cathedral. For me, the experiences of those days in the cathedral cabin were the highlight of the tour.

# 18

# THE FOURTH MAN

During an extended ministry tour in India, the itinerary called for a men's teaching session at an Anglican church. Simultaneously, my wife, Shirley, and I would be teaching a seminar for ladies and men respectively. With most traditional churches, the architecture is spectacular. As we approached the extensive grounds, we saw this one was no exception; the church was more like an abbey. Although we had been in the country for several weeks, it was still difficult to acclimatize to the heat, which was almost forty degrees Celsius or about one hundred degrees Fahrenheit, with high humidity. It was therefore relaxing to know that within these massive cloistered rock walls there would be a cool, refreshing breeze flowing through the sanctuary, making the several hours of teaching comfortable for everyone.

After arriving a few minutes early for the session, we had time to wander through the building and appreciate the design, commemorative plaques, and biblical stories vividly portrayed in the ornate stained-glass windows. That setting was so different from the rural and jungle settings of most meeting places we had experienced. The change from teaching in the fatiguing heat would be a welcome blessing. Secretly I found myself relishing that venue; by contrast, it would be much easier.

I settled myself in a cool, quiet corner and reviewed the

material for the session as many attendees began moving toward the front pews. Suddenly my attention was diverted to an elegantly garbed senior cleric coming in my direction. In broken English, he gestured toward those assembled at the front of the sanctuary, pointing out that they were all ladies who were waiting for my wife's session. Then he asked, "Would you please follow me?" As we did so, he led us across the quadrangle to an outside overhang of the complex that was in the direct sunlight and where two banks of about two hundred chairs awaited our arrival. Gone was my dream of teaching in comfort.

As I walked between the sublime and the ridiculous locations, holding my Bible and material that was prepared for that session, I distinctly sensed in my spirit a check by the Holy Spirit not to use my prepared materials. Instead, He dropped into my mind the thought, "Teach on the fourth man!" My instant reaction was, "What fourth man?" I had no material on the fourth man. Never had I prepared nor preached a message on the fourth man. Without preparation, how does one teach for three hours from a two-word title? Oh yes, the Scripture reference was there in Daniel, and so was my crowd, waiting for me to begin speaking.

Even as a child preacher, I had prayed and studied for hours wrestling with Scripture passages to design them into an interesting, progressive, and orderly message. Shortly after being saved at seven years old, it was a common event to lie on the grass on my stomach in the corner of the farm field with my Bible preaching to my dog, MacWhurter, who rested his head on his front paws for hours as I solemnly declared the Word. My father continually reprimanded me for preaching to the hundreds of hens in their houses. He said it "hindered their egg production." This childishness developed over the next few years into leading children to Christ on the way home from school, which my Father despised, feeling I was too immature for such an endeavour.

In Bible college, homiletics or preaching was a major subject that, when I understood it, enabled the best of my spirit and research to be presented in a moving manner that would challenge and persuade the listener. To stand behind the sacred desk without adequate preparation of heart, spirit, and mind and without a burning message for the heart of the hearer would be tantamount to a breach of my divine call to win the lost or disciple believers. In accepting the call to declare the whole "gospel of God" (Rom. 15:16 AV), the responsibility was mine to declare it to the best of my ability from "the unsearchable riches of Christ" (Eph. 3:8d AV). The fire of the message burning in my heart for that audience had to be delivered to that audience alone.

The true gospel message is seeded with God's revulsion for sin and sacrificial love for the sinner through His coming in Christ to shed His blood to cleanse us from sin. It is to declare His righteousness and His demand for holiness. It is to be laced with His mercy and grace. His resurrection power will enable the new convert to escape from his human weaknesses. The power of Satan is now broken forever through the work on the cross of Christ. Christ commissioned Saul, later to be known as the apostle Paul, saying, "I now send you, to open their eyes, *in order to turn them* from darkness to light, and *from* the power of Satan to God, that they may receive forgiveness of sins and an inheritance among those who are sanctified by faith in Me" (Acts 26:17–18 NKJV). The new believer may now be victorious through his new Master by overcoming sin and living in Him now as a new creature in Christ (2 Cor. 5:17).

The true spirit of the message will be born in the heart of the preacher by the Holy Spirit from the living Word. It will be delivered with His anointing, and the fire of that anointing will be carried to and felt in the spirit and conscience of all who are candidates of His work of divine grace.

As it is proclaimed, the anointed message, not as a second-hand word retrieved from another's writing or Internet site but born in prayer, praise, and study, will, by the Spirit, pierce the heart of the listener and accomplish His will.

May God help me never to lose the sense of my ministry vocation! My work is not to please or tickle ears, not to entertain or say what the audience wants to hear but by the Spirit, to preach an anointed and living word that they *must* hear to move them from where they are to where God wants them to be: "to make you wise for salvation through faith which is in Christ Jesus" (2 Tim. 3:15c NKJV). "For the word of God is living and powerful, and sharper than any two edged sword, piercing even to the division of soul and spirit, and of joints and marrow, and is a discerner of the thoughts and intents of the heart" (Heb. 4:12 NKJV).

On that outdoor abbey occasion, no such preparation time was given to me. After a brief introduction, the convenor gestured for me to begin.

Although it was only a few metres from my chair, the walk to the podium seemed like a long one. In those few seconds, my mind went through a thousand thoughts as it raced around the world. I relived the morning of God's supernatural intervention for ministry, taking me from Western evangelism to the third world; it is the same gospel but a different audience and in the supernatural power and demonstration of the Holy Spirit.

Then His emphasis to me seemed to be for a new anointing with the supernatural accompanying my preaching and teaching of His Word.

Now, many years later, that call has proven to be true. Also flashing through my memory was my unforgettable first Asian pastor's seminar when the Holy Spirit began teaching through my mouth without my mind having formed the thoughts. That experience is now still almost inconceivable to me but true. That fork in the road was His affirmation of the supernatural accompanying the new third-world chapter of my evangelistic ministry.

That first day of that seminar concluded in unimaginable, life-changing events, resulting not from human skill or mission ministry experience but from the operation of the gifts of the Spirit. As pastors prayed with and forgave one another of lifetime issues, deliverance and healings flowed. I literally became a bystander, an observer.

When one can find it in one's spirit to forgive another, it not only releases the other person but also cancels the guilt and removes the consequential physical, spiritual, and emotional obstacle on both sides, created by the issue. This mature scriptural action allows both parties to grow and flow together in God's fullest intended stature.

That outdoor abbey audience was a new challenge for me, another opportunity to step out of the boat and walk on water. I was faced with almost two hundred men for three hours of a seminar and without a single note or outline—just God! After my usual introductory remarks, I announced the subject title, "The Fourth Man." As they prepared their notebooks, they looked relaxed and waited to be fed by me, the senior Western teacher. Unknown to them, all I had was the title. I, too, was waiting to be fed.

As we opened our Bibles to Daniel 1, I drew the picture of Daniel and his three friends establishing their faith in the living God. In chapter 3, King Nebuchadnezzar created a massive golden image that all people, nations, and languages were required to fall down and worship. All of the king's leaders, governors, judges, and magistrates came and stood before the image. The instruction was given that when the musical instruments sounded, all would be required to fall down and worship the image the king had erected. The penalty for the person refusing to worship the image was to be cast immediately into a burning, fiery furnace. It was reported to the king that the three Jewish boys refused to bow down to the image.

By refusing to bow down to the golden image that Nebuchadnezzar set up, Shadrach, Meshach, and Abed-Nego ignited the king's fury. After demanding an audience with them, he asked if the report was true. They affirmed that it was. Although the king was willing to give them another chance, they declined by saying, ". . . our God whom we serve is able to deliver us from the burning fiery furnace, and He will deliver *us* from your hand, O king. But if not, let it be known to you . . . that we do not serve your gods, nor will we worship the gold image which you have set up" (Dan. 3:17-18 NKJV).

It was then the king commanded the furnace to be heated seven times hotter than usual and for his mighty men to bind the three young men and cast them, fully clothed, into the furnace. Even the men casting them into the furnace perished because of the excessive heat.

As the king watched for their death, he jumped to his feet in astonishment and asked his counsellors, "Did we not cast three men bound into the midst of the fire?" "True, O King," they answered. "Look!" he said. "I see four men loose, walking in the midst of the fire; and they are not hurt, and the form of the fourth is like the Son of God"; "Or *a son of the gods*" (Dan. 3:24-25, 3:25 footnote, NKJV).

In his exposition of the book of Daniel, J. E. H. Thompson in *The Pulpit Commentary* noted the following: "While we ought to guard against ascribing to the Babylonian monarch the idea that this appearance was that of the Second Person of the Christian Trinity, we are ourselves at liberty to maintain this, or to hold that it was an angel who strengthened these servants of God in the furnace."[43]

The king approached the mouth of the furnace and called by name each of the young Hebrews to come out of the furnace and to come to him, and he identified them as "servants of the Most High God" (Dan. 3:26 NKJV). All the dignitaries who had caused the trauma came and saw the unharmed servants. They witnessed that on their bodies the fire had no power. The hair of their heads was not singed. Their garments were not consumed in the flames. The smell of fire was not on them.

The king enthusiastically blessed their God, "who sent His Angel and delivered His servants who trusted in Him" and "that they should not serve nor worship any god except their own God!" (Dan. 3:28 NKJV).

He continued by making a decree that any people, nation, or language that spoke anything against their God would be cut in pieces. Their houses would be made an ash heap, because there was no other God who could deliver like this. Then he promoted them (Dan. 3:29-30). The king further declared to his world "the signs and wonders that the Most High God has worked for me" (Dan. 4:2 NKJV).

As the impromptu theme began to unfold in the abbey quadrangle on that scorching hot day, each significant point of the story was highlighted and applied in a practical way to the hearts of the hearers.

When the four young Hebrew men were transplanted to their new Babylonian culture, they identified themselves immediately as children of the Most High God. As children of God, to them that culture was a type of the world. They were, as we are, in the world but not of it (John 17:14-16). It is becoming increasingly more critical that believers early and intentionally identify themselves as children of God and with their Saviour and the teachings of His Word. The battle of the ages, life and death, sin and righteousness, was not waged in secret but in public on the world stage by God the Son, who sacrificially died once and for all on a Roman cross.

Morally, are the lines of demarcation fading? In our Christian lifestyle, in our worldly appetites and spiritual integrity, is black and white becoming grey? How much of our Bible has to be deleted to ease our consciences of worldly compromise or promote a blending of major religions? The multiplicity of new Bible versions or translations invariably inject diluted adjectives or terms in the name of advancement and improvement and at the same time, it seems, dull the two-edged sword of the Word.

Even more radical changes may be ahead as the emerging church, in the name of modernising and moving forward, continues to introduce so-called progress by reverting to the trappings of the ancient past in an attempt to reconcile formerly opposing faiths. Merging of that nature can only be accomplished with massive compromise, including the erosion of many cornerstone Scriptures, to the detriment of the Christian faith.

We need a clarion call to alert us to the foundational words of the gospel that are being insidiously dropped from many preachers' pulpit vocabularies. In keeping with community spirit, offensive words like the cross, the blood of Christ, the gospel, original sin, hell, holiness, morality, and righteousness are wrongly being replaced with smoother, warmer, less invasive socially acceptable and politically correct terms.

That day I reminded the pastors of the words of the apostle Paul: ". . . woe is me if I do not preach the gospel!" (1 Cor. 9:16d NKJV). To Timothy he gave a charge that can be applied today to every young person who is about to be ordained:

> I charge you therefore [*not before men, a governing body of a board of governors, faculty, or denominational presidents, but* (Author's emphasis)] before God and the Lord Jesus Christ, who will judge the living and the dead at His appearing and His kingdom: Preach the word! Be ready in season *and* out of season. Convince, rebuke, exhort, with all longsuffering and teaching [doctrine]. For the time will come when they will not endure sound doctrine, but according to their own desires, *because* they have itching ears, they will heap up for themselves teachers; and they [teachers] will turn *their* ears away from the truth, and be turned aside to fables. But you be watchful in all things, endure afflictions, do the work of an evangelist, fulfill your ministry (2 Tim. 4:1-5 NKJV).

This is an awesome charge. We who claim to be called of God are accountable finally not to the ecclesiastical hierarchy or the whims of social acceptability but to "God and the Lord Jesus Christ" (2 Tim. 4:1 NKJV). Cultures around the world change, but the Psalmist reminds us,

> *Forever, O LORD,*
> *Your word is settled in heaven* (Ps. 119:89 NKJV).

God Himself declared, "For I *am* the LORD, I do not change" (Mal. 3:6 NKJV).

Although the seminar had just begun and the pastors had settled in to note taking, there was a refreshing spirit permeating the gathering. In my own heart, I was searching for the reason to change material and how it would better serve that audience. What surprise had God planned for us?

We considered the Babylonian golden image and what it represented: something that was to be observed, respected, and worshiped, not only by the population but also by the servants of ". . . the Most High God" (Dan. 4:2b NKJV). This, to them, was idolatry in its highest form. Anyone or thing that came between the Hebrew children and the worship of their living God they considered as idolatry.

We took time in the session to consider what might be our "golden image" that is taking our adoration and worship away from our God. In answer, many major and not so major factors were voiced. Considering many pastors and church workers have very meagre possessions, I almost feared their response. Some spoke of putting the importance of building their assembly ahead of the worship of God. Others spoke of their children or wives or of material or financial things as golden image factors of temptation.

My mind crossed the globe to Western Europe and North America and shuddered at what, by comparison, would be the reaction of these Christian workers at our materialism and lifestyle choices. What or who would be our golden image? During those moments, they became quite introspective. Silently, no doubt, they searched their hearts for the more obvious and unspoken gods that might possibly impede the progress of their ministries. Was there a god that had to be dethroned if the power of the living God was to fill them and anoint their ministries to His highest and best purposes?

All the Western paraphernalia that we take for granted would certainly qualify with them as coming between the believer and his God. Those were moments when each one of us felt constrained to examine our hearts and affirm that indeed the living God was dominant in our worship of Him alone.

As they searched through the layers of life, the strata of choices that had been made over a lifetime, they knew they didn't walk there alone. In support, the fourth man walked with them. As the line of an old hymn says, there is "Nothing between my soul and my Saviour."

How vigilant the servant of God should be that nothing becomes an idol. Anything taking center stage that detracts from the purity of our worship of Him alone would qualify as such.

We need always to be alert so that nothing becomes even an "appearance of evil" (1 Thess. 5:22 AV). Then we will have this assurance: "Beloved, if our heart does not condemn us, we have confidence toward God" (1 John 3:21 NKJV).

King Nebuchadnezzar's demand to the three young men was unwavering: either bow or burn! This was the high price they paid for their nonconformity.

The pastors at the seminar understood that in a very real way. One of their colleagues in a rural village who recently stood up for his faith was murdered, chopped into small pieces, and then returned to his family. Another was set on fire and died in his small hut while he slept. Many are beaten within an inch of their lives and often left maimed.

As leaders of the dominant religion in another country were going to incinerate his church building, one of our pastors was told to leave it, but he and his family refused to leave. Kneeling in front of the platform by the communion table, he and his wife, their daughter, who was to soon be married, and the young married assistant pastor, who was also a father, were found burnt to death after the fire. That was the high price they paid for their nonconformity.

Paul in his letter to the Romans made this point clear: "And do not be conformed to this world, but be transformed by the renewing of your mind, that you may prove what *is* that good and acceptable and perfect will of God" (Rom. 12:2 NKJV).

Although being offered an audience with King Nebuchadnezzar and now facing certain death by refusing a second chance, the emphatic answer of the young Hebrews was, ". . . our God whom we serve is able to deliver *us* from the burning fiery furnace, and He will deliver us from your hand, O king. But if not, let it be known to you, O king, that we do not serve your gods, nor will we worship the gold image that you have set up" (Dan. 3:17–18 NKJV).

These pastors understood the three young men's predicament. In their own experiences, each of them continually faced ridicule and threats, sometimes of death, to them or their children. In the face of persecution, they developed faith in their living God. Today we need living faith to live; tomorrow we may need, and will have, dying faith to die. Jesus mentored the disciples with the following encouragement: "Therefore I say to you, do not worry about your life . . . do not worry about tomorrow, for tomorrow will worry about its own things. Sufficient for the day *is* its own trouble" (Matt. 6:25, 34 NKJV). Jesus Christ assures us, as He did the apostle Paul, "My grace is sufficient for you. My strength is made perfect in weakness" (2 Cor. 12:9 NKJV).

Although distracted by the burning heat and insects, the pastors listened intently as we discussed the furnace and the fire. It was not an imagined furnace or fire; it was real, and even the king's strong men were consumed by approaching it. Our furnaces are not imagined either; they are very real. Our fourth man is always present to walk with us.

In every seminar, there is a telling moment, a change of spirit and a deeper silence, almost as though our hearts are being arrested or challenged by a greater "still small voice" (1 Kin. 19:12 AV, NKJV). This was that moment. Each one listening had a fiery furnace of his own to face. The truth of the message was sinking in—that walking through their hottest fire and darkest night with them was their *fourth man.*

As the pastors listened intently, they knew their witness for Christ was also playing out in the public arena. Every move of their Christian lives was monitored, every gesture and every domestic action at home or school. One false move and their furnace could be stoked. Not long before, because a preacher was overheard saying from a loud speaker, "Our witnessing will take the town for Christ," that weekend almost every Christian church in the town was torched.

Publicly, the king, together with the dignitaries, recognized that the living God had displayed His power on behalf of His servants. Their bodies were unharmed, their hair was not singed, their clothes were not consumed, and the smell of fire was not on them. This was the work of the God of superlatives, the God of more than enough. Jesus Himself declared, "All authority has been given to Me in heaven and on earth" (Matt. 28:18 NKJV).

Sharing with the pastors from Daniel's vision, I further assured them that their fourth man, who is the Son of Man, had total authority and was in control of their every concern.

> *I was watching in the night visions,*
> *And behold One like the Son of Man,*
> *Coming with the clouds of heaven!*
> *He came to the Ancient of Days,*
> *And they brought Him near before Him.*
> *Then to Him was given dominion and glory and a kingdom,*
> *That all peoples, nations and languages, should serve Him.*
> *His dominion is an everlasting dominion,*
> *Which shall not pass away,*
> *And His kingdom the one*
> *Which shall not be destroyed* (Dan. 7:13–14 NKJV).

As the golden sun was beginning to set on our outdoor upper room, it was as though the Holy Spirit had softened and quieted our hearts. In the closing moments of the event, I had intended to pray. Typically, this means extended prayer, as the majority of the audience will line up individually to be ministered to in prayer. But more importantly, they were reminded that their fourth man was in their midst. He was walking between them to work His sovereign touch on their lives.

Each one began quietly to minister to one another. The Holy Spirit breathed His presence on each needy life, meeting needs only they knew existed. Heaven came down, and glory filled their souls. As God walked between them, miracles began to happen as hostilities were resolved and reconciliation resulted. They had fresh passion for their work and calling and a new commitment to serve, and they had shared testimonies with one another. The fourth man alone had done His work.

What, we may wonder, was wrong with the original intended text? Nothing! The concept of the fourth man was what the Holy Spirit needed to be shared.

All He required was a conduit, a voice through which to flow. Each of my thoughts during this sermon came more readily than if it had been prepared. Ministry is an ongoing learning experience; one never arrives. Holy Spirit ministry is supernatural; one only needs to hear His prompt, step out of the boat, and follow His direction.

Several hours later as we retraced our steps across the quadrangle, it was with the satisfaction and fulfillment that He does all things well. Despite four hours in the gruelling heat, the joy of the Lord had become my strength, and I felt energized with His anointing, fresher than if I had been allowed to teach in the cool abbey.

How marvellous it is to be an onlooker and watch God do His work! God Himself had spoken exactly what was needed for these His Hebrew children in their Babylon. As the fourth man, He had walked in the cloisters with them and ministered to their personal needs. So He will walk with us when we recognize Him as our fourth man.

# CONCLUSION

Everything you have read to this point is but the tip of the iceberg of what we have seen God do. The apostles Matthew and Mark both recorded what Jesus said from the Psalms:

> *This was the Lord's doing;*
> *It is marvellous in our eyes*
> (Ps. 118:23 NKJV; see also Matt. 21:42 and Mark 12:11).

Shirley and I feel the same about what we encounter as we witness God's marvellous *now*, which is the result of us making the right choices at each fork in the road.

About thirty years ago while I was sitting in a secular inspirational lecture in Vancouver, Canada, the speaker, Bob Beale, asked three opening questions: "What are you doing today that will be remembered in five years?" Then he asked, "What are you doing today that will be remembered in fifty years?" Finally, he asked, "What are you doing today that will be remembered in five hundred years?" For me the lecture finished at the start. That *was* the question. Focus on the most important choice! Life is about making major choices.

When God called us, it was a major choice to obey Him. Now books could be written—and may still be published—about the God of the supernatural in these past years. The following example says it all.

Two small boys lived on the edge of an Asian jungle. By waiting silently high on the branches of trees, they became adept at snatching tiny birds in flight. The elderly village wise man always sat on his special bench by the village gate. He answered everyone's questions; no question seemed too difficult for him to answer. The small boys had a plan. They would catch a bird, cage it between their cupped hands, and take it to the old sage. "Sir," they would say, "We have a bird caged in our hands; is it living or is it dead?"

If the wise old man said it was living, they would press their thumb on the tiny bird's chest and drop it dead at his feet. If his answer was "It's dead," they would open their cupped hands and release it. Either way they would prove the man of wisdom wrong. With their plan rehearsed, they stood before him, asking their question. "Sir, we have a bird cupped in our hands; is it living, or is it dead?" Slowly, with the wisdom of his years, he looked into the boys' eyes, then at their carefully concealed prize between their tiny fingers, and yet again looked into their eyes. He replied, "It will be whatever you want it to be."

Is this not also the wisdom of life? Is it not all about choices? In this writing, I have tried to be transparent about the major choices of life that I called forks in the road. I have tried to show the significance of right or wrong choices and their lasting rewards or consequences.

The boys had the wisdom of the sage to learn from, if they would. We have access to wisdom of the ages, wisdom beyond measure in "the only wise God" (1 Tim. 1:17d AV; Jude 25a AV).

The burden of my heart is that, in some small way, while endeavouring to be His servant by my writing, I may have become your servant for Jesus' sake. I desire to help you make a choice that will be remembered not only for five hundred years but forever. The choice is yours: "'. . . seek first the kingdom of God and His righteousness, and all these things shall be added to you'" (Matt. 6:33 NKJV).

Early in our overseas ministry, while I was in prayer, the Holy Spirit impressed upon me some thoughts that, by way of conclusion, I leave with you as a ministry prayer.

Lord, give me:

- The *eyes* of Christ to see their need.
- The *ears* of Christ to hear their cry.
- The *hands* of Christ to lift their load.
- The *feet* of Christ to walk with them.
- The *back* of Christ to bear rebuff.
- The *heart* of Christ to show His love.
- The *Spirit* of Christ to forgive.

I love you in the Lord Jesus; I am your servant for Jesus' sake.

# AFTERWORD

Thank you for journeying with me! For you the journey has been but a few hours; for me, it took a lifetime in preparation. Weaving the threads into what has become the fabric of this book has taken over one thousand hours, many of them in far-flung corners of the globe. In almost every mode of travel, my trusty laptop performed.

For a long time, many of my colleagues had encouraged me to put pen to paper to capture the notable events that God allowed us to witness as He moved on hearts and lives changed forever. Not until more recently was I persuaded to action. A senior brother challenged me with this statement: "When God takes you home, your voice will be silent, your active ministry finished forever. Then the only way your voice will speak encouragement to future generations will be through your writing. Show them where God can take them in supernatural ministry by leaving a road map detailing how He mentored you." *Living in the Supernatural Dimension* is my rookie attempt to comply.

Each stand-alone chapter is intended to touch a heartstring, evoke an "aha" moment. When the Holy Spirit speaks by gently prompting from Scripture or in your spirit, His desire is to move you from where you are to where is best for you.

Using a road journey as a metaphor of life may be less accurate than using a flowing river. In such a river, there is no standing still. The will to win by going against the current, if lost, carries one backward. God's plan for you is only to move ahead in victory to His destination for you.

*Living in the Supernatural Dimension* refers to forks in the road.

The journey of life can be a good, better, or best journey. To be in harmony with God's best means making the right choices at each major fork.

The crucial choice is allowing Christ to be Saviour, Lord, and Master. Receive His love and forgiveness, and become His child. Grow in your faith by a healthy relationship with Him, learning to walk in obedience to His Word. Speak to Him in prayer as you would communicate with a best friend. Live your life circumspectly as His child, confident of and walking in your divine inheritance.

You are loved today, at this very moment, regardless of your social position, situation, or emotions. God is as close to you as the calling of His name. Release your grip on the steering wheel of your life, and allow Him to be Master and take control of it. As a believer, perhaps your life has taken a difficult turn or you have missed a fork in the road. All is not lost, because He will never leave you. So just breathe His name, put your hand in His, and walk safely into the unknown.

# YOU ARE LOVED

When God first repositioned Shirley and me to evangelism in third world and developing nations, He planted a seed or concept in my spirit. It was this thought: "Be their servant."

For hundreds of years, as missionaries have left all and often lost everything, including their families, in order to labour in far-off lands, the stories are legendary of how the nationals perceived the messenger of the gospel.

Although we sometimes lived in jungle ministry at the level of the national, with a family sleeping often like cordwood on a bamboo mat spread on an earthen floor, God had more in mind about love and servant hood.

One evening, as several thousand people stood in an open field hearing the gospel, mostly for the first time, I sensed the Holy Spirit say very clearly, "Tell them you are here to love them and to serve them because of Me." In contrast with our Western comforts, God knew there were many things about our mission's assignment that were difficult. At times, it was hard to love and serve in the natural.

This statement was not about the natural but about the spiritual-love them as you would love Me; serve them as you would serve Me. Then I said in my opening remarks, "I love you in the Lord Jesus, and I am your servant for Jesus' sake." Saying it for the first time sounded dishonest. In the natural, it was almost impossible, but in the spiritual, it was possible. This was not about natural love but about His divine love flowing from us to them. They felt God's love, they understood it then, and they are still responding to it. They experienced His presence and touch on their lives.

Since that night, and for almost every public function, I communicate that statement of love and service. It puts my spirit and attitude on the line. That single statement, lived out before the people, has enabled me to be closer to them, to feel their pain, and to love them into a new or greater relationship with the living God.

I have said that to say this to you: God loves you, I love *you* in the Lord Jesus, and I am *your* servant for Jesus' sake.

Whatever life has thrown at you, however dark and sad your night may be, His light and His joy will come in the morning (Ps. 30:5).

He desires not only to be your Saviour but also for you to allow Him to be your Lord and Master, giving Him total control of your life. Then, as you walk in obedience to His Word, God will then open the windows of heaven and pour out on you an abundant blessing (Mal. 3:10).

Through our contact information below, you are invited in confidence to allow me to be your servant for Jesus' sake. In Christ you *are* loved. How may I help you?

We invite you to contact us. Please write to:
John & Shirley Abraham
P.O. Box 2190
Abbotsford, BC Canada V2T 3X8.
Or contact us online at: www.globalcanada.org

# ENDNOTES

1   M. B. Woodworth-Etter. *Signs and Wonders: God Wrought in the Ministry for Forty Years.* Abridged Ed. London: P. St. G. Kirke, 1916.

2   Thomas William Miller. *Canadian Pentecostals: A History of the Pentecostal Assemblies of Canada.* Edited by William A. Griffin. Mississauga, ON, Canada: Full Gospel Publishing House, 1994. Maria Woodworth-Etter is referenced eight times in Miller's Index (p. 450).

3   Aimee Semple McPherson is referenced nineteen times in Miller's Index (p. 441). For more on McPherson see Edith L. Blumhofer. *Aimee Semple McPherson: Everybody's Sister.* Grand Rapids, Mich.: William B. Eerdmans Publishing Co., 1993.

4   Miller, 102.

5   G. Campbell Morgan. *The Acts of the Apostles.* New York: Fleming H. Revell Co., 1924, 35.

6   Morgan, 50.

7   Robert Owens. "3. The Azusa Street Revival: The Pentecostal Movement Begins in America" in *The Century of the Holy Spirit.* Edited by Vinson Synan. Nashville. TN: Thomas Nelson, 2001, 39-68.

8   John Pollock. *Crusades: 20 Years with Billy Graham.* Special Billy Graham Crusade Edition. Minneapolis, MN: World Wide Publications, 1969, 16.

9   Pollock, 172, 183.

10  Sherwood Eliot Wirt, *Billy: A Personal Look at Billy Graham, the World's Best-Loved Evangelist.* Wheaton, IL: Crossway Books, 1997, 28.

11  Wirt cites Stephen Olford, 28.

12  Wirt cites Billy Graham, 28.

13  Wirt, 28.

14  Wirt cites Olford, who quotes Graham, 28-29.

[15]  Wirt cites Olford, 29.

[16]  Ibid.

[17]  Wirt cites Olford, who quotes Graham, 29.

[18]  Wirt, 29.

[19]  Wirt cites Olford, 29.

[20]  Wirt cites Olford, who quotes Graham, 29.

[21]  Wirt cites Olford, 29–30.

[22]  Wirt cites Olford, 30.

[23]  M. H. Reynolds, "Amsterdam 83" in *Foundation*. IV, No. 4: 4–11. See also Billy Graham's *Just As I Am: The Autobiography of Billy Graham*, 574–8.

[24]  Sterling W. Huston, *Crusade Evangelism and the Local Church*. Minneapolis, MN: World Wide, 1984, 22.

[25]  Huston cites Graham, 22. Graham is quoted in his "The Evangelist and a Torn World" in *The Evangelist and a Torn World: Messages from Amsterdam*, 15.

[26]  Sherwood Eliot Wirt. *Billy: A Personal Look at Billy Graham, the World's Best-Loved Evangelist*. Wheaton, IL: Crossway Books, 1997.

[27]  Pollock, 6.

[28]  Aarum, Wes. "Lou Peskett" in *The Evangelical Christian*. Feb. 1967, 15–16.

[29]  "The significance of **rhema** (as distinct from **logos**) is exemplified in the injunction to take 'the sword of the Spirit, which is the word of God,' Eph. 6:17; here the reference is not to the whole Bible as such, but to the individual scripture which the Spirit brings to our remembrance for use in time of need, a prerequisite being the regular storing of the mind with Scripture." (W. E. Vine, *An Expository Dictionary of New Testament Words*. Old Tappan, NJ: Fleming H. Revell Co., 1966), IV: 230.

[30]  Don & Katie Fortune. *Discover Your God-Given Gifts*. Old Tappan, NJ: Fleming H. Revell Co., 1987.

[31]  C. S. Lewis. *The Four Loves*. London: Geoffrey Bles, 1960.

[32]  Lewis, 106–132.

[33]  Lewis, 42–68.

[34]  Lewis, 69–105.

[35]  Lewis, 133–160.

[36] Numbers used randomly to protect the privacy of individuals.

[37] Matthew Henry. *Commentary on the Whole Bible.* New York: Fleming H. Revell Co., n.d., v. 5, 72.

[38] R. P. Spittler. "GLOSSOLALIA" in *The New International Dictionary of Pentecostal and Charismatic Movements.* Rev. & enl. Ed. Stanley M. Burgess, Editor. Grand Rapids, MI: Zondervan, 2002, 670.

[39] Spittler, 670.

[40] Ralph W. Harris. *Spoken by the Spirit: Documented Accounts of "Other Tongues" From Arabic to Zulu.* Springfield, MO: Gospel Publishing House, c1973.

[41] Harriet Beecher Stowe. *Uncle Tom's Cabin.* London: The Collector's Library, 2004.

[42] Charles S. Price. *The Lonely Cabin on the Forty Mile: A Marvellous Story of the Grace of God.* Los Angeles, CA: Free Tract Society (Inc.), n.d., 1–8.

[43] J. E. H. Thompson, "Daniel" in *The Pulpit Commentary.* New Ed. Edited by H. D. M. Spence and Joseph S. Exell. V. 29. London: Funk & Wagnalls Co., 1896, 110.

# REFERENCES

Aarum, Wes. "Lou Peskett" in *The Evangelical Christian*. Feb. 1967, [15]-16.

Blumhofer, Edith L. *Aimee Semple McPherson: Everybody's Sister.* Grand Rapids, MI: William B. Eerdmans Publishing Co., 1993.

Fortune, Don & Katie. *Discover Your God-Given Gifts.* Old Tappan, NJ: Fleming H. Revell Co., 1987.

Graham, Billy. *The Evangelist and a Torn World: Messages from Amsterdam.* Minneapolis, MN: World Wide Publications, 1983.

_____. *Just As I Am: The Autobiography of Billy Graham.* San Francisco, CA: HarperSanFrancisco, Zondervan, 1997.

Harris, Ralph W. *Spoken by the Spirit: Documented Accounts of "Other Tongues" From Arabic to Zulu.* Springfield, MO: Gospel Publishing House, 1973.

Henry, Matthew. *Commentary on the Whole Bible.* New York: Fleming H. Revell Co., n.d.

Huston, Sterling W. *Crusade Evangelism and the Local Church.* Minneapolis, MN: World Wide, 1984.

Lewis, C. S. *The Four Loves.* London: Geoffrey Bles, 1960.

Miller, Thomas William. *Canadian Pentecostals: A History of the Pentecostal Assemblies of Canada.* Edited by William A. Griffin. Mississauga, ON, Canada: Full Gospel Publishing House, 1994.

Morgan, G. Campbell. *The Acts of the Apostles.* New York: Fleming H. Revell Co., 1924.

Owens, Robert. "3. The Azusa Street Revival: The Pentecostal Movement Begins in America" in *The Century of the Holy Spirit.* Edited by Vinson Synan. Nashville: Thomas Nelson, 2001, 39-68.

Pollock, John. *Crusades: 20 Years with Billy Graham.* Special Billy Graham Crusade Ed. Minneapolis, MN: World Wide Publications, 1969.

Price, Charles S. *The Lonely Cabin on the Forty Mile: A Marvellous Story of the Grace of God.* Los Angeles, CA: Free Tract Society (Inc.), n.d., 8 p.

Reynolds, M. H. "Amsterdam 83" in *Foundation.* IV, No. 4: 4-11.

Spittler, R. P. "GLOSSOLALIA" in *The New International Dictionary of Pentecostal and Charismatic Movements.* Rev. & Enl. Ed. Stanley M. Burgess, Editor. Grand Rapids, MI: Zondervan, 2002.

Stowe, Harriet Beecher. *Uncle Tom's Cabin.* London: The Collector's Library, 2004.

Thompson, J. E. H. "Daniel" in *The Pulpit Commentary.* New Ed. Edited by H.D.M.Spence and Joseph S. Exell. V. 29. London: Funk & Wagnalls Co., 1896.

Vine, W. E. An *Expository Dictionary of New Testament Words.* Old Tappan, NJ: Fleming H. Revell Co., 1966.

Wirt, Sherwood Eliot. *Billy: A Personal Look at Billy Graham, the World's Best-Loved Evangelist.* Wheaton, IL: Crossway Books, 1997.

Woodworth-Etter, M.B. *Signs and Wonders: God Wrought in the Ministry for Forty Years.* Abridged Ed. London: P. St. G. Kirke, 1916.

# INDEX OF NAMES AND LOCATIONS

Colombo | 209

Colossian | 189, 243

Comforter | 150, 176. See also Holy Spirit

Corinthian | 25, 97, 149, 158, 164, 190, 242

Cork [Eire] | 58

Cornelius, William | xx

Creator | 17, 182, 221, 250, 256

Cunard's Saxonia | 16

## D

Damascus | 130

Daniel [Biblical figure] | 117, 259, 262, 263, 269, 281, 284

David and Goliath | 6. See also David; Goliath

David [King of Israel] | xi, 6, 20, 100. See also David and Goliath; Psalmist

De Hahn, M. R. | 6

Disneyland | 231

Doherty, Sam | 7

Douglas, Fred | 8

## E

Earls Court [London] | 31

Eastern | 52, 86, 121, 159

Eben | 109

Eden | 92, 221. See also Garden of Eden

Edmonton | 41, 46, 54, 55

Edmonton Airport | 55

Egypt | 42, 59

Egyptian | 58, 59, 110

Eire | 50. See also Cork

Elliott, Sam | 8

Elrose [Sask.] | 22

England | 37

English | 38, 76, 80, 88, 112, 198, 213, 246, 259

Englishman | 147

Ephesians | 98, 149, 173, 177, 249, 250, 252, 257

Equator | 141

Eston College | xx, 15, 47. See also Full Gospel Bible Institute

Ethiopian | 217

Eve. See also Adam

Eve [Biblical figure] | 58, 221

Examining Ordination Board | 29

Exell, Joseph S. | 281, 284

## F

Faith Academy [Manila, Philippines] | 70

Father | 80, 86, 87, 99, 150, 208, 214, 244, 259. See also God

First Nations | 49

Fortune, Don | 283

Fortune, Katie | 81, 280

Fourth Man | 258, 259, 262, 266, 269–271

Friend | xx, 4, 6, 7, 8, 15, 19, 36, 37, 39, 43, 44, 49, 54, 58, 62–64, 70, 75, 76, 110, 145, 154, 162, 168, 171, 174, 182, 207, 208, 222, 233, 246, 262, 276

Frontenac | 17. See also Chateau Frontenac

Frontier Lodge | 41

Full Gospel Bible Institute | xx, 15, 40, 47. See also Eston College

## G

Galatians | 25

Gamaliel [teacher of the law and Pharisee in the Sanhedrin] | 28

Garden of Eden | 92. See also Eden

Ghi, Andrew | xix

Gilchrist, Tom | 8, 10

Glegg, Lindsay | xix

Glidden [Sask.] | 22

God | ix, xi, xiii, xiv, xv, xvi, xix,
    xxiii, xxiv, 3, 6, 8–13, 16–21,
    24–27, 29, 34, 37, 40–63,
    69, 70, 72–77, 81, 85,
    86–101, 106–110, 113–120,
    124–129, 132–135, 140,
    144, 145–156, 159, 162–
    165, 169–187, 192–196,
    199–201, 205, 208, 209,
    212–215, 217–219, 222–
    227, 232–235, 237–255,
    260–279, 262, 283, 284. See
    also Father; Lord; LORD;
    Majesty; Most High God;
    Potter; Righteous Judge;
    Rock; Saviour

Godhead | 152. See also Trinity

God-man | 222. See also Jesus Christ

Goliath | 6. See also David and
    Goliath

Good Shepherd | 80, 129, 247. See
    also Jesus Christ

Gospel Hall | 2, 214. See also Plym-
    outh Brethren Gospel Hall

Graham, Billy | xx, 23–25, 27, 30,
    31, 35, 38, 47, 240, 279,
    280, 283, 284

Greek | 52, 88, 150, 159

Griffin, William A. | 279, 283

## H

Ham, Mordecai | 27. See also Ham,
    Mordecai F.

Harringay [London] | 31

Harris, Ralph W. | 213, 281, 283

Heathrow Airport [London] | 44

Hebrew | 58, 59, 80, 124, 242, 263,
    264, 266, 267, 270

Henry, Matthew | 195, 281, 283

Higginbottom, Martin | 31

High Priest | 80. See also Jesus Christ

Hildenborough Hall [Kent] | 24

Holy One of Israel | 242. See
    also Jesus Christ

Holy Spirit | xi, xiv, xv, xvii, xxiv,
    6, 10–14, 20–22, 24, 25,
    27, 37, 50, 52–55, 62, 65,
    69, 72–74, 77–81, 84,
    86–88, 90, 97, 102, 107,
    112, 114–116, 125, 126,
    128, 131, 132, 133, 144,
    146, 148–151, 154, 155,
    158–162, 164–171, 175,
    176, 180, 181, 184, 186,
    190–194, 200, 201, 205,
    207, 212, 217, 228, 233,
    234, 245–250, 253, 257,
    259–261, 269, 272, 275,
    277, 279, 284. See also Com-
    forter; Paraclete; Promise of
    the Father; Spirit

Hong Kong | 71, 120, 197, 199. See
    also China

Huston, Sterling W. | 280, 283

Hutchinson, Cecil | 8

## I

India | 258

Indian Ocean | 132, 135

Indo-Asia | 125

Indonesia | 119, 132, 146, 212

Indonesian | 139, 147, 213

Ireland | 2, 19, 35, 38, 40, 49, 57,
    121, 235

Irian Jaya | 119. See also Province of
    Papua

Irish | 19, 38, 43, 44, 51

Isaac [son of Abraham] | 107

Isaiah [Biblical prophet] | 62, 63,
    66, 76, 90, 193, 240, 244,
    253

North American | 221
Northern Ireland | 2, 35, 38, 121, 235
Northern Saskatchewan | 19

# O

Odeon | 32
Olford, Stephen | 24, 279
OMF International | xix. See
    also China Inland Mission
Oregon | 49, 56
Outreach to Industry | 31
Owens, Robert | 279, 284

# P

Paisley, Harold | 3
Palatka [Fla.] | 23
Pangman [Sask.] | 15, 47
PAOC | xvi, xvii, xx, 70, 130, 161,
    209. See also Pentecostal As-
    semblies of Canada
Papua | 119
Paraclete | 150. See also Holy Spirit;
    Spirit
Paul. See also Saul
Paul [Saint, apostle] | 11, 24–26, 28,
    51, 52, 76, 80, 87, 93, 97–99,
    107, 130, 148, 149, 152, 158,
    160, 164, 173, 177, 182, 189,
    190, 208, 229, 243, 244,
    249–254, 256, 260, 265, 267,
    268
Pentecost | 11, 14, 21, 78, 148–150,
    153, 160, 192
Pentecostal | xi, xvi, xx, 9–14, 13, 21,
    120, 130, 153, 161, 209, 235,
    240, 279, 281, 284
Pentecostal Assemblies of Canada |
    xi, xx, 13, 120, 130, 161, 209,
    235, 279, 283. See also PAOC
Pentecostal Assemblies of Sri Lanka
    | 130

Pentecostals | 13, 21, 153, 279, 283
People's Church [Surrey, B.C.] | 49
Persia | 117
Peskett, Lou | 280, 283. See also Pes-
    kett, Louis
Peskett, Louis | 40, 41. See also Pes-
    kett, Lou
Peskett, Shirley | 45, 54. See also Abra-
    ham, Shirley; Mills, Shirley
Peter [Saint, apostle] | 12, 20, 39, 89,
    103, 116, 243, 249, 254–256
Pharaoh's | 58
Philip [Saint, apostle, evangelist] |
    217
Philippians | 182, 243
Plymouth Brethren | 2. See
    also Brethren
Plymouth Brethren Gospel Hall | 2.
    See also Gospel Hall
Pollock, John | 279, 284
Pontypridd [Wales] | 24
Portadown [Northern Ireland] | 8
Portland [Oregon] | 49, 51, 52, 56
Potter | xxiv, 20. See also God
Price, Charles S. | 235, 281, 284
Pritchard, Lorne | 44
Promise of the Father | 150. See
    also Holy Spirit
Province of Papua | 119. See
    also Irian Jaya
Psalmist | 96, 216, 244, 265. See
    also David

# Q

Quebec City | 16, 17

# R

Radio Luxemburg | 5
Rank, J. Arthur | 32
Ratz, Calvin | 70. See also Ratz,
    Calvin C.

Ratz, Calvin C. | xx. See also Ratz, Calvin

Redeemer | 59, 242. See also Jesus Christ

Reynolds, M. H. | 280, 284

Righteous Judge | 150. See also God

Robb, Stanley | 8

Roberts, Oral | 6

Rock | 110. See also God; Jesus Christ

Roman | 149, 189, 264, 267

Romans | 149, 267

Rome | 26

Russia | 209

Russian Assemblies of God | 209

Ruth [Biblical figure] | 59, 89, 243

## S

Saskatchewan | 15, 17, 19, 22, 40, 42, 44, 45

Saskatchewan River | 22

Saskatoon [Sask.] | 17, 29, 44

Satan | 4, 58, 78, 144, 237, 249–252, 255, 256, 260. See also Lucifer

Saul | 254, 260. See also Paul

Saul [King of Israel] | 254, 260

Saviour | xiii, 28, 34, 43, 77, 81, 133, 142, 144, 155, 159, 195, 208, 218, 222, 228, 232, 243, 264, 267, 276, 278. See also God; Jesus Christ

Saxonia | 16. See also Cunard's Saxonia

[Sayers], Shirleen (Abraham) | ix, 69, 70, 78, 141

Schlamp, Wally | 45

[Sczebel,] Rosanne | 45

Sczebel, Wally | 45

Second Person | 263. See also Jesus Christ

Seventh Avenue Full Gospel Church [Edmonton, Alta.] | 45

Shadrach | 262. See also Abed-Nego; Meshach

Shanghai | xv

Shea, George Beverly | 23

Singapore | 139, 141, 147

Singapore International Airport | 139

Sloan, Joshua | 8

Son | 23, 89, 144, 175, 216, 222, 223, 263, 264, 269. See also Jesus Christ

Son of God | 23, 263. See also Son of Man

Son of Man | 269. See also Son of God

South Canary Islands. See also Canary Islands

South China Sea | 83, 107, 241. See also China

South Saskatchewan River | 21

Southeast Asia | 197. See also Asia

Spence, H. D. M. | 281

Spirit | xi, xiii–xvi, xxiv, 6, 10–14, 20–22, 23, 25, 27, 37, 42, 45, 50, 52, 54–56, 61–63, 65, 66, 69, 70, 72–74, 77, 79–82, 84, 86–88, 90, 97, 99, 102, 107, 110, 112, 114–116, 125, 126, 128–132, 144, 146, 148–151, 153, 155, 157–161, 164–171, 175, 176, 180, 181, 184, 186, 190–194, 200, 201, 205–207, 212, 213, 217, 228, 233, 234, 238, 239, 245–250, 253, 255–257, 259–261, 269, 272, 275, 277, 279, 280–282, 283. See also Holy Spirit

Spittler, R. P. | 213, 281, 284

# INDEX OF SCRIPTURE REFERENCES

## NEW TESTAMENT

Lightning Source UK Ltd.
Milton Keynes UK
UKOW04f1123071113

220597UK00001BA/36/P